D1327729

The Ethical Mysticism of Albert Schweitzer

The Ethical Mysticism
of Albert Schweitzer

*A Study of the Sources and Significance
of Schweitzer's Philosophy of Civilization*

By Henry Clark

With Two Essays by Albert Schweitzer

Beacon Press   Boston

Acknowledgments

Grateful acknowledgment is extended to the following publishers: A. & C. Black Ltd. and The Macmillan Company for permission to quote from *The Decay and Restoration of Civilization* and *Civilization and Ethics* (published in the United States by The Macmillan Company as *Philosophy of Civilization*), *The Quest of the Historical Jesus*, *The Mysticism of Paul the Apostle*, *The Theology of Albert Schweitzer for Christian Inquirers*, *On the Edge of the Primeval Forest*, *More From the Primeval Forest*; The United States Conference for the World Council of Churches, Inc., for permission to quote from *Christendom*; The American Humanist Association, Yellow Springs, Ohio for permission to quote from *The Humanist*; George Allen & Unwin Ltd. for permission to quote from *Christianity and the Religions of the World*; The Christian Century Foundation for permission to quote from *The Christian Century*; the publishers of the *Saturday Review* for permission to quote from that periodical; The New American Library of World Literature, Inc., and Henry Holt and Company, Inc., for permission to quote from *Out of My Life and Thought*; Paul Haupt Verlag of Berne, Switzerland, for permission to quote from *Ehrfurcht vor dem Leben*; and Harper & Brothers for permission to quote from *Inside Africa* and *God's Grace and Man's Hope*.

To My Esteemed Teachers at

Duke University
Union Theological Seminary
University of Berne
Yale Divinity School

The deepest difference, practically, in the moral life of man is the difference between the easy-going and the strenuous mood. When in the easy-going mood the shrinking from present ill is our ruling consideration. The strenuous mood, on the contrary, makes us quite indifferent to present ill, if only the greater ideal be attained. The capacity for the strenuous mood probably lies slumbering in every man, but it has more difficulty in some than in others in waking up. . . .

The capacity of the strenuous mood lies so deep down among our natural human possibilities that even if there were no metaphysical or traditional grounds for believing in a God, men would postulate one simply as a pretext for living hard, and getting out of the game of existence its keenest possibilities of zest. Our attitude towards concrete evils is entirely different in a world where we believe there are none but finite demanders, from what it is in one where we joyously face tragedy for an infinite demander's sake. Every sort of energy and endurance, of courage and capacity for handling life's evils, is set free in those who have religious faith. For this reason the strenuous type of character will on the battle-field of human history always outwear the easy-going type, and religion will drive irreligion to the wall.

—WILLIAM JAMES, in
The Moral Philosopher and the Moral Life

Preface

Earnest conviction that Albert Schweitzer is a great thinker as well as a great man led me to write this book. In it I have tried to explain clearly and thoroughly the structure of Schweitzer's philosophy, and to exhibit the principal reasons why his thought is of great significance today.

Obviously, no book *about* Schweitzer can substitute for those written *by* him. When the doctor was in Oslo in 1954 to receive his Nobel Peace Prize, I had the good fortune to meet him and ask him the question, "Where should I go and under what particular professors should I study in order to get the best possible education in your thought?" His reply to my question is my own advice to others who want to know more about Schweitzer, for he exclaimed: "Read my books! No one can express the ideas of a man so well as he has expressed them himself in his writings!"

Nevertheless, I am persuaded that a secondary source is needed to orient the serious reader of Schweitzer's writings to their context and ramifications. For example, the uninitiated reader could become bewildered by *Civilization and Ethics*, the work which contains the fullest statement of Schweitzer's philosophical position. *The Quest of the Historical Jesus* and *The Mysticism of Paul the Apostle* can be appreciated adequately only with an awareness of their seminal significance in the field of New Testament scholarship. Even Schweitzer's masterful autobiography gains new power when read with knowledge of its author's specific intellectual concerns and achievements.

Schweitzer does not have all the answers, but he deals with the most critical questions of our time, and where he presents answers they deserve a wide hearing and sober consideration. His earliest books, written more than half a century ago, have brought about a revolution in theology. The negative significance of "thoroughgoing eschatology" has been forced upon the attention of most New Testament scholars, but the positive

significance of Schweitzer's understanding of Jesus has not
been fully explored by theologians. The central theme of his
major philosophical writings, "the decay and restoration of
civilization," is a problem of concern to all thinking men—yet
many of Schweitzer's ideas about this problem are damned with
faint praise, drowned in a sea of sentimental adulation, or ignored. Schweitzer's urgent appeal for an end to nuclear weapons
testing has not been communicated to enough citizens. His
views on colonialism have seldom been subjected to systematic
exposition and criticism. In short, previous works on Schweitzer
have left much to be discovered about Albert Schweitzer's contributions to the philosophical, theological and social thought
of Western civilization.

I have not confined this book to an exposition and critique
of those ideas which are explicit in Schweitzer's writings. I have
also analyzed some of the ideas implicit in his writings, ideas
which offer exciting opportunities for further elaboration. But
my fundamental aim has been to provide an analysis of Schweitzer's thought which I hope will stimulate the reader to enter
into a profound dialogue with Schweitzer: to face with Schweitzer the elemental questions of human existence and to consider
appreciatively but critically his answers.

If this book succeeds in awakening in the reader a desire
to study Schweitzer, and in providing an acquaintance with the
background of his thought which will lead to a higher degree
of comprehension of what Schweitzer says, I shall be content.

I am grateful for the support and guidance which has been
given me in my work on Schweitzer by many persons. Through
the generosity of the Woodrow Wilson Scholarship Program
and the Danforth Foundation, I was able to pursue my academic
training in this country. The generosity of the Rotary Foundation made possible my year of special study and research in
Europe, during 1957–1958. My appreciation goes out to all of
the teachers who have influenced and helped me; and especially
to Professors Martin Werner and Fritz Buri of the University
of Berne, to Professors John C. Bennett, Reinhold Niebuhr and
Daniel Day Williams at Union Theological Seminary, and to
Professors H. Richard Niebuhr, Liston Pope and William Lee

Miller of Yale Divinity School. Herr Richard Kik, head of the Schweitzer Freundeskreis in Heidenheim an der Brenz, Germany, rendered invaluable assistance by supplying me with articles on Schweitzer from the private publication which he edits, articles which I would have been unable to obtain otherwise. Dr. Herbert Phillips, head of the Albert Schweitzer Education Foundation in Chicago, has been extremely kind in allowing me to participate in several important conferences of Schweitzer scholars sponsored by the Foundation, and in furnishing me with several important documents pertaining to Schweitzer. Professor Robert Spivey of Williams College, Alan Levensohn and Karl Hill of Beacon Press have greatly assisted me by their criticism of the manuscript. And I am grateful to my wife, Nancy Hurst Clark, for her many hours of typing and proofreading, her suggestions and her encouragement.

HENRY CLARK

Contents

The Ethical Mysticism of Albert Schweitzer

The Ethical Mysticism of Albert Schweitzer

I. Schweitzer and His Public

1. Adulation and Rejection

Albert Schweitzer is regarded as a great man by most of those who know his life or his writings, but few of even these have thoroughly and critically explored either the depths of his thought or the significance of the complex relationship between his life and his thought.

On the one hand his admirers intone their panegyrics without more than a superficial analysis of the intellectual stature of the "Jungle Doctor." Often there is virtually no attempt to assess the peculiar limitations and shortcomings of Schweitzer the man or Schweitzer the thinker. As John Gunther so pungently stated it:

> He himself is quite conscious of his faults, and mentions in one of his books that he has often been "arrogant" and "lacking in love," and that he has even "hated, slandered, and defrauded." In plain fact, the old man has several frailties. His venerators are horrified if these are mentioned; they want their Great Man whole, untattered and undiminished. . . .[1]

I do not say that uncritical tributes should never have been written. After all, there *is* something dazzling about the real accomplishments and the moral grandeur of Albert Schweitzer. He is, as Churchill has called him, a "Genius of Humanity." One might even agree with those who call him "the great man's great man" (Hagedorn), "almost, if not quite Olympian," "a universal man in the sense that Leonardo da Vinci and Goethe were universal men" (Gunther), and say of him, as Einstein has, "Nowhere have I ever found such an ideal union of goodness and passion for beauty as in Albert Schweitzer."[2]

But appreciative estimation has all too frequently passed over into rampant adulation, oversimplifying when not actually distorting Schweitzer's complex thoughts. Feschotte explains to his unsuspecting readers that the New Testament concept "Son of Man" is "a synonym for Messiah, invented by the prophet Daniel," [3] when as a matter of fact Schweitzer's whole interpretation of Jesus depends on the radical differences between apocalyptic and messianic expectations. Wolfram certainly overdramatizes Schweitzer's belief that "truth, love, peaceableness and goodness are that power over all powers." [4]

"Reverence for life," the phrase used by Schweitzer to condense the significance of his ethical mysticism, is open to both misinterpretation and criticism on the ground that it is sentimental. Schweitzer himself has written and done much to justify such criticism. But surely Schweitzer admirers have exaggerated this sentimentality in the doctor's thought by using the phrase as a magic wand of ethical efficacy and by popularizing Schweitzer as the nice old man who goes about picking worms off paths.[5]

One admirer who felt that his life had been revolutionized by Schweitzer's books predicted that when reverence for life became widely known and practiced, it would bring about a revolution in ethics comparable to that wrought by Einstein in physics.[6] Magnus Ratter's book on Schweitzer, which George Seaver called "undoubtedly the most informed and penetrating study of Schweitzer's life and thought that has yet appeared in English," [7] passed entirely into adulation, as voiced in this paragraph, and others like it:

> To anticipate the verdict of posterity, to enhalo a living man, is to challenge the world: and we challenge it. As it was declared to Victorian England that the natural supernaturalism of Goethe would take children from the mines, redeem men from selfishness and extrude the cancer from industrial life, so we declare to Georgian England that Reverence for Life will deepen the spiritual life of the individual, can free Europe from the dread of war and has power to create an ideal society. . . .[8]

Schweitzer's very name is often used as a magic wand. The title page of Hermann Hagedorn's *Prophet in the Wilderness*, a book about Schweitzer, features a quotation from Gandhi:

"If a single man achieves the highest kind of love it will be sufficient to neutralize the hate of millions." Marcus Bach, after relating how thrilled he became as he watched Schweitzer "affectionately caring for his aged cat, which had already lost its teeth," goes on to exclaim:

The longer I was with Schweitzer the more I believed in St. Francis of Assisi. And it may be that until the masses of men retain such childlike trust and affection for life on every scale, we never will see the kingdom of God on earth.[9]

Faith in Schweitzer sometimes attains a religious intensity. Pierhal, not the first to imply that Schweitzer considers himself a saint, implies just that by quoting out of context Schweitzer's account of the following conversation between himself and his African helper, Joseph:

One day, in my despair at some of the natives who had once more been drawing polluted water, I threw myself into a chair in the consulting room and groaned out: "What a blockhead I was to come out here to doctor savages like these!" Whereupon Joseph quietly remarked: "Yes, Doctor, here on earth you are a great blockhead, but not in heaven." [10]

But Schweitzer's immediately following lines on page 102 of *More From the Primeval Forest* remove any impression that he considers himself a saint and in fact give quite a practical and humble point to the story: "He likes giving utterance to sententious remarks like that. I wish he would support us better in our efforts to hinder the spread of dysentery!"

Hagedorn is not alone in comparing Schweitzer with Jesus, but he does present an exceptionally flamboyant portrait in *Prophet in the Wilderness:*

In the parsonage at Gunsbach, one bright Whitsunday morning, Albert Schweitzer lay in bed listening to the birds singing in the first warmth of the new year. Such a morning! . . .
The rapture of living lifted him clear out of himself so that the Voice he had fled from and sought to silence spoke as it had never before spoken . . . "You must pay."

Yes, but how *did* one pay for such benefactions, so freely given? How . . . had . . . Jesus . . . paid? [Text as printed.]

A carpenter's shop till he was thirty. His skill with tools; the hills of Judea, the meadows, the Lake, sunrises, sunsets and the young moon; his mother, his brothers and sisters, his friends. All these wholly to enjoy . . . until he was thirty; then God, and Man, for as long a time as might be granted him.[11]

An even less edifying appreciation of Schweitzer is exhibited in Clement C. Chesterman's poem entitled "An Elephant in Ebony," which appeared in the book *To Dr. Albert Schweitzer* and contained passages as extravagant as:

> This elephant, conceived in ebony
> Will symbolize as best it can
> Albert Schweitzer, Superman.[12]

It is regrettable that so many books and articles about Schweitzer have been published which do little more than reiterate the timeworn praises, some of them inaccurate and many of them irrelevant, retracing old paths of eulogy until not a shred of living growth is left among them! These renditions of adulation perform a very partial and impermanent service to Schweitzer. Their tendency is to elevate him onto an irrelevant pedestal of romantic heroism, a pedestal which isolates his public image from the real roots of his thought. Such treatments impede the dissemination and influence of Schweitzer's truths, while they perpetuate his fallacies and illusions by protecting them from criticism even while publicizing them.

It is the ingredient of truth in adulatory portrayals of Schweitzer which makes them so misleading. One does think of St. Francis when one encounters Schweitzer. One would do well to consider in all vividness what Albert Schweitzer gave up in order to carry out his desire to serve men directly. And people who hear about Schweitzer in this fashion do acknowledge something great about him, so that when asked on a TV program "who they would most like to be," they might indeed say, "That man in Africa, Albert Schweitzer!" [13] They may even approach a higher level of understanding and say, as an unlettered American road foreman did in 1942, long before Schweitzer became widely renowned in this country, " 'Schweitzer is great because he had the courage to do what we would do if we had the courage.' " [14]

Until people comprehend *why* Schweitzer possesses an ethical vigor lacking in most men, until they understand and follow Schweitzer's injunction to think deeply about the human condition and about the responsibilities and possibilities of their own personal existence, they will continue to say glibly that they admire him and would like to be like him, without having either the discrimination to know what is worth adopting from Schweitzer and what is not, or the *convictions* to motivate them "to do what we would do if we had the courage."

Uncritical adulation of Schweitzer prevents any true understanding of his thought. As Homer Jack has written:

> Those who understand Schweitzer best admire him because he is a man, not a god. They know that, because he is a man, he is not infallible and indeed makes many mistakes as other men do. Some of his supporters, it is true, try to defend his every idea and thus make a cult out of him. Dr. Schweitzer strongly discourages such slavish behavior. [15]

Schweitzer's disavowal of hero-worship is illustrated by his reply to the founders of the Albert Schweitzer College in Churwalden, Switzerland, when they asked him for permission to use his name: he granted permission only on the condition that neither he nor his thought would be shown any partiality in the courses taught there. [16] Thus, Schweitzer's own wishes in regard to his reputation and influence coincide with the obvious demands of scholarship and balanced thinking in ruling out the adulatory attitude exhibited in Norman Cousins's statements: "Respect the image of Schweitzer that exists in the souls of people," and, "If Albert Schweitzer is a myth, the myth is more important than reality." [17]

While avoiding an unthinking praise of Schweitzer, we must avoid equally an unthinking dismissal of the man and

his thought. Much or all of Schweitzer's thought has been
termed "irrelevant" or even has been totally ignored by many
leading theologians, who might have recognized much of their
own thought or learned much which they had not thought, had
they carefully studied Schweitzer. Schweitzer's philosophy of
ethical mysticism, which he himself considers his most important
accomplishment, is frequently ignored even by those theologians
who study and acclaim his scholarly studies of the New Testament. Reinhold Niebuhr applied the adjective "irrelevant" to
Schweitzer's ethical mysticism, when in the fall of 1956 he
sought to discourage me from undertaking a detailed study of
Schweitzer's thought. I have encountered this reaction to
Schweitzer in others. John Baillie, the Scottish theologian, has
said to me of Schweitzer as an ethical theorist: "All I remember
is that after hearing him deliver the Gifford Lectures in French
in 1934, I was awfully sick and tired of hearing about 'respect
de la vie.' " [18]

Contemporary theological literature abounds with such
thoughtless rejections of Schweitzer the philosopher and systematic theologian. Though Emil Brunner has some sympathy with
Schweitzer's concern for lower forms of life, he nevertheless
states flatly that:

> Every kind of ethics is sentimental and finally inhuman whose
> principle is "reverence for life," that is, an undifferentiated conception
> of life itself. . . . Albert Schweitzer's *Kulturphilosophie* . . . whose
> main conception is that of "reverence for life," is a curious and re-
> markable hybrid, composed of the pantheistic mystical attitude towards
> life, represented by *Guyau* and *Fourier,* on the one hand, and the
> Kantian humanistic personalism on the other. Schweitzer's own life-
> work is the most convincing proof of the inadequacy of this concept
> for the basis of an ethical system, since he, as a doctor, is obliged to
> kill a million forms of life in order to preserve human life, and knows
> that in so doing he is acting ethically.[19]

Oscar Cullmann and Peter Vogelsanger agree with Brunner
that there is an inconsistency between Schweitzer's life and his
announced conclusions as a thinker. Vogelsanger praises him
for having rediscovered the primacy of the eschatological

emphasis in the New Testament, but calls his subsequent efforts to de-eschatologize the Gospel and "build up an ethics without Jesus . . . unbiblical." [20] Cullmann agrees:

It is difficult to understand why Albert Schweitzer—and above all, his disciples—while rejecting theologically the element that, from a historical point of view, they have recognized as the center of the New Testament faith, nevertheless persist (in a manner that strikes us as completely inconsistent) in claiming to hold the same faith.[21]

Karl Barth has by no means ignored Schweitzer's ideas. He even contends that "reverence for life" must not be dismissed lightly, as it often has been, on the ground that it is "sentimental." He has called the principle "superb" and entitled a lengthy section of his *Dogmatik* by the phrase. Yet at the same time he criticizes severely the form these insights have taken in Schweitzer's books. Barth believes with Cullmann that the insights achieved by Schweitzer in his biblical studies are inconsistent with his ethical mysticism.[22] Specifically, Barth attacks his exposition of "reverence for life" for being both impractical and insufficiently theological. It is impractical because, as anyone who has ever had direct responsibility for nourishing and housing people knows, there is no harm in cutting down trees, plucking flowers or tearing off leaves.[23] It is insufficiently theological because for Schweitzer the cosmic principle of *life* usurps the authoritative position that rightfully belongs to "God's command." [24]

But the critics just quoted verge on obstinacy in their failure to comprehend Schweitzer's meaning. As H. Beintker has pointed out, it is as great an error to reject Schweitzer from the standpoint of "exegesis-centered theology" or to assume that his interpretation is merely a vapid amalgam of "ethics, humanism, and loving brotherliness" as it is to follow him slavishly.[25]

2. *The Appreciation of Schweitzer*

There are reasons why Schweitzer has not been given the attention he deserves as a serious thinker.

Many of the most substantial writings by or about him have either never been translated into English or never brought forth from the obscurity of esoteric periodicals.

Insubstantial and even misleading writings about him are all too available. How many people form their first impression of him from pictorial articles in popular magazines? They receive the false impression that he, though still brilliant, has put scholarship behind him to devote his full time to his hospital. They are led to believe that he has lost touch with the contemporary intellectual world.

But in reality Schweitzer has maintained contact with the academic communities of Europe by frequently visiting his friends there; and he has kept abreast of modern thinking by reading in Lambarene important new European books which are sent to him there. He recently chided a guest at his Gunsbach home, when the guest displayed surprise at his familiarity with a current theological work:

> Yes, you are surprised that I know about this, aren't you! The learned theologians here in Europe are thinking, "The jungle doctor sits in his hospital down there in Africa and doesn't know what we are thinking and writing up here." Well, let me tell you something—I read it all! [1]

Serious thinkers often neglect Schweitzer's thought because of the formidable ambiguities and apparent contradictions in his writings. How can he be both rational and mystical? Why does he omit reference to God in some of his writings, while dwelling on Christ and the Holy Spirit in others? How can his humanistic concern for civilization be related to his reverence for the lower forms of life, or his wish for civilized progress be reconciled with his failure (until recently) to speak out on the important political issues confronting civilized men today?

Some of these critical questions about his thought can be resolved through a detailed analysis of his words and ideas. Others concern paradoxes which he consciously intends as the most adequate possible statements of complex truths, which would be distorted by too easy a resolution of the tension between the conflicting aspects of the truth in question. Yet other serious questions about his thought address themselves to unconscious and irresolvable paradoxes in his thinking. It is a task of this book to clarify some of the ambiguities in his thought, and further to elucidate the wisdom of some of his paradoxes.

My debt to many competent and scholarly writings about Schweitzer's thought should be obvious. Of books which describe his life as well as the general significance of his thought, George Seaver's justly popular *Albert Schweitzer: The Man and His Mind* deserves special commendation. Of books which deal with his philosophy of life, Oskar Kraus's early work, published in 1926, and Gabriel Langfeldt's recent book are the most penetrating. The latter work inquires whether Schweitzer ought to be regarded as a Christian or not. It should provide rewarding reading to those who find my treatment of the same question either sound or very unsound, since Langfeldt and I draw opposite conclusions from much the same evidence.

But no prior analysis of Schweitzer's ethical mysticism has justly recognized and analyzed its intricate structure. Nor has there been published an appraisal of the significance of his thought which satisfactorily demonstrates its ties with the past and its extraordinary relevence for the present and for the future of civilization. The present study is directed toward these important, difficult and neglected aspects of Schweitzer's ethical mysticism.

II. The Sources of Schweitzer's Thought

3. Signs of Decay in Western Civilization

To appreciate fully the implications of Schweitzer's ethical mysticism, we must examine the background from which his thought emerged and the circumstances which motivated his first work toward a philosophy of civilization. He himself has given us a vivid account of the occasion of his first interest in working out a systematic philosophy of civilization. He writes:

> My first incitement to take up this subject I had received in the summer of 1899 at the house of the Curtius family in Berlin. Hermann Grimm and others were conversing there one evening about a sitting of the academy from which they had just come, when suddenly one of them—I forget which it was—came out with: "Ach, we are all nothing but 'Epigoni' [descendants of great forebears who live on the greatness of the past without contributing anything to it]!" It struck home with me like a flash of lightning, because it put into words what I myself had felt.[1]

As early as fifteen years before World War I had shocked the people of Europe out of their complacent confidence in the upward march of history, Schweitzer was among the few prophetic souls who sensed that decay had set in and was far advanced. The war merely confirmed what had long been visible to perceptive eyes.

What were the symptoms of decay? To answer that question, we must keep in mind the definition of "civilization" which Schweitzer uses as a criterion by which to judge his age. "Civilization," he declares, "I define in quite general terms as spiritual and material progress in all spheres of activity, accompanied by an ethical development of individuals and of mankind."[2] Or, as it is described in *The Decay and Restoration of Civilization*, "it realizes itself in the supremacy of reason, first, over the forces of nature, and secondly, over the dispositions of men."[3] The two important points to be noted are these: the legitimacy, indeed, the indispensability of progress in technological mastery of nature is asserted, and "the ultimate object of civilization" is seen to be "the spiritual and moral perfecting of individuals."[4] The failure of European civilization is not in the field of material progress; on the contrary, the trouble is that the control of reason over the moral disposition of men has not kept pace with its control over nature, and consequently the equilibrium between technological and spiritual progress has been destroyed.[5]

The symptoms of decay, then, are discernible in the qualities of human personality and the types of interaction between persons which characterize the modern world. The first sign of decay, warns Schweitzer, is that increased urbanization and mechanization have brought about separation from the soil, overorganization, overspecialization and a loss of independence and creativity in daily work, which add up to widespread dehumanization of men and women today.[6] Schweitzer finds much wisdom in the Chinese proverb which predicts that men who constantly use machines may soon begin to carry on all their affairs like a machine and thus develop a machinelike heart.[7] Not only do people become accustomed to treating one another as strangers, they even use the new communication media to manipulate one another by means of various kinds of propaganda.[8] Even when interpersonal relations today remain above this level of perversion, they are usually so superficial as to be subhuman:

> How completely the want of thinking power has become second nature in men today is shown by the kind of sociability it produces. When two of them meet for a conversation each is careful to see that the talk does not go beyond generalities or develop into a genuine exchange of ideas. No one has anything of his own to give out, and everyone is haunted by a sort of terror lest anything original should be demanded from him.[9]

A still more distressing sign of decay, in Schweitzer's estimation, is the decline of ethical idealism among the populace of most countries. People have become so callous that they no longer seem capable of voicing righteous indignation against the inhumane ideas that are openly announced and discussed in every land.[10] People have become so cynical that they accept a Machiavellian pursuit of national self-interest on the part of every government as something to be taken for granted.[11] People have become so skeptical about ideals that they readily abandon their hopes for the future of mankind and settle for lesser goals that can be secured without risking disappointment or further disillusionment.[12] The spiritual vitality of Europe is being sapped by pessimism.[13]

Christianity ought to have been a countervailing power in society, to shore up civilization against all the forces which were undermining it. But what Schweitzer saw of Christianity in Europe and Africa gave him little cause to hope that the church was fulfilling this mission. World War I proved decisively that religion was no longer a force in the spiritual life of the age, but even earlier signs pointed to the same verdict.[14] The church had succumbed to "a kind of modern worldliness" in measuring its success in terms of statistical advancement and other external standards of organizational achievement.[15] This inordinate concern for institutional advancement led to an unsavory rivalry among various denominations—and Schweitzer noted that this rivalry "confuses the [African] native and hinders the spread of the Gospel." [16]

Christianity was also prone to stress dogma too much and ethical spirituality too little. Being a Christian ought to mean being "possessed and dominated by a hope of the Kingdom of God, and a will to work for it, which bids defiance to external reality."—but the energy which Christians ought to expend in realizing spiritual ideals in civilization is all too often squandered in a selfish concern for individual redemption.[17] Schweitzer met in his own experience these tendencies in present-day Christianity. His application to work in Africa was almost rejected because the Paris Missionary Society held suspect his unorthodox theological views. He relates that some officials "objected even to the acceptance of a mission doctor who had only correct Christian love, and did not, in their opinion, hold also the correct Christian belief." [18] But the greatest shock came when he announced to his friends his decision to become a doctor in Africa:

My relatives and my friends all joined in expostulating with me on the folly of my enterprise. . . .

In the many verbal duels which I had to fight, as a weary opponent, with people who passed for Christians, it moved me strangely to see them so far from perceiving that the effort to serve the love preached by Jesus may sweep a man into a new course of life, although they read in the New Testament that it can do so, and found it there quite in order. I had assumed as a matter of course that familiarity with the sayings of Jesus would produce a much better appreciation of what to popular logic is nonrational, than my own case allowed me to assert.[19]

Schweitzer also regards the rise of nationalism as one of the most virulent manifestations of decay. He deplores nationalism for disrupting a people's sense of truth and slashing the bonds of brotherhood which should exist among all men.[20] He attacks the loss of objectivity (particularly in regard to a sense of history) which occurs when a nation begins to search for a means of justifying the dictates of *Realpolitik* by "decking them out in a kind of tinsel idealism." [21] He rejects the hunting up of spurious "spiritual affinities" between countries which find it expedient to unite politically, along with the drumming up of far-fetched pretexts for hostility. He sneers at "national civilization" as an unreal abstraction conceived in the minds of politicians to advance their own selfish purposes at home and abroad.[22]

Other symptoms of decline can be observed in the realm of intellectual and esthetic activity. There was a time, argues Schweitzer, when educated persons refused to give credence to ideas that were candidly superstitious—but now such ideas are tolerated and embraced even in cultured circles.[23] This fact indicates that the loss of respect for truth has penetrated into the very core of European civilization. The confusion of mind of

its privileged classes is also reflected in the prevailing love of
"dissonance, in tones, in lines and in thought" that permeates
museum and lecture hall. In Schweitzer's opinion, this love
of dissonance reveals how far away from "right thinking" the
spirit of the age is: "for right thinking is a harmony within
us." [24]

And if the failure of mind and spirit is a symptom of a
rotting civilization, it is even more a cause. Indeed, Schweitzer's
whole *Philosophy of Civilization* might be subtitled "A Description of the Failure of Thought in the Past, and a Prescription for
Sound Ethical Philosophy in the Future." The most important
stimulus motivating Schweitzer to work out his philosophy
systematically was his conviction that civilization is impossible
without a firm intellectual foundation, and that the most basic
cause of the decline in which Europe found herself at the turn
of the century was the inadequacy of nineteeth-century theology
and philosophy.

In search for the reasons why civilization was decaying in
Western society, Schweitzer found himself drawn into a radical
questioning of the presuppositions which had hitherto supported
Western thinking. The symptoms of decline were all condensed
in the fact that the integral bond which had formerly united
ethics with an affirmative attitude toward existence was gradually dissolving. This had not resulted in an immediate loss of
the desire for progress in civilization, but it had produced an
externalization and a disorientation of the desire for progress.[25]
But the root of the illness lay even deeper. When Schweitzer
probed further he discovered that the dissolution of moral
tissue was being caused by shallowness of thought. The modern
attitude—in which optimistic affirmation of life remained, but
from which ethics were disappearing—arose from thought that
was "noble and enthusiastic but not deep":

The intimate connection of the ethical and the affirmative
attitude towards life was for it a matter of feeling and experience
rather than of proof. It took the side of life affirmation and of ethics
without having penetrated their inner nature and their inward
connection.

This noble and valuable view, therefore, being rooted in belief rather than in thinking which penetrated to the real nature of things was bound to wither and lose its power over men's minds.[26]

For Schweitzer the eighteenth century was the golden age of philosophy. It was par excellence the age of reason, the age of optimism, the age of classical balance and order. To be sure, the philosophers and theologians of this period took an insufficiently rigorous attitude toward the problems of civilization and ethics—that is why their synthesis between ethics and belief in progress fell apart before the end of their century. But their instincts were sound, and theirs was the last century in which the power of ideals held sway over the less worthy forces of "realism," which assumed dominance in the nineteenth century.

One of Schweitzer's most interesting appraisals of the intellectual situation at the turn of the century is contained in an untranslated essay, "Philosophy and General Education in the Nineteenth Century," published in 1900.[27] It is brief and is not profound, but many of the themes which he was to elaborate in subsequent books and essays may be discerned in it. In this early essay, we see his concern for the fragmentation of thought in the nineteenth century, a concern that was to become characteristic of his later thinking. Related to this fragmentation, and equally deplorable, was the insistence of most intellectuals that each academic discipline should be autonomous—independent of, and unrelated to, the quests for truth being carried out by other disciplines. Commented Schweitzer:

This is a time that is utterly lacking in philosophic education. The individual disciplines have emancipated themselves: either they feel no need to share in one organic world-view, or else they maintain that they will create for themselves a private philosophy. "Science is power"— that is the slogan which seems to carry the day. But people forget to add that science is not education. We learn from our century that even while scientific knowledge is advancing, the number of educated persons may diminish.[28]

Interestingly enough, Schweitzer accused theology of having isolated itself from other branches of learning and of having thus lost its vitality. This charge is unusual, since many twentieth-century theologians have pilloried nineteeth-century theology for having had *too much* intercourse with secular thought and having thereby lost the uniqueness of the church's gospel. There is ample evidence to support both interpretations. What is characteristic of Schweitzer is that he sided with scientific scholarship against a conventional piety which seeks refuge from the onslaughts of rational investigation in the fortress of traditional dogma. In discussing David Friedrich Strauss's highly controversial work on the life of Jesus, Schweitzer mentions "the feeling of repulsion which German apologetic theology inspired in every genuinely honest and thoughtful man by the methods which it adopted in opposing Strauss." [29] Beyond doubt, he feels a similar scorn for any person who endeavors to protect a static faith by isolating it from reason.

Schweitzer praises sophisticated German theology, especially its inquiry into the problem of the historical Jesus, as "a great, a unique phenomenon in the mental and spiritual life of our time," [30] but he is frankly critical of its errors. *The Quest of the Historical Jesus* catalogues the ways in which Hegelians, Kantians, romanticists and other thinkers have projected their own philosophical presuppositions into their treatments of the life of Jesus. Of Wolfgang Kirchbach's long-forgotten volume, Schweitzer comments:

> Worthless as [it] is from an historical point of view, it is quite comprehensible as a phase in the struggle between the modern view of the world and Jesus. The aim of the work is to retain His significance for a metaphysical and non-ascetic time; and since it is not possible to do this in the case of the historical Jesus, the author denies His existence in favor of an apocryphal Jesus.[31]

Going on, then, to attack the whole lot of metaphysicians and moralists who are attempting to use the historical Jesus for their purposes, Schweitzer writes:

> Men who have no qualifications for the task, whose ignorance is nothing less than criminal, who loftily anathematise scientific theology instead of making themselves in some measure acquainted with the

researches which it has carried out, feel impelled to write a life of Jesus, in order to set forth their general religious view in a portrait of Jesus which has not the faintest claim to be historical, and the most far-fetched of these find favor, and are eagerly absorbed by the multitude.[32]

Schweitzer admires in German scholarship its attempts to overcome dogma with truth. He contends that "the historical investigation of the life of Jesus did not take its rise from a purely historical interest; it turned to the Jesus of history as an ally in the struggle against the tyranny of dogma."[33] At its best, the study of the life of Jesus was ennobled by a "pure faith in the truth, not seeing whereunto it wrought."[34] At its best, this endeavor was "a uniquely great expression of sincerity, one of the most significant events in the whole mental and spiritual life of humanity."[35] But despite these worthy intentions, liberal theologians were unable to find the true historical Jesus because of their determination that He be a particular type of spiritual hero, "the Messiah, who preached the ethic of the Kingdom of God, who founded the Kingdom of Heaven upon earth, and died to give His work its final consecration."[36] In Schweitzer's memorable words,

The study of the life of Jesus has had a curious history. It set out in quest of the historical Jesus, believing that when it had found Him it could bring Him straight into our time as a Teacher and Saviour. It loosed the bands by which He had been riveted for centuries to the stony rocks of ecclesiastical doctrine, and rejoiced to see life and movement coming into the figure once more, and the historical Jesus advancing, as it seemed, to meet it. But He does not stay; He passes by our time and returns to His own. What surprised and dismayed the theology of the last forty years was that, despite all forced and arbitrary interpretations, it could not keep Him in our time, but had to let Him go. He returned to His own time, not owing to the application of any historical ingenuity, but by the same inevitable necessity by which the liberated pendulum returns to its original position.[37]

Because of cowardly isolation, barren speculation and inadequate historical research, nineteenth-century theology had failed to provide either the ethical enthusiasm or the sound rational religious faith needed by civilization. At its worst, Christianity lacked intellectual integrity and breadth of moral vision; at its best, it still lacked the emotional fire, the spiritual thrust, of the eschatological faith proclaimed by Jesus. Schweitzer's earliest, and perhaps his greatest, contribution to theological studies was this emphasis upon eschatological faith, together with his formulation of a Christology characterized by both integrity and ethical power.*

Philosophy, although it too was represented by men of brilliance, had also failed to meet its obligations to civilization. The failures of theological and philosophical thought were closely related, since as Schweitzer had stated in his essay on "Philosophy and General Education in the Nineteenth Century," there can be no morality or religion without good education— and good education is impossible without philosophy.[38]

* See ch. 17.

4. Schweitzer's Debt to Nineteenth-Century Thought

Discussion of Schweitzer's views on nineteenth-century philosophy must begin with Kant, whom Schweitzer considers the dominant philosophical figure of the entire age.[1] It was Kant who initiated the downfall of the naïve optimistic-ethical world-view of the eighteenth century by his insistence that morality be based upon something more solid than inclination or "moral sentiment."[2] His awareness that ethics must spring from "inward compulsion" was a step in the right direction, and he even rendered a service to ethics by his "challenge to profounder reflection on the nature of the ethical and the ethical destiny of man."[3] But "profundity is gained at the cost of vitality," for what actually happened was that Kant destroyed the directness, the simplicity, which had been the glory of eighteenth-century ethics, without re-establishing a morality with sufficient *content* or a sufficiently *compelling* character.[4]

Kant replaced the eighteenth century's emphasis upon "sympathy" as the natural source of morality with his own cold precept of a purely formal objective moral law that exalted the feeling of duty over the natural feeling of compassion that one creature often has toward others.[5] A related flaw in Kant's ethical theory—in Schweitzer's view—is the fact that nonhuman creatures are excluded from the "kingdom of ends" prescribed by Kant's ethics.[6] Kant erred in attempting to combine ethical idealism with epistemological idealism. Schweitzer means by this that Kant tried to build his theory of ethics upon a questionable theory of knowledge: he tried to make morality dependent upon the postulates of God, free will and immortality. Since two of these three postulates (God and immortality) cannot be satisfactorily demonstrated, the entire edifice of moral obligation crumbles.[7] The main gist of Schweitzer's criticism is that Kant's "edifice complex," i.e., his concern to build a foolproof speculative system explaining everything, led him to an ethics lacking in concreteness and vigor.

The same tendency to lose ethical vitality in speculation is exhibited in a much worse degree by three outstanding thinkers

who follow Kant. Fichte carries epistemological idealism to
absurd extremes: he defines ethics as "activity which aims at
subjecting the material world to reason," [8] but he also implies
that ethical action does not differ from the natural course of
events. Everything that occurs is a manifestation of "the
world-spirit's impulse to activity." [9] Schleiermacher also allows
himself to get bogged down in what Schweitzer terms "supra-
ethical" contemplation: he conceives of ethics as a primarily
descriptive discipline, not an activating force.[10] The emascu-
lation of ethics by metaphysical speculation reaches a climax in
Hegel's glorification of the state and in his identification of the
rational with the real. After Hegel, it was inevitable that
general education would despair of philosophy and that other
intellectual disciplines would dissociate themselves from philosophy.[11]

The second major school of ethical philosophy in the
nineteenth century is that of naturalistic thinkers who attempted
to deduce ethics from sociology or biology. The critical flaw
in this school of thought was its inability to see that true
ethics must spring from the heart of the individual, neither
from the customs and legislation of society nor from the brute
force of the "survival of the fittest." Under the influence of this
school, progress was conceived materialistically, and the spiritual
dimension of civilization began to be neglected as never before
in history.[12]

When he traces the development—or the degeneration—of
utilitarianism from Bentham through Mill to Marx, and when he
shows the relationship between utilitarianism and social Darwinism, Schweitzer perceives a progression which might be called
"the irony of utilitarianism." The movement began by abjuring
all interest in nature-philosophy. The utilitarians wanted to be
completely *practical*, to seek nothing more profound than the
greatest happiness of the greatest number, a goal to be
discovered through a calculus of pleasures and pains. But the
calculus of pleasures and pains implied a biological conception
of happiness, and this conception led to social Darwinism's
glorification of nature as a quasi-divine metaphysical principle.
Schweitzer draws from the story this moral:

In its attempt to secure a basis for itself and to think itself out completely [pure utilitarianism] changes into biological-sociological utilitarianism. . . . Although it pretends to be only the practical ethics of human society, it has become a product of nature. . . . No ethics can avoid trying conclusions with nature-philosophy.[13]

Schweitzer devotes even closer criticism to the moral philosophies of Darwin and Spencer. He finds that both of these evolutionists explain and finally replace altruism by a gradually more enlightened egoism. For them, ethics expresses neither natural sympathies nor instincts of benevolence, but only man's evolving realization of the strength to be gained from union with one's own kind, a union requiring mutual interpersonal restraints, civilities and kindnesses. The theory conflicts with Schweitzer's belief that moral obligation is rooted in the sensitive heart of the thoughtful individual. The evolutionist theories would rob ethics of all nobility.

Schweitzer's second criticism of Spencer and Darwin is that naturalistic interpretations of ethics allow realism to triumph over idealism, at least in the present stage of evolution, when altruism has not yet evolved. Altruism in a fully developed form will come in due time, but in the meanwhile men cannot and really should not try to hasten the process along by earnest moral striving. Thus social Darwinism echoes Hegel's assurance that whatever *is*, in the course of history or nature, is rational and right: and both systems are equally supra-ethical.[14]

Another path taken by nineteenth-century ethics led to the philosophy of values and pragmatism. Schweitzer objects strenuously to the implication that ethics might be based on knowledge of what is *valuable for* man (i.e., "useful to," or even "needed by" man) rather than on what is *true about* men. Such a theory would relativize the notion of truth and demolish it, encouraging once again the substitution of the principle of realism for ideals. Moreover, the sense of sincerity would be blunted, and this would be a fatal blow to ethics.[15]

Finally, the excesses of Schopenhauer and Nietzsche are considered. Schweitzer finds much to admire in these two thinkers, and others who fully appreciate the need for ethics to be grounded in the subjective experience of the individual rather than grounded in acquiescence to the morality of society. He admires these two philosophers' avoidance of "abstract cosmic speculations." [16] But Schopenhauer terminates his movement of thought in the supra-ethical, since his stress on pity as the essence of the ethical is really no more than an expression of pessimistic world-denial. One pities other creatures just as one pities oneself: for being doomed to existence in a sorry world that cannot offer happiness for anyone. Nietzsche errs in being too subjective. By focusing all of his attention upon self-fulfilment, he neglects the moral obligations of individuals to others. Nietzsche is one of the greatest of all thinkers in his ability to plumb the depths of life-affirmation, but his thought becomes unethical because of his failure to show how true life affirmation should broaden into world-affirmation.[17]

Schweitzer's criticisms of the shortcomings of previous ethical philosophies constitute but one side of his philosophical development. He also absorbed many methods and principles from some of the philosophers he criticized. Even when he swims against the current of the larger intellectual movements of the nineteenth century, he is unconsciously swept along by them, and perhaps owes more to them than he is willing to acknowledge.

His doctoral dissertation was a study of Kant, the philosopher of the past who probably most influenced him. Schweitzer came under Kant's sway indirectly through Neo-Kantianism's impact upon late nineteenth-century German theology. It was Neo-Kantianism which emphasized *morality* as the crucial ingredient in the Christian life, and, consciously or unconsciously, Albert Schweitzer became a representative of this school of thought. Kant's thought stamped Schweitzer's thought in two more direct respects: it imparted to him the conviction that ethics must be founded on rational thought, and it reinforced his own doctrine of essential human selfhood.

The direct influence of the rational aspect of Kant's ethics is revealed by a comparison of Kant's statement of purpose in his *Fundamental Principles* with Schweitzer's like statement in the preface to *Civilization and Ethics*. Kant writes that he is undertaking a metaphysic of morals because of his conviction that "all moral philosophy rests wholly on its pure part. When applied to man, it does not borrow the least thing from the knowledge of man himself (anthropology), but gives laws a priori to him as a rational being." He is persuaded that this is a momentous undertaking, "because morals themselves are liable to all sorts of corruption as long as we are without that clue and supreme canon by which to estimate them correctly." [18] Schweitzer shares Kant's confidence that "in moral concerns human reason can easily be brought to a high degree of correctness and completeness, even in the commonest understanding." [19] These two cardinal presuppositions underlie Schweitzer's entire philosophical undertaking.

The second important idea which Schweitzer may well have discovered in Kant, or at least had impressed upon him by Kant, is his understanding of man as a creature who has a high moral destiny built into the structure of his being. In *Fundamental Principles* Kant made reference to "the end that nature has in view in regard to humanity." In *Religion Within the Bounds of Reason Alone* he developed this idea into the following chain of reasoning. Man was created good; that is, his original constitution was good, and he was created for a good end.[20] This originally good constitution is more accurately described as an "original capacity for good . . . which consists in respect for the moral law." The goal of the moral life is to raise this capacity to its utmost purity by making the moral law the "supreme principle of all our maxims, by which it is adopted into these not merely in combination with other springs [to conduct] . . . but in its entire purity as a spring *sufficient* of itself to determine the will." [21] How is this goal achieved? On the level of action, it is achieved by the gradual cultivation of "firmness of purpose in following duty." When duty has become a habit, it is called "virtue, as far as legality is concerned, which is its *empirical character* (*virtus phaenomenon*)." [22] This "does not require any *change of heart*, but only a change of morals," and that is not enough. Purity of will must be attained on the level of inward disposition, through a transformation of heart that will make a man "not merely a *legally* but a *morally* good (God-pleasing) man, that is, virtuous in his intelligible character (*virtus noumenon*)."[23] It should be emphasized that although "contending against vices singly, leaving the general root of them untouched" is certainly not the essential element in ethics, nevertheless, good acts, and progressively more of them, are essential in the ethical life:

> that is, when a man reverses the ultimate principle of his maxims by which he is a bad man by a single immutable resolution (and in so doing puts on a new man); then so far he is in principle and disposition a subject susceptible of good; but it is only in continued effort and growth that he is a good man. . . .[24]

We shall encounter the influence of this Kantian doctrine of "the end that nature has in view in regard to humanity" many times as we analyze Schweitzer's ethical mysticism.

From the voluntarists and the vitalists of Germany and France, Schweitzer derived the key concept of his thought system: will-to-live. In discussing his predecessors' uses of this concept, I shall establish what I believe is the correct basis for comprehending the meaning of this term in Schweitzer's ethical mysticism.

Will-to-live is a term that is associated with a school of philosophical speculation known as voluntarism, of which Schopenhauer is probably the foremost German exponent.[25] He is undoubtedly the writer from whom Schweitzer adopted the term, for Schweitzer praises him as the first to perceive that "the essence of things in themselves, which is to be accepted as underlying all phenomena" is will-to-live.[26] So will-to-live is— in its first aspect—the force, the energy, the power that is active in all things which have being; it is the ultimate reality of the cosmos, and all existing things exist only so long as and because will-to-live is operating in them. When speaking of will-to-live in this cosmic sense, Schweitzer often calls it (as in the above quotation) "universal will-to-live" or "infinite will-to-live," and sometimes he substitutes "Creative Force" or "Creative Will." Will-to-live is—in its second aspect—"the first fact of thought," the most immediate datum of self-consciousness in human beings. And in Schweitzer, as in Schopenhauer, the reality of all phenomena is inferred to be will-to-live because the fundamental reality of one's own self is experienced as will-to-live.[27]

But for Schopenhauer the will-to-live, both within the individual and in the universe, was a blind, purposeless drive; therefore, he agreed with many Eastern sages that the only way to escape from the torment of this insatiable force is to deny it, to retreat from desire by becoming detached from the world. Schweitzer parts company from Schopenhauer at this point, for two principal reasons. First, Schweitzer does not regard will-to-live as a simple, indivisible entity: when he speaks of will-to-live in human beings, he regards it as having a higher and a lower dimension, a spiritual and a material aspect, and he speaks of a "higher life-affirmation" which involves the partial negation of the will-to-live in the interest of "self-perfection." And second, he does not agree with Schopenhauer's opinion that asceticism is higher than ethics, or that "everything which helps to deaden the will-to-live" is good.[28] He believes, on the contrary, that life is intrinsically good and ought to be affirmed.

It is in regard to life-affirmation that Schweitzer takes a leaf from Nietzsche's notebook. He agrees with Nietzsche that life itself is honored in the affirmation of any individual life, and that this is true, in a profound teleological sense, because will-to-live is not only a drive to *be,* but a drive to be *fulfilled.* As Nietzsche proclaimed, human will-to-live is not an uninhibited savage spontaneity, but a disciplined will-to-power in the sense of a demand for power over oneself, for *self-mastery.* Thus Schweitzer lauds Nietzsche for condemning the superficiality of morality which springs from the needs of society instead of from the inner demand of the individual will-to-live for self-perfection: "Individual morality comes before social morality. Not what it means for society, but what it means for the perfecting of the individual, is the first question which has to be put." [29]

However, in Schweitzer's view, Nietzsche went astray in failing to accept the fact that *higher* life-affirmation does require "the repressing of natural impulses and natural claims on life, and is thereby in some way or other connected with life negation." [30] Schweitzer admits that Nietzsche's later writings reflect an exaltation of the demonic "superman, who asserts himself triumphantly against all fate, and seeks his own ends without any consideration for the rest of mankind"—but he tries to absolve Nietzsche of blame on the grounds that the poor man was already half-insane when he penned these depraved works. [31]

Nietzsche's misunderstanding of higher-life-affirmation was corrected to a significant degree by Georg Simmel, a Berlin professor under whom Schweitzer studied for a short period of time while still an undergraduate. According to Martin Werner, dean of Schweitzer's European interpreters, Simmel helped to implant in his young student's mind the conviction that will-to-live manifests itself in man as a drive towards *self-transcendence*. [32] This means that self-perfection seeks to overcome the *actual* self of any given moment, in order that one may become the higher self that he is *potentially*. [33] Self-transcendence leads one into a mystical unity with the universal will-to-live, an all-encompassing spiritual force which bears a striking similarity to Bergson's God, whom Bergson defines as life itself acting in all things. Schweitzer and Bergson agree further that the cosmic force is not blind but purposive, and that there is a sharp dichotomy between matter and spirit. [34]

Schweitzer credits two relatively obscure French thinkers, Fouillée and Guyau, with having appreciated more than did others of their time the notion that devotion of oneself to the nurture of other persons is not a surrender of the self (as Nietzsche would have contended), but rather "a manifestation of its expansion." [35] Fouillée is applauded for his dictum, "Act towards others as if you became conscious of them at the same time as you become conscious of yourself." [36] Guyau is considered notable for having emphasized that "real living consists not only in receiving, but in giving out of oneself as well." [37] Thus does Hume's notion of sympathy receive a heightened expression. [38] This expansion of the self through altruism differs from utilitarianism's equation between altruism and enlightened egoism in that this ethic of self-devotion has its source in spiritual meditation on the meaning of one's own experience of his life, whereas the utilitarian ethic is a product of merely prudential calculation. In Kantian terms, this is to say that Fouillée and Guyau present a categorical imperative that is experienced inwardly, whereas utilitarianism offers only a hypothetical imperative dictated by a desire for outward happiness.

Possibly Schweitzer's greatest intellectual affinity is with a predecessor who was neither an academic philosopher nor a radical voluntarist: Goethe. Whether Schweitzer adopted any specific terms or concepts from Goethe remains quite uncertain, although the doctor's great admiration for Goethe's *Wilhelm Meister* has led many of Schweitzer's readers to assume that his concept of "reverence" was drawn from that work. Both the marked similarity between the thought of the two men and Schweitzer's expression of his debt to Goethe in very sweeping terms suggest that Schweitzer's praise for the famous author's insights is in large measure a statement of his own position. Surely Schweitzer's own understanding of human will-to-live as a compound of matter and spirit is revealed in this comment on Goethe's view:

Looking with the eyes of the spirit upon nature, as it is within ourselves, we find that in us also there is matter and spirit. Searching into the phenomena of the spirit in us, we realize that we belong to the world of the spirit, and that we must let ourselves be guided by it. . . . The spirit is light, which struggles with matter, which represents darkness. What happens in the world and within ourselves is the result of this encounter.[39]

The terminology employed by Schweitzer to express his ethical mysticism is also derived from the German philosophic tradition. An explanation of his use of the terms "world-view" and "life-view" will clarify the perspectives that dominate his thought; an explanation of his use of the term "ethical world-and life-affirmation" will clarify the intention which motivates and guides his activity as moral philosopher.

WORLD-VIEW AND LIFE-VIEW

According to Lee Ellerbrock, an American Schweitzer scholar whose mother tongue is German, the word *Lebensanschauung* (life-view, view of life) refers to the subjective outlook of any human being as to "what his life means to him and what purpose he wishes to give to his life." [40] In a more general sense it refers to the conception that one has of the meaning of human life as a whole. The important thing to note here is that a life-view is restricted in scope and that it is the result of a free decision on the part of the individual concerned. [41]

The reference of the German word *Weltanschauung,* variously rendered as "world-view," "view of the world," "theory of the universe" and "conception of the universe" in the English version of Schweitzer's *Philosophy of Civilization,* is normally expanded to include the entire cosmos and all that it contains. A world-view would normally include a life-view: one's interpretation of the structure and meaning of the universe would define one's conception of human life, including one's interpretation of his personal existence. But Schweitzer is at pains to repudiate this conventional meaning of "world-view" and to develop a different conception, more limited in scope and more thoroughly ethical in content. To do this, he uses the German word *Totalweltanschauung* in the opening chapter of his work to designate the kind of world-view which he regards as impossible of attainment. [42] He believes that Western ethical philosophy has gone wrong in seeking to achieve a life-view by elaborating such a "total view of the universe." Ethical philosophers should have confined themselves, as he proposes to confine himself, to the limited world-view which can grow out of a life-view. A "total" or "closed" world-view is fraudulent precisely because it purports to ground itself in *certain knowledge* of the universe and purports to constitute an explanation of all cosmic mysteries. Opposed to such a world view is Schweitzer's "open" world-view, which is based upon a prior life-view and which claims to illuminate only the relationship of the individual man to Cosmic Reality. [43]

ETHICAL WORLD- AND LIFE-AFFIRMATION

"Affirmation" conveys more than mere "acceptance." It implies ratification or confirmation by the affirming person. The affirmer of world and life is he who says, "Yes!" to the existence of the whole creation and his existence in it. He need not be entirely happy with the details of the created world or the details of his own existence. Still, he will not maintain that it would have been better had the universe not come into being at all. Nor will he cry with Milton's Lucifer, "I will not serve!" and seek to extricate himself from life altogether. He believes that "life is worth living," as we commonly say.

And *ethical* world- and life-affirmation has an additional aspect which raises it above even ratification and confirmation: it involves active participation in the effort to help life flourish in the world. Since the "world" includes all forms of life, Schweitzer often uses the single term "world-affirmation" to imply ethical self-devotion to one's fellow creatures.[44]

Schweitzer's residual intellectual debts to the nineteenth century, over and above the technical philosophic debts which have been discussed, cluster together under his belief in progress. His idealistic optimism about the possibilities for progress in human affairs is an obvious product of late nineteenth-century liberalism.[45] He rejoices that he is privileged to be a worker for the "coming Era of Peace," and he speaks of the Kingdom of God as a possibility within history.[46] He admits that there would be little hope for progress "if the man of today is taken as an example of the race"; however, he leaves room for hope by asserting that contemporary man is a "pathological phenomenon." [47] His very definition of civilization includes "a belief in progress that is destined to include all men, and the recognition of duties and responsibilities for the individual and society which such a belief involves.[48] He even ventures to predict that "Sooner or later there must dawn the true and final Renaissance which will bring peace to the world." [49]

Schweitzer's hopes for civilization depend in large measure upon his analysis of the capacity of human reason to think its way clearly to the truth, and the further capacity of the human individual, having attained truth, to act upon it and do the good. He concedes that mankind is falling into material as well as spiritual misery because of its renunciation of thought, but he remains optimistic because of his unshakable faith that "the spirit generated by truth" can triumph over "the force of circumstances." [50] In his Nobel Prize address of 1954 he affirmed that:

> The human spirit is not dead; it lives on in secret. Compelled to live on without that knowledge of the world which would correspond to its ethical character, it has contrived to do so. It had understood that it must base itself on nothing but the essential character of man. Now, independent of all other knowledge, it is the stronger for that independence.[51]

But is this hidden spirit of humanity strong enough? Schweitzer answers in the affirmative: "I am convinced, intellectually convinced, that the human spirit in our time is capable of creating a new attitude of mind: an attitude based upon ethics." [52] And in a recent letter to some young people in Germany, who expressed their skepticism as to whether he was familiar enough with their problems to understand them, he replied that it was his fervent hope that they would preserve their faith in humanity. He enjoined them to forget the injustices and follies of the past and present, and to concentrate on realizing their membership in another, better, more spiritual world, "striving after the inward piety which Jesus directed us to in His words." [53]

Yet Schweitzer is no blind optimist. He is an exponent of what D. D. Williams has called "liberalism at its best" [54] in that he most indubitably does not expect progress to come easily or automatically. He explicitly rejects the notion that "the miracle" will certainly come to pass of its own inner compulsion "in a steady and slow development." [55] His "willing and hoping are optimistic," but his "knowledge is pessimistic." [56] He is aware of the fact that social evils are caused not only by bad institutions but also by bad men, and when he speaks in religious language he owns that men are not merely weak or ignorant but *sinners*.[57] He realizes, then, that there is no certain correlation between knowledge and virtue, that human reason is not an all-sufficient power for good in the world. In 1950 Schweitzer warned:

> We are at the beginning of the end of the human race. . . . So long as its capacity for destruction was limited, it was possible to hope that reason would set a limit to disaster. Such an illusion is impossible today, when its power is illimitable. Our only hope is that the Spirit of God will strive with the spirit of the world and will prevail.[58]

The foregoing analysis of the background from which Schweitzer's ethical mysticism emerged gives us some helpful insights into the problems which he hopes to solve and the goals which he hopes to reach in his endeavor to frame a more adequate moral philosophy. His chief problem will be to combine the compelling authority of Kant's altogether rational, altogether objective system, with the profound and ardent subjectivity of men such as Schopenhauer and Nietzsche. He will be seeking an ethic which grows out of the individual's experience of his own will-to-live; on the other hand, he must come out with an *ought* that makes the self-expansion of self-devotion a necessity of thought, and therefore equally binding on all rational beings. He will not be satisfied with an ethic which excludes sub-human forms of life from the circle of compassion, for such an ethic has been condemned as disgracefully partial. Finally, since he regards the present state of Christianity as an aberration, a falling away from its former devotion to the ideal of the Kingdom of God, he will hope to find an ethic which can revitalize the church by restoring to it a vital notion of the Christian life.

III. The Structure of Ethical Mysticism

5. Ethical Mysticism in Outline

The detailed analysis of Albert Schweitzer's ethical mysticism must begin with a sketch of the broad outlines of the system, as Schweitzer himself has drawn them. This sketch will include a description of the argumentation by means of which Schweitzer attempts to establish reverence for life as a "necessity of thought"; i.e., that attitude which any thinking man will achieve if he engages in what Schweitzer calls "elemental thinking." It will include also a discussion of the three principal characteristics of reverence for life: rationality, absoluteness and universality.

Elemental thought is thought "which starts from the fundamental questions about the relations of man to the universe, about the meaning of life, and about the nature of goodness." [1] Such thinking has been rendered impossible throughout the history of Western philosophy because of Western man's erroneous assumption that world- and life-affirmation must be logically deduced from knowledge about the world. From this assumption it followed that an intelligent purposive meaning must be attributed to the universe as a whole before the meaningfulness of human life can be established. Western thought erred in deriving its life-view from its world-view.[2] This approach is futile since our knowledge of the world gives no grounds for belief that the universe is "working purposefully" toward any "coordinated, definite end" whatsoever, much less toward the same end for which mankind is striving.[3] Schweitzer writes:

If we take the world as it is, it is impossible to attribute to it a meaning in which the aims and objects of mankind and of individual men have a meaning also. Neither world- and life-affirmation nor ethics can be founded on what our knowledge of the world can tell us about the world. In the world we can discover nothing of any purposive evolution in which our activities can acquire a meaning. Nor is the ethical to be discovered in any form in the world-process. . . . To understand the meaning of the whole—and that is what a [total] world-view demands!—is for us an impossibility. The last fact which knowledge can discover is that the world is a manifestation, and in every way a puzzling manifestation, of the universal will-to-live.[4]

The enlightened mind's first step is an act of resignation: it relinquishes its longing for complete knowledge about the universe. All world-views claiming to explain "the whole" of the world-process are necessarily "artificial," pretentious "fabrications" illegitimately projecting human wishes onto the clouded screen of the cosmos. The first stage in the ascent to enlightenment is the "learned ignorance" of the wise man, who acknowledges the barriers beyond which he may not venture.[5]

But skepticism concerning knowledge of the world, Schweitzer insists, must not produce cynicism.[6] An optimistic-ethical outlook on *life* does not depend upon an optimistic-ethical interpretation of the *world*. Life-view is prior to world-view, despite the contrary teaching of previous philosophers. He who turns his attention away from the world into himself, into his own inner experience, and meditates deeply upon the reality he finds there, will emerge with a life-view that justifies world- and life-affirmation as well as ethics:

The solution is not to try to get rid of dualism from the world, but to realize that it can no longer do us any harm. This is possible, if we leave behind us all the artifices and unveracities of thought and bow to the fact that, as we cannot harmonize our life-view and our world-view, we must make up our minds to put the former above the latter. The volition which is given in our will-to-live reaches beyond our knowledge of the world. What is decisive for our life-view is not our knowledge of the world but the certainty of the volition which is given in our will-to-live. The eternal spirit meets us in nature as mysterious creative power. In our will-to-live we experience it within us as a volition which is both world- and life-affirming and ethical. . . . World-view is a product of life-view, not vice-versa.[7]

Schweitzer speaks with such naive, matter-of-fact assurance of the ability of an individual to find all that he needs for a "noble and valuable" life-view within himself, we are almost persuaded that he does not realize what an audacious claim he is making. He concurs with Goethe in the belief that man must be moral because of an "inner necessity" which is "a part of his being." [8]

His explanation of the steps by which thought directed inward reaches its goal is equally naive and matter-of-fact. Schweitzer holds that these steps are the natural course taken by "elemental thinking" in the mind of a reflective person who has been freed from intellectual "artifices and unveracities." [9] The primary datum of self-conscious reflection is not Descartes' "I think, therefore I exist"—it is rather "the more elemental and much more comprehensive 'I am life which wills to live in the midst of life that wills to live.' " [10] A by-product of this initial act of thought is a deepened sense of resignation, resignation in the face of all the elements of existence which, even if one can *know* them, one cannot *control*.

The second step toward ethical wisdom is to acknowledge reverence for one's own will-to-live. All of us must be endowed with "an instinctive reverence for life," since even the "pessimistic facts of knowledge" about the world do not suggest suicide to the normal man. "So long as we are comparatively in our right mind" we must reject this option, for we have "an instinctive feeling of repulsion from such a deed." [11] Schweitzer's treatment is distinctive in its application of "reverence" to the admittedly *instinctive* drive for self-preservation.

Schweitzer summarizes the import of the first two steps of elemental thinking in the following memorable passage:

> Thus if we ask, "What is the immediate fact of my consciousness?". . . we find the simple fact of consciousness is this, I will to live. Through every stage of life, this is the one thing that I know about myself. I do not say, "I am life"; for life continues to be a mystery too great to understand. I only know that I cling to it. I fear its cessation—death. I dread its diminution—pain. I seek its enlargement—joy.[12]

The third step of elemental thought is the definition of the good as the maintenance, furtherance and fullest development of life.[13] And this definition of the good must be applied to other forms of life as well as to oneself:

What shall be my attitude toward this other life which I see around me? It can only be of a piece with my attitude toward my own life. If I am a thinking being, I must regard other life than my own with equal reverence. For I know that it longs for fullness and deepness of development as deeply as do I myself.[14]

Such an attitude toward life is already ethical since ethics "grow out of the same root as world- and life-affirmation, for ethics, too, are nothing but reverence for life."[15]

The first specific characteristic of the philosophy of reverence for life is its *rationality*. Schweitzer affirms that reverence for life is a "necessity of thought" and that whoever earnestly "explores the depths of thought must arrive at this point." "To be truly rational is to become ethical."[16] When Schweitzer is confronted with the question why reverence for life was not long ago recognized to be the basis of rational thought, if it is such a reasonable and necessary attitude, he answers that "thought fears such an ethic." And he is more interested in affirming the truth of reverence for life than in discussing why more thinkers have not seen the truth:

This is an absolute and reasonable ethic. Whether such-and-such a man arrives at this principle, I may not know. But I know that it is given inherently in the will-to-live. Whatever is reasonable is good. This we have been told by all the great thinkers.[17]

By the *absoluteness* of the ethic of reverence for life Schweitzer means that ethics must always be striving for the ideal, never resting content with what is merely possible. He uses the term "absolute" as opposite not to "relative," but to the "practicable." He admits that reverence for life is an ideal that cannot be perfectly realized, but he believes it important that an absolute claim be placed upon men to be ethical. His ethics contain no casuistry of specific rules for every foreseeable situation, no maximum or minimum limits to what we must or must not do. His ethics simply confront us with the fact that "we are responsible for the lives about us." [18]

The third specific characteristic of reverence for life is its *universality*. Here Schweitzer's ethics show originality, for as he himself remarks sadly in both *Civilization and Ethics* and *Indian Thinkers,* virtually all Occidental philosophers, and many Oriental philosophers as well, have limited ethical concern to human relationships.[19] Schweitzer grants that "We happen to believe that man's life is more important than any other form of which we know," but he adds that such comparative evaluations cannot be proved and that above all we must never allow ourselves to believe of any form of life, "This has no value!" [20] And he refuses to draw a sharp line between the living and the nonliving, even stating in one passage that ice crystals fall within the province of wills-to-live which must be reverenced. "In and behind all phenomena there is will-to-live." [21]

This recognition of volition or "will-to-live" in all phenomena orients Schweitzer's ethics toward mysticism. *Voluntarism* combines with the *universality* of reverence for life to make his ethics *mystical,* not merely systematic. His system of ethics is *ethical mysticism,* for it offers the possibility of union with the infinite: "Whenever my life devotes itself in any way to life, my finite will-to-live experiences union with the infinite will in which all life is one." [22]

Mystical unity with the infinite is attained through serving and cooperating with the Creative Will of the universe, not through attempting to understand it.

> Only by serving every kind of life do I enter the service of the Creative Will whence all life emanates. . . . It is through community of life, not community of thought, that I abide in harmony with that Will. This is the mystical significance of ethics.[23]

How can Schweitzer treat reverence for life as both mystical and rational? How can anything mystical be a "necessity of thought?" Rationality and mysticism are complementary, not contradictory, in his view. He believes that thought becomes artificial, and therefore irrational, when it seeks to establish ethics upon a nonmystical basis of certain knowledge about the universe. Further, thought is superficial, and therefore again irrational, when it neglects to "penetrate to the depths." Thought must push forward into a suprarational "experience of the universe" which is rooted in rationality, yet goes beyond it. "The ethical mysticism of Reverence for Life is rationalism thought to a conclusion." [24]

Schweitzer's inquiry, which began in the renunciation of any hope for a knowledge of the world which could support an optimistic-ethical world-view, and continued by affirming the life-view inherent in the finite will-to-live, finally arrives at a mystical relatedness to the universal will-to-live, a relatedness which assures a word-view of ethical world- and life-affirmation. The inquiry arrives at a conclusion which Schweitzer states concisely:

From an inner necessity, I exert myself in producing values and practising ethics in the world even though I do not understand the meaning of the world. For in world- and life-affirmation and in ethics I carry out the will of the universal will-to-live which reveals itself in me. I live my life in God, in the mysterious divine personality which I do not know as such in the world, but only experience as mysterious Will within myself.[25]

6. The Ethic of Self-Perfection

We have seen in the outline of ethical mysticism that Schweitzer's starting point in philosophical reflection is the awareness, "I am will-to-live in the midst of other wills-to-live." Reverence for life includes reverence for one's own life. Therefore the preachers of life-denial, Schopenhauer and the Indian philosophers, are in the wrong.[1] As Nietzsche insisted, life itself (the universal will-to-live, the Creative Force in all phenomena) is honored in one's affirmation of his own life, and to deny one's own will-to-live is to dishonor in one's own existence as a free being the purposes of Creation.[2] Inclusive of but larger than life-affirmation is world-affirmation: concern for the welfare of all life which manifests itself in the world. Since individual lives and life-affirmation often come into conflict with one another, world-affirmation necessarily introduces life-negation within one's affirmation of his own life. But life-affirmation which does not expand into world-affirmation is no better than life-denial.[3] "Life-affirmation and life-negation are both for a certain distance ethical; pursued to a conclusion they become unethical." [4] "The ethical is a mysterious combination of the two." [5]

The goal of self-perfection, different for each individual but still the destiny toward which all life and especially human life should move, is equilibrium between the healthy affirmation of one's own life and the ethical disciplining of one's own life, in the interest of other lives. This ideal conceals an ambiguity, if not a contradiction, in Schweitzer's thought: the prime agent in self-perfection is sometimes identified as the human self, but at other times it is identified as an outside force, the Holy Spirit.

That the Holy Spirit is the prime agent in human perfection is indicated in a letter from Schweitzer to a group of English children in which he speaks of "God's voice of love speaking to us in the secret places of our hearts." [6] A more considered statement on the efficacy of the Holy Spirit is found in a usually neglected sermon by Schweitzer.[7] He likens the Spirit to a river which only gradually becomes strong enough to fill the hearts of men and manifest its force in them. "It is difficult, of course, to open our hearts to the Holy Spirit. The Holy Spirit is strange to us. It wishes to control our lives. . . . We must seek to possess it." The implication that the Spirit is not to be identified with anything already given in man's nature is made even stronger in these sentences: "The Holy Spirit is not the spirit of ordinary men. *We become another kind of being.* Indeed we must be born again through the Holy Spirit" (author's italics). It is the Holy Spirit which "brings happiness to our hearts."

Yet Schweitzer often seems to propound a doctrine of immanence. He consistently interprets Goethe in this light, as when he understands the message of Goethe to be "Let man fulfill the good that is in his personality and thereby become truly himself." [8] Even in the sermon on the Holy Spirit there are sentences which imply that man himself is the key agent in the process of rebirth. The reference to "ordinary men" suggests men who simply have not become enlightened enough or energetic enough to realize the potentialities that exist within them already. After the sentences quoted above Schweitzer declares, "We must decide that we will be different from others. Every day we must fight . . . everyone of you must strive. . . ." And in certain passages of *Civilization and Ethics* he emphasizes that the perfection towards which the will-to-live strives is a characteristic that belongs to it by definition, a characteristic with which "it is endowed." In man, particularly, "the craving for perfection is given" in our very being. We cannot ascertain how or why this striving originated within us, but one thing is certain: "it is given with our existence. We must act upon it if we would not be unfaithful to the mysterious will-to-live which is within us." [9]

Whatever the source of the impulse to self-perfection, it can be stated with certainty that, for Schweitzer, this impulse is not a self-seeking ideal, but is rather a "higher life-affirmation" which "exerts itself to take up life-negation into itself in order to serve other living beings by self-devotion, and to protect them, even, it may be, by self-sacrifice." [10] In the struggle toward self-perfection, I must "recognize it as the destiny of my existence to be obedient to this higher revelation of the will-to-live in me."[11] It is this "higher revelation" that differentiates human will-to-live from animal or vegetable will-to-live:

> Nature knows only a blind affirmation of life. The will-to-live which animates natural forces and living beings is concerned to work itself out unhindered. But in man this natural effort is in a state of tension with a mysterious effort of a different kind, namely, the urge to self-devotion.[12]

Let us now turn from the origins and form to the specific content of Schweitzer's ideal of self-perfection.

The claim of the self to its own right for reverence is considered legitimate. Schweitzer once dismissed some overly aggressive American reporters who had quizzed him for hours by reminding them that his will-to-live deserved some consideration too, and that what it craved at the moment was some privacy and relaxation.[13] One's sense of responsibility to other life should make one frugal and diligent, but rigid ascetic disciplines of a monastic sort are not recommended by Schweitzer. He rides third-class trains because there is no fourth-class (although now he must ride second-class because there is no longer any third-class!), but he has never stated that everyone who reverences life must do the same. "The ethics of reverence for life . . . offer us no rules about the extent of the self-maintenance which is allowable."[14] Schweitzer is married. He has imported to Lambarene certain European foods which are common in Europe but an expensive treat in the tropics.[15] Self-perfection does require an unswerving devotion to duty, a devotion such as that which has separated Schweitzer from his family for a good part of his life. It involves a vocational asceticism that

> forbid[s] me to still my conscience with the reflection that, as the more efficient man, by quite legitimate means I am advancing myself at the cost of one who is less efficient than I. . . . It bid[s] me think of others, and makes me ponder whether I can allow myself the inward right to pluck all the fruit that my hand can reach.[16]

Full self-development requires contact with nature. Schweitzer shares with many men of his own generation, and with some social critics of a younger generation, great concern lest the industrializing and organizing of life should separate men from the soil in which they have their roots and from the air which is necessary to both the life of the body and the life of the spirit.[17] From direct contact with nature (the firsthand study of flora and fauna, open air walks and relaxing meditation) comes awareness that nature's mysteries and beauties are not exhausted by the description of natural laws which scientific man so confidently elaborates. Schweitzer is grateful to a high-school science teacher for leading him to revere the forces of nature as ultimate mysteries before which man must stand in wonder.[18]

A series of "common virtues" are also part of Schweitzer's definition of self-perfection: honesty, self-control, patience, gratitude, forgiveness, humility and diligence and thoroughness in the performance of daily tasks.[19]

Honesty is one of the virtues which Schweitzer prizes most highly, and in his understanding of this trait are included its corollaries: sincerity, and faith in the power of truth to conquer falsehood and dissimulation.[20] His genuinely profound understanding of honesty manifested itself in the way he met the challenge made by the Paris Missionary Society against his heretical tendencies. Instead of taking an inflexible "Here I stand; I can do no other" stance before the committee as a whole (a tactic which he knew would lead to his rejection), he visited each member separately and really opened up his heart in private.[21] The allegation often heard, that he violated his promise to the society to be "mute as a carp" if they allowed him to go under its auspices, is incorrect. As he relates in his autobiography, he was released from this promise to the society by its local representatives, who were very little interested in the "questions of dogma on which the Missionary Society's committee in Paris had laid so much weight," and with whom Schweitzer felt himself "united in the piety of obedience to Jesus, and in the will to simple Christian activity." [22] It might be mentioned, though, that Schweitzer is flexible enough in the matter of practicing justifiable deception to overcome the exigencies of some difficult situations. For example, when he and his wife were being moved from Africa to a prison camp in France during World War I, they sewed money into the lining of their coats in order to avoid its being confiscated by the guards! [23] On another occasion, he is reported to have helped an American visitor get a seat in a concert which he was giving that had been completely sold out, by distracting the attention of the ticket taker long enough for his friend to slip in! [24]

Self-control is pivotal. Schweitzer himself had considerable difficulty in cultivating this, apparently, for he relates that as a child he had to resolve to quit playing cards because of the violent outbursts of temper the game involved him in! [25] He gave up smoking because he felt that the habit was mastering him to an extent that was not good for his independence as a person.[26] But Schweitzer does not allow self-control to weaken the warm bonds of compassionate love which bind persons together. He reports that as a doctor he is unable to discipline himself to forget one patient who has been treated and go on to another who has not yet been treated, or to conserve his energies in a spirit of utilitarian efficiency by putting his patients out of his mind when he is away from them.[27] It is difficult to determine whether he wishes he could control himself to that extent. His well-known prejudice against the utilitarian spirit [28] indicates that in his opinion he would be doing violence to his humanity to carry self-control so far.

Patience is another important common virtue. Schweitzer learned its importance very early: he had joined with other village boys in tormenting an old Jewish gentleman, but was soon made to feel ashamed of himself by the calm forbearance of the old man.[29] Schweitzer has had occasion in later years to appreciate patience, both in himself and in others. He had to endure what he describes as an almost unbearable torture at the hands of the well-meaning friends who tried to dissuade him from going to Africa.[30] He is very grateful for the patience once shown his wife and himself while they were prisoners. The police in charge of moving them to another camp came at an earlier hour than expected, but graciously allowed the

Schweitzers to gather together their possessions before moving.[31]

Gratitude, too, is essential to self-perfection. Schweitzer frequently complains of ingratitude in the natives with whom he works. He laments that these "children of nature," accustomed to sustaining their lives by filling their needs from the bounties of nature, fail to understand that the resources of the hospital are limited and that every beneficiary must contribute to the needs of the hospital.[32] Gratitude was one of the chief motives Schweitzer expressed for his decision to go to Africa. It is also the word he consistently uses to describe his attitude toward his own good health and his opportunities to carry out his vocation.[33] The doctor's expression of gratitude to his wife for her willingness that he turn down a chair at the University of Zurich, offered him in 1920, to return to Lambarene is touching: "I have never ceased to be thankful that she made the sacrifice of agreeing, under these circumstances, to my taking up once again the work at Lambarene." [34]

Forgiveness is incumbent upon every person because everyone is in need of forgiveness.[35] But Schweitzer is aware that forgiveness can be superficial and may act as the cloak of unresolved resentment or hostile pride.[36]

It is axiomatic that *humility* is essential, especially for those who have had the good fortune to be free enough from the responsibilities of life to follow through with their destined self-devotion to others.[37] This is a trait which Schweitzer seems to exhibit marvelously well in his own life. Fritz Wartenweiler relates how Schweitzer, as a young man preaching in St. Nicholas Church in Strasbourg during the period 1901-1913, used to preface many of his remarks from the pulpit with apologies for his lack of experience and requests for a charitable attitude on the part of his hearers.[38] Another Strasbourg citizen who knew Schweitzer as a young professor recalls that he was unusually prompt, polite and respectful of his students' personalities, always endeavoring to convey his ideas without forcing his own personality upon others.[39]

His humility is often indistinguishable from his concentration upon the task or purpose at hand. Many have first recognized in Schweitzer's concentration his full intellectual and moral stature. Archibald T. Davison made this recognition when he observed him filling in as conductor during a rehearsal:

> Turning his back squarely upon both orchestra and chorus, one hand thrust in his trousers pocket, his head back, staring up into the dark of the Salle Gaveau, his arm moving in awkward sweeps and unorthodox directions, it was quite obvious that if he gave himself a thought—which I doubt—it was only to consider himself the agent who should bring the music to life. . . . Above all, there was complete detachment; entire absorption in the sound of the music. To this day I can remember the intense admiration I felt for Schweitzer's indifference to externals.[40]

For years, Schweitzer refused to allow a movie about his life to be made; when he finally consented, he insisted on writing the script himself to insure that there was no hero worship in it.[41] When notified that he had received the Nobel Peace Prize, he commented, "No man has the right to pretend that he has worked enough for the cause of peace or to declare himself satisfied"—whereupon he broke off the interview to tend to a patient with a broken leg.[42]

Finally, *diligence* and thoroughness in the performance of one's daily tasks is a vital part of self-perfection.[43] This is not a surprising ideal in Schweitzer, brought up as he was in an Alsatian Protestant parsonage in the nineteenth century. His own diligence was revealed in the thoroughness and freshness which characterized his lectures even after his resolve to become a doctor.[44] Diligence is further evident in the painstaking scholarship of his books on Bach, the historical Jesus and Pauline mysticism.[45] Unfortunately, the same thoroughness does not strike the reader of his two volumes on the philosophy of civilization—but perhaps it should be said in Schweitzer's defense that he expressly disavows the meticulous scholarly approach in these two volumes, hoping to illuminate the significant content of the history of thought and the predicament of modern civilization by stressing only the aspects which he considers important for ethics and life-affirmation.

Schweitzer places great emphasis on the importance of the inner development of man's intellectual, aesthetic and spiritual potential. Intellectual development includes study of what other men have thought in the past: "To read a good book is to become a man." [46] Even more essential in one's development as a full-fledged human being is thought concerning the meaning of existence. Such "elemental thinking" about nature, God and man is not only a *means* towards the ultimate end of more responsible citizenship in the world community; it is also an *end* in itself. [47] Even if thought terminates in despair or a false theory of the universe, it is better to have grappled with the fathomless questions of life and not solved them properly than never to have meditated on them at all. [48] "Thinking is a harmony within us." [49] To accept thoughts from others without digesting and testing them thoroughly oneself is a betrayal of one's true being. [50] And thinking elementally is possible for all human beings, no matter how simple their culture or their training may be. Elemental thought may even be easier for people less affected by modern industrial civilization. [51]

Apprehension of the nondiscursive truths of art may be inferred as an important element in the inner development of the individual from Schweitzer's lifelong activity as musician and literary critic. His lectures on Goethe are noteworthy; his monumental work on Bach is considered by many to be his greatest achievement in the field of letters. [52] It is apparent from his autobiography that he considers his work in organ building one of the most worthwhile endeavors of his career; [53] one commentator even calls this work a form of reverence for life! [54] That Schweitzer allows time in his busy schedule at Lambarene for practice on his pedal-piano indicates his high evaluation of aesthetic experience. His conviction that great art is more than a purely formal arrangement of tones, words or colors and lines is conveyed in many passages:

What so fascinates us in this piece [the *Well-Tempered Clavichord*] is not the form of the build of the piece, but the world-view that is mirrored in it. It is not so much that we enjoy the *Well-*

Tempered Clavichord as that we are edified by it. Joy, sorrow, tears, lamentation, laughter—to all these it gives voice, but in such a way that we are transported from the world of unrest to a world of peace, and see reality in a new way, as if we were sitting by a mountain lake and contemplating hills and woods and clouds in the tranquil and fathomless water.[55]

Whoever has once felt this wonderful tranquility has comprehended the mysterious spirit that has here expressed all it knew and felt of life in this secret language of tone, and will render Bach the thanks we render only to the great souls to whom it is given to reconcile men with life and bring them peace.[56]

Schweitzer quotes Bach himself to support his thesis that music is of cosmic significance to those who understand it. He cites with approval a passage in which the great composer declares that figured bass should produce "an agreeable harmony for the glory of God and the justification of the soul," adding that "where this is not kept in mind there is not true music but only an infernal clamor and ranting." [57] Schweitzer links music with the depths of inwardness that are, as we have noted, a vital part of his ideal of self-perfection by pointing out that Bach's music can only be appreciated by those who "attain a composure and an inwardness" that will enable them to establish contact with "the deep spirit which lies hidden within it." [58] He remarks that "Bach's cantatas and Passions are not only children of the Muse, but also children of leisure." [59]

Composure and leisure bring us near *quietness*, another essential aspect of the ideal of inner development. Schweitzer's chief objection to modern materialism and overorganization is that under such conditions life loses its quietness. The constant assault of noise, advertisement, propaganda and gadgets is detrimental or even fatal to inner development.[60] In addressing the missionaries at the Selly Oak Conference in 1925, he warned:

We do not have enough inwardness, we are not sufficiently preoccupied with our own spiritual life, we lack quietness; and this not only because in our exacting, busy existence it is difficult to obtain, but because, ignoring its importance, we do not take pains to secure it, being too easily contented with living our lives as unrecollected men who merely aim at being good.[61]

This concern for quietness and inner development saves the often pragmatic doctor from the activist fallacy of overemphasizing externals. Still, he is equally careful to avoid an exclusive stress upon the contemplative life; indeed, his entire stress upon the *ethical* nature of his mysticism is directed against religion and philosophy which are merely contemplative.

In Schweitzer's conception of self-perfection, quietness is related closely to *resignation* in the face of the inevitable frustrations encountered by will-to-live and will-to-love. But this resignation is neither cynical and rebellious, nor yet quietistic. It is not cynical since "True resignation is not a becoming weary of the world, but the quiet triumph which the will-to-live celebrates at the hour of its greatest need over the circumstances of life." [62] In part, resignation means an inner liberty which has certain affinities with the Stoic ideal of *apathia*: one must become inwardly detached from the external circumstances of life, over which he has so little control, and in so doing he will gain "strength to deal with everything that is hard in his lot" plus deep tranquility and purification. Thus resignation is "the spiritual and ethical affirmation of one's own existence," and only the man who has achieved it is capable of genuine world-affirmation.[63] In part, then, resignation is actually a kind of exaltation, for it represents "the triumph of our will-to-live over whatever happens to us." [64]

Yet resignation must not be thought of as a quietistic retreat into the harmony of one's inner selfhood, or into a belief that "whatever is, is right." It is, on the contrary, a necessary step in the direction of ethical action—because no one who has failed to take this step will be able to devote himself *consistently* to others. [65] Resignation is inward detachment from the world which is instrumental in enabling one "to work in the world as an instrument of God." [66] "The profoundest inner freedom from the world is that which man strives to attain in order to become an ethical personality and as such to serve the world." [67]

Why is such inward detachment necessary for ethics? It is necessary to "raise us above all considerations of possibility or impossibility" in our ethical action.[68] It is also necessary to enable the individual who senses keenly the weight of suffering which oppresses the world to bear this mystery, yet all the while, in W. H. Auden's words, "show an affirming flame." In a moving passage, Schweitzer testifies:

> I experience in its full weight what we conceive to be the absence of purpose in the course of world happenings. *Only at quite rare moments have I felt really glad to be alive.* I could not but feel with a sympathy full of regret all the pain that I saw around me, not only that of men but that of the whole creation. From this community of suffering I have never tried to withdraw myself. It seemed to me a matter of course that we should all take our share of the burden of pain which lies upon the world [69] [author's italics].

Resignation is intimately related to the final aspect of self-perfection, which also forms the link between self-love and ethical love in Schweitzer's thought: active compassionate suffering. Albert Schweitzer speaks with authority and from experience when he describes the depths of one's being which remain unplumbed unless one has passed through arduous toils, conflicts and suffering. As he has remarked, "You *can* burn a candle at both ends if the candle is long enough!" [70] His years of medical study were a constant battle with exhaustion.[71] Many of his letters to friends in Europe mention that he is writing them late at night, when dead tired. Some of his letters are even broken off in the middle because of some interruption, and mailed without being finished.[72] As Schweitzer has grown older, the burden of weariness has quite naturally become increasingly heavy, as the following report on Lambarene during the years of World War II reveals:

> . . . due not only to the long sojourn in the hot, close equatorial climate, but to the excessive work and overstrain, henceforth we had

to draw on our last reserves of energy in order to meet the demands of the Hospital. Not to fall ill—to keep fit for work—this was our constant, daily care. It was clear to all that not one of us must collapse, for there could be no replacements for a long time. . . . So we carried on.[73]

Schweitzer's health has been remarkably sound, but he has now and again been afflicted with painful physical maladies resulting from his work.[74] He has subjected himself to the hazards of medical experiment in order to make certain that drugs were safe for his patients.[75] He has suffered the loneliness of separation from his family. His natural reticence was bruised, so he reports, by the necessity of having to explain his reasons for the decision to go to Africa, as well as by the necessity of having to solicit funds for the hospital.[76] The loss of financial independence is one of the "three great renunciations" which caused him great anguish at the time of his decision, the other two grievous losses being his activities as musician and teacher.[77]

But there is nothing good about suffering per se; in fact purposeless pain is worse than death.[78] It is *compassionate* suffering that crowns the fulfilment of the self. Compassion is necessary to self-perfection because it insures that one's will-to-live does not operate "unhindered" but "always within special relations of solidarity with others." [79] Compassion is the only avenue of genuine heroism that is open to a man—for genuine heroism is not an adventurous attack upon some lofty citadel visible to the eyes of men; it is not "doing something special." It is rather simply the undertaking of what seems to be one's duty "as a matter of course" and "with sober enthusiasm":

Only a person who can find a value in every sort of activity and devote himself to each one with full consciousness of duty has the inward right to take as his object some extraordinary activity instead of that which falls naturally to his lot. Only a person who feels his preference to be a matter of course, not something out of the ordinary, and who has no thought of heroism, but just recognizes a duty undertaken with sober enthusiasm, is capable of becoming a spiritual adventurer such as the world needs. There are no heroes of action: only heroes of renunciation and suffering.[80]

Compassion has cosmological significance. This is apparent from a careful analysis of the implications of Schweitzer's voluntarism. If the universal will-to-live is the fundamental metaphysical reality which underlies all phenomena in the universe, then all individual wills-to-live are united because of the fact that they all partake of the same vital cosmic essence. Yet these individual wills-to-live are not one; they are separate and *separated* from each other. Not only that: they are engaged in continual *conflict* with each other. Compassion is the healing force which seeks to end this warfare, this "division of life against itself" (*Selbstentzweiung*—literally, "self-cutting-in-two"). And whenever one life devotes itself to the nurture of any other life, its finite will-to-live "experiences union with the infinite will in which all life is one." [81] Now, since the universal (or infinite) will-to-live is for Schweitzer another way of saying "God," then the pinnacle of self-perfection is compassion, for it is the inward prerequisite for union with God.[82]

The mystic's union with God has usually been conceived as a rapture, but Schweitzer has said that he could feel "really glad to be alive" only upon rare occasions.[83] In a recent letter to an intimate friend he remarked: "I have success in my life, but no one knows how difficult my life is and how dearly I pay for it." [84]

Does Schweitzer's compassion stem from a joyless ethic of duty? There are very strong praises of dutifulness in his discussions of the motivation for compassionate self-devotion. But he grants that "happiness and success" are legitimate goals of the will-to-live, though he strictly limits their legitimacy and scope:

At the moments when I should like to enjoy myself without restraint, reverence for life wakes in me reflection about misery that I see or suspect, and it does not allow me to drive away the uneasiness I feel. . . . It is an uncomfortable doctrine which the true ethics whisper into my ear. You are happy, they say; therefore you are called upon to give much. Whatever more than others you have received in health, natural gifts, working capacity, success, a beautiful childhood, harmonious family circumstances, you must not accept as being a

matter of course. You must pay a price for them. You must show
more than average devotion of life to life.[85]

The theme of *noblesse oblige* occurs again in his account
of his decision to go to Africa, and prompts him to state that
everyone who has experienced the benefits of modern medical
care has an obligation to help spread abroad such benefits,
either by training himself to serve as a doctor or nurse in
uncivilized areas or by contributing to the financial support of
those who do.[86] This theme appears in the closing words of
his autobiography, where he closes a catalog of his blessings with
an expression of thanksgiving that "I can recognize as such
whatever happiness falls to my lot, accepting it also as a thing
for which some thank offering is due from me." [87]

Even as a child Schweitzer was sensitive to the difference
between his own modestly privileged status as son of the village
pastor and the condition of other boys. Once when a boy
he had beaten in a fight taunted him by crying, "Yes, if I got
broth to eat twice a week, as you do, then I should be as strong
as you are," little Albert refused to eat his broth for several
days.[88] He aroused the ire of his father once by refusing to
wear an overcoat warmer than the wraps possessed by other
children.[89] The motive of Schweitzer's father in wanting his
son to wear the fine overcoat that had been cut down to size for
him was chiefly his desire that his son look his part as a member of
the pastor's family.[90] Paul Schweitzer, younger brother of
Albert, testifies to the fact that his father did not emphasize
particularly the duty of a Christian to pay for his blessings by
taking upon himself the sufferings of others.[91]

The note of duty resounds even more strikingly in those
passages where Schweitzer speaks of self-devotion to the natives
of Africa as a sort of atonement for the wrongs which white
men have inflicted on Negroes for centuries:

> Whatever benefit we confer upon the people of our colonies is
> not beneficence but atonement for the terrible suffering which we
> white people have been bringing upon them ever since the day on which
> the first of our ships found its way to their shores.[92]

His plea for reverence for animals is sometimes coupled with a tribute to their value to men and some reference to the debt we owe them.[93]

Schweitzer's compassion is more than an ethic of duty, however prominent duty and altruistic negation of self are in his thinking. Self-perfection is self-*fulfilment*, self-*affirmation*, and is, in fact, "the higher life-affirmation." The ideal of self-perfection contains within itself, as "a natural manifestation of the will-to-live," the ideal of self-devotion, because the self actually enlarges and enriches itself by "overlapping other human existences" through service to them. "Self-devotion is, therefore, not a surrender of the self, but a manifestation of its expansion." [94]

Schweitzer's remark that he is seldom glad to be alive must be evaluated in the context of his sensitivity to the burden of pain that so mysteriously prevents life from being completely happy or completely comprehensible. In numerous other passages he speaks of the deep joy that he has been privileged to know through his self-devotion to others. Sometimes he even says that unwillingness to launch out into the depths of self-giving compassion is the reason for our failure to know inward peace and happiness.[95] Of the role of compassion in deep happiness he says:

As a being in an active relation to the world, he [*i.e.*, the man whose compassion has been deepened by resignation] comes into a spiritual relation with it by not living for himself alone, but feeling himself one with all life that comes within his reach. He will feel all that life's experiences as his own, he will give it all the help he can possibly give, and will feel all the saving and promotion of life that he has been able to effect as the deepest happiness that can ever fall to his lot. . . .

Existence will thereby become harder for him in every respect than it would be if he lived for himself, but at the same time it will be richer, more beautiful, and happier.[96]

7. Social Ethics

A social dimension of ethics and love proceeds directly from self-perfection, since for Schweitzer one's highest self-realization involves a necessary element of self-devotion to others. By defining self-perfection to include an element of altruism, Schweitzer progresses toward a solution of the problem which plagued all previous ethical systems postulating self-perfection as the ultimate goal of human effort: The lack of adequate content.

An equally serious defect has marred ethics dominated by social considerations: their inclination to be "in too much of a hurry to reach practical results." [1] This defect is in large part cured by Schweitzer's insistence that altruism must spring from "inward necessity."

What exactly does he mean by "self-devotion"? Since reverence for life is a universal ethic, one which affects all life, we might expect it to include a concern for all of the institutions of organized society which affect life so crucially. But this is not the case: self-devotion is concerned only with "the mutual relations between man and man" which comprise "the ethics of active self-perfecting." [2] Social ethics are not equal in importance with and a mutual implication of self-perfection, but merely one form, and a subordinate form, of self-perfection. In fact, social ethics do not deserve the family name "ethics" at all. The active and passive ethics of self-perfection form "the ethics of ethical personality," which is qualitatively superior to "the ethics of ethical society." [3] This is true for Schweitzer because the former is "personal, incapable of regulation, and absolute"; whereas the latter comprise a "system established by society for its prosperous existence" that is "supra-personal, regulated, and relative." [4] Innumerable passages could be cited to document his convictions about "the essential difference between the morality of ethical personality and that which is established from the standpoint of society." [5]

The fundamental objection to social ethics is that any social ethic tends to sacrifice individuals and groups of individ-

uals to the general welfare.[6] Though society does serve ethics by
expressing the elementary principles of morality in legal codes,
this should not be interpreted to mean that individual men
should learn from society what is right and what is wrong. When
that happens, genuine ethics are lost, for only the thoughtful
individual is capable of discovering and practicing true morality.[7]
Any influence of social considerations on the ethic of ethical
personality is pernicious.[8]

> The morality of ethical personality, then, and the morality which
> is established from the standpoint of society cannot be traced back
> the one to the other, and they are not of equal value. The first only
> is a real ethic; the other is improperly so called.[9]

> The objective, standard morality of society . . . is never a true
> code of ethics, but merely an appendix to ethics.[10]

A pronounced individualism characterizes Schweitzer's
treatment of self-devotion: "Ethics is the activity of man
directed to secure the inner perfection of his own personality." [11]
Ethics can be defined as "the maintaining of life at the highest
point of development—my own life and other life—by devoting
myself to it in help and love," [12] with the understanding that
"life" means primarily the *self*, not merely the orgnizations to
which one belongs and the government which represents one.
Ethics are concerned "with conduct which springs from inward
necessity" and "a man must be ethical from inner necessity." [13]
Schweitzer is critical of utilitarian morality because it originates
in society, and no morality can be genuine which "originates
outside the individual." [14] He stated in a speech on Goethe that

> the greatest measure of love will be attained when each one realizes
> the love, the special love, that is within him. More love will then
> exist, coming naturally out of the individual, and along with it
> more happiness, than if we try to force the individual to sacrifice his
> personality, and only permit him to be something that is good for
> the whole.[15]

Community "ethics," in reality unethical, are identified with
materialism: "The ethics of materialism consists in saying: You

must live for the good of the community. . . . Can a man understand the purpose of his life when he says: I live for the good of the community? No!" [16]   Any other communal code would be unethical, since: "The criterion of a real code of ethics is whether it allows their full rights to the problems of personal morality and of the relation of man to man." [17]   Schweitzer's individualism is one of the factors that leads him to respect resignation and to write: "Inability to understand resignation and the relations prevailing between ethics and resignation, is the fatal weakness of modern European thought." [18]   Individualism further leads him to respect elemental thinking, which is necessary to prepare the individual for ethical activity by making him inwardly detached, necessary for the creation of ethical ideals which will lead to true civilization, and necessary for the moral empowerment of the individual.

The importance of thought for the development of civilization-furthering ideals is attested by the fact that unless the will-to-progress has been deepened beyond the materialistic or utilitarian level, it will not

possess the requisite insight to distinguish the valuable from the less valuable, and strive after a civilization which does not consist only in achievements of knowledge and power, but before all else will make men, both individually and collectively, more spiritual and more ethical.[19]

Individual thought is essential because without a "basic principle of the moral" any handling of practical questions is a "mere groping here and there." [20]   Thought is needed to combat the "practical realism" of twentieth-century society. Thought alone can create the "ethical ideals" which will be "so powerful that men say: we will use them to control reality. We will transform reality in accordance with these ideals." [21]   Only thought can overcome the unfortunate "maturity" which dominates the thinking of so many in our day, who have become disillusioned about ideals.[22]   Only thought can overcome the loss of faith in the power of thought that marks the spirit of our age.[23]   In sum, thought purges the spirit of an age from superstitions, dogmas and the downright immoralities of ancient custom and present practice.[24]

   This emphasis upon thought is predicated on the assumption that truth is unitary. Schweitzer considers pragmatism "dangerous" because it imperils this cardinal tenet by asserting that "every idea that helps me to live is true." Such a way of thinking must be rejected, for "if there is a double truth, there is no truth. The sense of sincerity is blunted . . . [and] when this fundamental is shaken, there is no spiritual life remaining." Pragmatism is wrong because it "permits men to take their ideals from reality." [25]

   Individual thinking is necessary for empowerment because "living truth"—truth which is "capable of uniting itself with [a man] to the very marrow of his being"—"is that alone which has its origin in thinking." [26] The "acceptance of authoritative truth, even if that truth has both spiritual and ethical content," will not suffice since thought must well up "unfettered" and "sincere" from the depths of the individual consciousness of a man. Whatever truth there may be in the thoughts he takes over secondhand from other sources will be "externalized and rendered torpid." [27] Schweitzer implies that thought is its own ethical justification, quite apart from any fruits it might bear:

   To be energetically occupied with the basic principle of the moral, even though it leads in the direction of the universal and apparently abstract, always brings with it results which are of a practical value, even if the solution of the problem itself is not thereby advanced beyond a certain point.[28]

The very existence of "a will-to-live which is filled with reverence for life and devotion to life" is an intrinsically valuable fact, a fact that is "full of importance to the world." [29]

   Every moral decision is an occasion for growth in spirituality on the part of the agent concerned: and the creation of a purified humaneness within individuals is more important than the attainment of any immediate factual results.[30] Schweitzer can take such a stand because he is fully persuaded of the power of truth to radiate out into society with unseen but nevertheless effective power. He feels that "the ethical disposition of the mind or spirit has not merely importance for the man himself, but is at the same time a power which goes forth from him." [31] He does not question the reality of this "radiation of kindliness."

Schweitzer's ethical mysticism is not a mysticism of contemplation; it is a "deed-mysticism." His "ethics of perfection of heart contain the principle of love and within that principle lies the impulse to activity." [32] He is antagonistic to any form of mysticism which allows "the danger that the mystic will experience the eternal as absolute impassivity, and will consequently cease to regard the ethical existence as the highest manifestation of spirituality." [33] Of such mysticism he comments, "Mysticism is not the friend of ethics but the foe." [34] Even pity, if it is "merely deliberative," is impotent and therefore supra-ethical rather than ethical.[35] Nor is thought itself ethical when it has no tendency toward deeds. Schweitzer's many affirmations of the sufficiency of thought in itself, some of which are quoted just above, must not be interpreted as divorcing thought from action. These affirmations are in part hyperbolic expressions of the extreme importance of thought, and in part reminders that thought is the first step toward action. As Planck has remarked, Schweitzer's stress on individual meditation is in large measure an indirect strategy designed to bring about the highest degree of optimistic life-affirmation and ethics.[36] Schweitzer cannot be misinterpreted when it is borne in mind that thought which is genuine and mysticism which is genuine must result in ethical activity.

He emphasizes the necessity for independence of action as well as independence of thought. His ideal of independent action profoundly influenced his own personal search for a way to render "direct service" to his fellow creatures. He abandoned the thought of working with tramps and discharged prisoners because such work could best be done "in collaboration with organizations." He felt, "What I wanted was an absolutely personal and independent activity." [37] Independent action is for him no mere gesture, but a mode of activity as culturally effective as it is personally uplifting:

We stand shuddering at the way the *Zeitgeist* is going: but if there were in Europe only a hundred thousand men scattered out a bit in all nations and stations of life, from princes to street cleaners, who dared to be natural in the sense of Jesus, then a general change of public opinion would take place in a few years.[38]

The same justification of independent activity is expressed in his comment to a visitor at Lambarene: "Everything great, in Africa as elsewhere, is always the work of one man. The action of a community can only be that of an accessory." [39]

One corollary of faith in the power of individual thought and action is a suspicion of any "scientific" or "organized" means of putting into effect the ethical ideals created by individual thinking. As Reuber and Grabs have pointed out, Schweitzer is fond of warning against the widespread tendencies of all nations today to look for their salvation in new institutional magic of one kind or another.[40] He even criticizes the construction of public parks as being "artificial." [41] "True power for the state as for the individual is to be found in spirituality and ethical conduct." [42] Only "in proportion as society takes on the character of an ethical personality, does its code of morals become the code of ethical society." [43]

Schweitzer has spoken out in recent years against further nuclear testing. However, his characteristic position in regard to political problems has remained one of aloofness. Pierhal states that Schweitzer's lack of faith in the effectiveness of "manifestoes" or "such declarations" prevented his protesting aggressively against Hitler.[44] His reply to people who urged him to condemn the Third Reich was simply, "My place is not in politics." [45] A similar remark on the same issue is reported by Hunter:

> I represent no political program. But I think that the highest good for men is freedom and that too much socialization wrongs the individual spiritually and materially. The dignity of man, of the individual, is the important thing.[46]

And when an inquisitive visitor to Lambarene tried "to draw him out on Europe's politics," Schweitzer parried the question

by remarking, "I am concerned with ethics." [47] His admission
that he has virtually no knowledge of African affairs outside his
own area of Africa, and his failure to mention African nationalism in his writings, are noted by Gunther.[48] In a personal conversation, Schweitzer said of political controversy, "No polemics,
no fighting with my opponents, but just living and working in
calmness and perseverance." [49]

Though Schweitzer's attitudes toward civil and political
laws are sometimes ambivalent, it is clear that he always prefers
private ethics to public law. He frequently approves the ends
of public laws but prefers that these ends be attained through
voluntary individual action rather than public legal coercion.
That society cannot exist without restrictions upon the activities
of its members he acknowledges. But he argues that the individual's sacrifice of personal liberties can and should be voluntary. This "doctrine of self-sacrifice" is preferred to the "doctrine of being sacrificed by others," under which the "sociological morality" of collective mankind deprives individuals of their
freedom and prosperity by subjecting them to legal restraints.[50]
The priority of ethics and the individual are always implied when
Schweitzer faintly praises the law or appeals to law. His recent
condemnation of nuclear testing, which contains an appeal to
international law, is made on ethical grounds and is directed to
individuals. His published comments on the subject of law always implicate ethics, as in this passage from his preface to
Civilization and Ethics:

> Law and ethics spring up together from the same idea. Law
> is so much of the principle of respect for life as can be embodied in
> an external code; ethics are what cannot be so embodied. The
> foundation of law is humanity.[51]

Schweitzer's ethical emphasis leads him to individualistic preferences in specific areas of law, such as the law of ownership:

> In the question of possessions, the ethics of reverence for life are
> outspokenly individualistic, in the sense that wealth acquired or
> inherited should be placed at the service of the community, not
> through any measures taken by society, but through the absolutely

free decision of the individual. They expect everything from a general
increase in the feeling of responsibility. Wealth they regard as the
property of society left in the sovereign control of the individual.[52]

His individualism becomes suspect in many of its applications, as when he approves low wages and substandard levels of
living in colonial areas. He offers his opinion that managements
of lumber camps along the Ogowe feed their workers "as best
they can." He states that natives who work for white traders
in the African river area are certainly not exploited: "Nowhere
in the world . . . is the total cost of labor higher in proportion
to the work done than in the primeval forest." [53] Yet in the
same passage, Schweitzer approves "the fine balance of profit"
made by one contractor. In his book, *On the Edge of the
Primeval Forest*, he discusses "the labor problem" and the "serious conflict between the needs of trade and the fact that the
child of nature is a free man." [54] He is less concerned that the
Negro laborer be underpaid, than that he be overpaid, paid in
unsuitable commodities, and lured away from tribal morality
and simple innocence. He speaks of the "taxes and new needs,"
including "useless trifles and rum," which "can make a Negro
work more than he used to," and which "make him anxious for
money and for enjoyment, but not reliable or conscientious." [55]
Schweitzer ends his discussion of the African's working conditions by stating that the native is "worth something" only when
he is living in his village, where the moral influence of family
and tribe prevent his "going to the bad." He describes colonies
of Negro laborers away from their families as "centers of demoralization," yet grants that "such colonies are required for
trade and for the cultivation of the soil, both of which would
be impossible without them." [56] A curious paradox in Schweitzer's thought is manifested here: on the one hand, the ethic of
reverence for life is said to "arise from inner compulsion" and
to be determined by a "will to action"; on the other hand, this
ethic "can leave on one side all problems regarding the success of
its work." [57] Thus Schweitzer is compelled to voice concern
about the disruption of the African style of life caused by trade,

but he rather complacently accepts the abuses of the trade system as something which cannot be avoided.

The positive content of "the ethics of ethical personality" is more important to Schweitzer than his ethics' perfunctory and even negative relations to social, legal and economic problems.

Nothing is more positive in Schweitzer's ethics than his doctrine of "giving yourself to others as a human being." The doctrine is similar to Buber's "I-Thou" approach to interpersonal relations in stressing the necessity for the profound devotion of the very core of one's being to others. The doctrine is a protest against the tendency in modern life for individuals to become accustomed to treating each other as "strangers" to whom one can be utterly indifferent.[58] Many of Schweitzer's most convincing passages urge men to struggle against dehumanization.

The hidden forces of goodness are embodied in those persons who carry on as a secondary pursuit the immediate personal service which they cannot make their lifework. The lot of the many is to have as a profession, for the earning of their living and the satisfaction of society's claim on them, a more or less soulless labor in which they can live out little or nothing of their human qualities, because in that labor they have to be little better than human machines. Yet no one finds himself in the position of having no possible opportunity of giving himself to others as a human being. The problem produced by the fact of labor being today so thoroughly organized, specialized, and mechanized depends only in part for its solution on society's not merely removing the conditions thus produced, but doing its very best to guard the rights of human personality. What is even more important is that sufferers shall not simply bow to their fate, but shall try with all their energy to assert their human personality amid their unfavorable conditions by spiritual activity. Anyone can rescue his human life, in spite of his professional life, who seizes every opportunity of being a man by means of personal action, however unpretending, for the good of fellow men who need the help of a fellow man. Such a man enlists in the service of the spiritual and the good. No fate can prevent a man from giving to others this direct human service side by side with his lifework. If so much service remains unrealized, it is because the opportunities are missed.[59]

[The ethics of reverence for life] demand that every one of us in some way and with some object shall be a human being for human beings. To those who have no opportunity in their daily work of giving themselves . . . it suggests their sacrificing something of their time and leisure, even if of these they have but a scanty allowance. It says to them . . . Open your eyes and look for a human being, or some work devoted to human welfare, which needs from some one a little time or friendliness, a little sympathy, or sociability, or labor. There may be a solitary or an embittered fellow-man, an invalid or inefficient person to whom you can be something. Perhaps it is an old person or a child. Or some good work needs volunteers who can offer a free evening, or run errands. Who can enumerate the way in which that costly piece of working capital, a human being, can be employed? More of him is wanted everywhere! Search, then, for some investment of your humanity. . . .[60]

By this ideal of "being a man for the good of fellow men," Schweitzer means first that one should *care* about others. The employer who is forced to discharge an employee or to choose between two men for one job must treat the rejected one humanely, showing his concern and offering all possible help and encouragement in the finding of another position. Schweitzer means, secondly, that one should give himself genuinely to his neighbor in *conversation*—and this not only in face-to-face contacts, but also in letters and published material. Grabs quotes Schweitzer as recommending that one should "put himself into his letters," not just write mechanically or in too businesslike a fashion.[61] He remarked to a recent visitor, "Writing takes a lot out of a man." [62] The rigorous honesty with which he expounded his radical views on the New Testament,[63] even at the cost of much inward suffering over the misunderstanding he knew would be created and the loss of face his work would result in for certain admired professors (especially his beloved Holzmann), is a manifestation of his integrity in self-giving. The same unflinching regard for sincerity is evident in his openness to all questions from his classes of candidates for confirmation.[64]

Schweitzer calls for a genuine sharing of selves, especially in face-to-face personal encounters. He regrets the almost subhuman shallowness of the inane chatter typical of present-day social intercourse.[65] Intelligent and sincere conversation is important, not only for spiritual reasons, but for the utilitarian purpose of creating a new kind of public opinion. The intelligent public opinion which is so desperately needed can be formed only through the "natural" method of spreading ideas, communication by personal exchanges. Natural or personal communication is likened to David's simple but effective sling, while Goliath's heavy and ineffective weapons have their counterpart in today's "unnatural" methods for communicating ideas by radio, by the press and within organized pressure groups.[66] Schweitzer used the unnatural media of radio to broadcast his appeal against nuclear testing only because he felt that the issue was being concealed by those in control of mass communications.[67]

To experience the fullest dimension of human fellowship, one must break through conventional patterns and open oneself to friends, making them aware that they can be free to do the same.[68] Schweitzer's reluctance to speak from a manuscript when adressing an audience is no doubt a manifestation of this desire for communication in depth.[69] However, one must respect the right of another person to certain areas of privacy in his personality which must not be violated. This conviction caused Schweitzer to suffer from his contacts with friends who demanded that he explain to them all the reasons for his decision to go to Africa. He greatly resented "so many people assuming a right to tear open all the doors and shutters of my inner self!" [70] He holds psychoanalysis suspect for the same reason.[71] On the other hand, free and voluntary sharings of the self are essential to personality and health. Barthel suggests that Schweitzer's stress upon the importance of personal relatedness grew out of his feeling that a very few individuals, by their free and honest sharing of themselves, had stimulated and brought forth his own latent spirituality.[72]

Schweitzer's own life illustrates the meaning of giving oneself to others, especially in daily contacts. Skillings marvels that Schweitzer, when in his home town of Gunsbach, "busy as he is, always has time for visitors." [73] A Britisher who entertained him in his home comments on Schweitzer's relaxed interest in teaching his host's seven-year-old daughter to play the piano.[74] A German pastor, who skinned his knee while riding a bicycle through Gunsbach in 1955 and came to Schweitzer as the nearest doctor, relates a charming story of the latter's stimulating conversation, warm hospitality and "gentle hand" while treating the wound.[75] When Schweitzer came to America in 1949 to speak at the Goethe Festival in Aspen, Colorado, he created some anxiety in the hearts of the schedule-conscious program heads by his habit of holding impromptu seminars with any and all interested parties who came to his table in the cafeteria.[76]

There are those who do not see Schweitzer's personification of his teachings in quite so favorable a light. None has been more critical in print than John Gunther:

> Dr. Schweitzer is a profound moralist, but he has comparatively little interest in human beings as such, Africans or otherwise. . . . Discipline, though not overtly exercised, is somewhat strict; everything, as I heard it put, is "noted." Discussion at mealtimes or in the evening hardly exists, and acolytes do not sit at the feet of the master to absorb wisdom—because he seldom talks. His aloofness is remarkable, and he has small contact with most of his workers. Of course his mind is far too elevated for casual chitchat. . . .
> He seems to be fonder of the animals in Lambarene than of the human beings, and perhaps—who knows?—they reward him more.[77]

Yet Gunther qualifies this impression in later sentences to the effect that "he can be magically charming on occasions and is literally worshipped by his old associates," that "His laughter—when he laughs—is a striking indication of his inner sweetness," and that "Schweitzer is a most incisive, alert and authoritative conversationalist. . . . The epigrammatic quickness of his mind is as astonishing as its spiritual breadth and profundity." [78]

Schweitzer's ideal of self-devotion involves the giving of one's hands as well as one's heart and mind. We have an ethical obligation to those who are less fortunate or less able to care for themselves than most people. This ideal he achieves chiefly by his work at Lambarene, but there are other illustrations of it in his life. When Schweitzer considered how he might offer his direct service to other men, he thought at one time of "taking charge of abandoned or neglected children and educating them." [79] (His "pay for your blessings" doctrine was present in his plan to make the children so benefited "pledge themselves to help later on in the same way children in similar positions.") Even hopeless hospital cases should be treated with sympathy in the hope of easing their misery. That is standard practice in the hospital at Lambarene,[80] and characteristic of Schweitzer's practices at other times. While a medical student, the time of his life when he was fighting a continual battle with fatigue because of an incredibly full schedule,[81] he played music for an hour each day to an elderly lady. At another time he sat as model for an elderly lady whose disease was incurable but whose interest in painting preserved her desire to continue living despite her sufferings.[82] Schweitzer's attitude of mercy extends to criminals and socially unacceptable individuals such as tramps. While considering working with ex-convicts and tramps, he joined with a Strasbourg minister in a program designed to aid such persons. Schweitzer reports with approval that this minster was never satisfied to give the applicant a trifle of money and send him on his way. He investigated the reality and legitimacy of the poor person's needs, after which he offered generous help, even over a long term.[83] Schweitzer carries a similar attitude into his medical and social work, and he advocates generous and liberal policies even for penal institutions.[84]

Charitable distribution of financial aid is a vital means of self-devotion. Schweitzer once worked in the program of benevolence carried on by a student association in Strasbourg known as the Diaconate of St. Thomas. While engaged in this work he visited poor families every week and distributed aid to them. The money for this benevolence had to be collected by the members of the diaconate from the well-to-do families of Strasbourg. For the young Albert, the task of soliciting funds was a painful one, but he comments that this experience later proved valuable to him when he was forced to do the same for his hospital. He learned to use tact and restraint, and he learned how to accept a refusal good-naturedly.[85]

Casual, spontaneous expression of the spirit of helpfulness

is also a part of self-devotion. When Schweitzer was in America in 1949 (at which time he was seventy-two), he abruptly excused himself from a conversation in the train station in order to help a lady carry her bags.[86] At Aspen, Colorado, during the same year, Schweitzer created considerable astonishment by offering to escort one of his visitors—a man much younger than he—back to his own cabin late one evening.[87]

Schweitzer's kindness toward all those with whom he comes in contact is related to the most famous aspect of his ethic of self-devotion: his reverence for nonhuman life. The universality of Schweitzer's reverence for life gives his ethical mysticism a cosmic dimension. Will-to-live is active throughout the cosmos. By devoting oneself to all forms of life, without distinction, one relates oneself to the infinite will-to-live, to the cosmos, to God.

8. The Cosmic Dimension

The individual and social forms of self-devotion are incomplete until they attain a cosmic dimension, within which they unite with each other to form one unitary ethic which is *mystical*. Ethical mysticism brings the individual who practises elemental thinking into relationship with the cosmos: a relationship which is more than intellectual or social, a relationship which is personal, loving and mystical. Indeed, the ethical individual is in much closer relationship with the living cosmos than with political, economic and legal organizations. It is only through his personal relationship with the cosmos that his "social" relationships acquire their fullest meaning.

Schweitzer repeatedly warns that self-devotion and self-perfection are incomplete until rooted in man's relationship to the cosmos. A merely activist ethic, which drives men out into the world to serve their fellow creatures without first allowing them "to come to their right senses" and gain awareness of "a spiritual inward relation to Being," can be but a weak and superficial ethic.[1] Not until ethics "embrace the whole Universe is an ethical world-view really possible."[2] As self-devotion to others depends upon relationship with the cosmos, so self-perfection reaches out to the cosmos. To attain self-perfection, one must enter into "true relationship to the Being that is in him and outside him."[3] It is in the *activity* of the individual's self-dedication to Being that self-devotion and self-perfection unite.[4] Any attempt to attain self-perfection through a passive self-dedication to Being inevitably estranges the ideal of self-perfection from the ideal of self-devotion to life and the infinite will-to-live. Neither ideal can realize itself on any scale that is less than cosmic, and on the cosmic scale of mystical unity with the infinite will-to-live they are united.

The critical flaw of most previous ethical systems was their inability to escape from the "circle of the passive." Within this circle the "spiritual inward devotion to Being" is "directed to an abstract totality of Being instead of to real Being."[5] The distinction between Being and real Being suggests the two chief problems which arise in connection with the cosmic dimension of Schweitzer's ethical mysticism.

The first problem concerns the specific nature of the Cosmic Reality with which we seek to be mystically related. Inquiry into the nature of this Cosmic Reality leads us to examine the ontological and theistic aspects of Schweitzer's thought.

The second problem concerns the mode of our relatedness to Cosmic Reality. Consideration of this problem leads us to examine the significance of the human will and the relationship between the human will and the possibility of ethical action.

The nature of Cosmic Reality is not indicated by Schweitzer's use of the term "Being," which he uses only because the term is traditional in discussions of mysticism and because it is convenient in distinguishing his mysticism from other mystical systems. He seldom uses the term except when distinguishing his living ethical mysticism from static or "dead" mysticisms which seek to attain an essential union with the Divine Essence. He does not mention "Being" when constructively describing his own ethics. The term does not occur in his carefully worded summary of his entire system which is found in the preface to *Civilization and Ethics.*

Schweitzer explicitly states that there is no such thing as an "Essence of Being," an "Absolute" or a "Spirit of the Universe," adding that these and "all similar expressions denote nothing actual," but are merely abstractions. "The only reality is the Being which manifests itself in phenomena." [6] Because this is so, it is inconceivable that an individual should be able to "enter into connection with the totality of Being." [7] And from this it follows that there can be no real interrelationships "except those of one individual being to another." [8] In Schweitzer's words:

It is only through the *manifestations* of Being, and only through those *with which I enter into relations,* that my being has any intercourse with infinite Being. The devotion of my being to infinite Being means devotion of my being to all the manifestations of Being which need my devotion, and to which I am able to devote myself [9] [author's italics].

Now if, concludes Schweitzer, we view phenomena as "real Being" and devote ourselves actively to them, we have succeeded in uniting the ethics of self-perfecting and the ethics of altruism —and we have succeeded in relating ourselves to Cosmic Reality.[10]

The question arises of what Schweitzer can mean by "God," since he emphatically rejects "the Essence of Being, the Absolute, the Spirit of the Universe, *and all similar expressions.*" This question assumes additional importance when we consider Schweitzer's comments on humanism, in a letter to the American Humanist Association:

> My full sympathy is given to the movement which you represent: Humanism. The world thinks it must raise itself above humanism; that it must look for a more profound spirituality. It has taken a false road. Humanism in all its simplicity is the only genuine spirituality. Only ethics and religion which include in themselves the humanitarian ideal have true value. And humanism is the most precious result of rational meditation upon our existence and that of the world.[11]

Taken alone, this passage implies that Schweitzer means something humanistic when he writes or says "God." But other passages, and in particular the central logic of his cosmic mysticism, imply something more than this.

In 1923, Oskar Kraus, a professor of philosophy at the University of Prague who was acquainted with Schweitzer personally and who had an earnest desire to understand his friend's philosophical thought, wrote to Schweitzer complaining about the indefiniteness of the concept of God in his ethical mysticism. The letter which Kraus received in reply remains one of Schweitzer's most illuminating pronouncements on this problem:

> . . . It has always been my practice not to say anything when speaking as a philosopher that goes beyond the absolutely logical exercise of thought. Therefore I do not speak of "God" in philosophy, but of the "universal Will-to-Live," which meets me in a twofold guise: as creative will outside me; as ethical will within me. To be sure, the tentative conclusion which you speak of [that Schweitzer is

a pantheist] may readily be drawn, but I am very doubtful as to whether drawing this conclusion is a matter for philosophy, or whether to do so would be advantageous for one's world-view. Consequently I prefer to limit myself to a description of the process of thought and to let pantheism and theism remain in undecided conflict within me. For that is the bare fact of experience I keep coming back to.

But if I am speaking the traditional religious speech, then I make use of the word "God" in its historical preciseness and lack of preciseness, just as I also in such cases say "love" instead of "reverence for life." For here the idea is to convey the familiar thought in its direct vitality and in its relation to traditional piety. In following this custom I am not making any concession either to nature philosophy or to religion. For in both cases the content remains the same: abandonment of knowledge concerning the world and establishment of the primacy of the universal will-to-live which is experienced within me. . . . "Being deeply stirred by the ethical will of God" is the main thing. . . .

My destiny and my determination is to think and to live so as to demonstrate how much ethics and how much piety can exist in a world-view which dares to remain an unclosed system. That which we absolutely agree on is this: the character of the world-view, what I call "the quality of the world-view." And that is the main thing.[12]

From this it seems that the nature of Cosmic Reality is better defined as "universal will-to-live" than as "Being" or anything else. This supposition is consistent with those assertions of Schweitzer to the effect that the fundamental datum of consciousness is awareness of oneself as will-to-live, and that "the last fact knowledge can discover is that the world is a manifestation . . . of the universal will-to-live."[13] It is further substantiated by his assertion that "the whole world is a manifestation of *forces*, that is to say of mysteriously manifold will-to-live"[14] [author's italics]. The supposition that the universal will-to-live is the elemental Cosmic Reality for Schweitzer is also confirmed by the fact that whereas "Being" is a static entity in his opinion, the universal will-to-live is a *dynamic force*—and "beings" are *forces*, individual wills-to-live which are a part of universal will-to-live.

This insight, even if valid, does not resolve a more basic

ambiguity in Schweitzer's notion of Cosmic Reality: the "two-fold guise" in which the universal will-to-live presents itself. In the epilogue to his autobiography, Schweitzer says:

> Anyone who has recognized that the idea of Love is the spiritual beam of light which reaches us from the Infinite . . . ponders, indeed, on the great questions: what is the meaning of the evil in the world; how in God, the great First Cause, the will-to-create and the will-to-love are one; in what relation the spiritual and the material life stand to one another. . . .
>
> Every form of living Christianity is pantheistic in that it is bound to envisage everything that exists as having its being in the great First Cause of all things. But at the same time all ethical piety is higher than any pantheistic system, in that it does not find the God of Love in Nature, but knows about Him only from the fact that He announces Himself in us as Will-to-Love. . . . Theism does not stand in opposition to pantheism, but emerges from it as the ethically determined out of what is natural and undetermined.[15]

(The tension between pantheism and theism in Schweitzer's thought is preserved in English translation by using "Will-to-Love"—or more rarely, "Will of Love"—whenever Schweitzer refers to Cosmic Reality as "Ethical Personality" or "God," and by using "will-to-love" when he speaks of this concept in a more generalized sense.)

Schweitzer expresses the same view in his Selly Oak lectures in which he describes the "ultimate problem of religion" as the mysterious split in the nature of Cosmic Reality implied by the fact that "in Nature we recognize [God] as impersonal creative Power, in ourselves we recognize Him as Ethical Personality." [16] These two manifestations "do not coincide. They are one; but how they are one, I do not understand." [17]

Schweitzer recognizes that such an unresolved conflict in one's thought would seem a terrible embarrassment to most metaphysicians trained in the rationalistic tradition of the West. But he is not afraid to face this embarrassment. Indeed, he considers a frank avowal of the hopelessness of escape from this paradox to be the beginning of wisdom. In any case, as he reiterated in his letter to Kraus, the "quality of the world-view" is "the main thing," and "being stirred deeply by the ethical will of God" is a quality which he believes can be achieved without knowledge. This mode of thought Schweitzer applies to the problem of God, distinguishing the relatively inadequate and the relatively adequate or determinative sources of knowledge about God and feeling toward God:

> Now, which is the more vital knowledge of God? The knowledge derived from my experience of Him as ethical Will. The knowledge concerning God which is derived from Nature is always imperfect and inadequate, because we perceive the things in the world from without only. . . . In myself, on the other hand, I know things from within. The creative force which produces and sustains all that is, reveals itself in me in a way in which I do not get to know it elsewhere, namely, as ethical Will. . . . All the mysteries of the world and of my existence in the world may ultimately be left on one side unsolved and insoluble. My life is completely and unmistakably determined by the mysterious experience of God revealing Himself within me as ethical Will and desiring to take hold of my life.[18]

The priority of God as Ethical Personality over God as impersonal will-to-live is confirmed in other passages. Schweitzer assures us that "it is only through love that we can attain to communion with God. All living knowledge of God rests upon this foundation: that we experience Him in our lives as Will-to-Love." [19] Schweitzer agrees with Kant that "The whole thought structure reaches its summit in the concept of God as moral personality." "God is the Ruler of the World in so far as He is giver of the moral law." [20]

But it must also be inferred from the correspondence with Kraus that Schweitzer's notion of Cosmic Reality cannot be simply resolved into an affirmation of God as Will-to-Love *instead of* God as will-to-live. "It suffices . . . to know that in some mysterious way, forever eluding investigation, they are one." [21] It is God as Ethical Personality who is source of and inspiration for ethical affirmation of other wills-to-live. However, it is God as universal will-to-live who is revered in the process of affirming these individual manifestations of will-to-live. Schweitzer's most memorable expression of this dialectical unity is his well-known simile of the Gulf Stream:

> There is an ocean—cold water without motion. In this ocean, however, is the Gulf Stream, hot water, flowing from the Equator towards the Pole . . . no scientist can explain it. Similarly, there is the God of love within the God of the forces of the universe—one with Him, and yet so totally different. We let ourselves be seized and carried away by that vital stream.[22]

This definition of Cosmic Reality as the twofold dynamic force which operates in the world to create infinite manifestations of will-to-live and in the heart of man to create reverence for these infinite manifestations, confronts us with the problem of man's mode of relatedness to Cosmic Reality.

Direct monistic union with the Essence of Being, God-mysticism, is impossible in Schweitzer's view. Such God-mysticism is even undesirable. No "living religion" could be derived from it, but only "a passive determination of man's being, an absorption into God, a sinking into the ocean of the Infinite." Schweitzer equates God-mysticism with deadness of spirit.[23]

The relatedness which is both possible and eminently desirable is a twofold "becoming-one of the finite will with the Infinite," twofold because the finite will experiences both a passive quiescence in the Infinite (resignation) and a "being-taken-possession-of by the will of love, which . . . strives in us to become act [i.e., the act of altruistic self-devotion]." [24]

Such relatedness or "becoming-one with the Infinite" is attainable through a particular aspect of selfhood: "the finite will." This finite will is capable of experiencing the mystical union as both quiescence and activity, both of which are indispensable in ethical man's relatedness to Cosmic Reality. If Cosmic Reality is a force rather than an essence, if it is will-to-live and will-to-love, and if the fundamental datum of our experience of ourselves is will-to-live, then it is in the realm of the will that we can expect to find mystical relatedness to Cosmic Reality. This Schweitzer states dramatically in the last sermon

he preached in St. Nicholas Church in Strasbourg before going
to Africa for the first time:

> But the last question . . . is concerned with only one thing:
> What happens with our will? How is it in the Will of God? And the
> highest knowledge which man can attain is the longing for peace,
> that our will becomes one with the infinite Will, our human will with
> the Will of God.[25]

We might through our finite wills achieve mystical relatedness to God as Will-to-Love by also willing love. But how do
we achieve meaningful relatedness to God as universal will-to-
live? We need to inquire further into what it means to will
love: it means that we, having become "conscious of other will-
to-live," become "desirous of solidarity with it." [26] And how
do we achieve such solidarity? Only by devoting ourselves to
the individual manifestations of will-to-live which need our devotion. And this is precisely what is meant by "being-taken-
possession-of by the will of love which . . . strives in us to become act." Becoming one with the infinite Will of God implies
both "solidarity" with universal will-to-live in its individual
manifestations and union with God as Will-to-Love, which in
us "desires to become one with other will-to-live." [27]

> For in world- and life-affirmation and in ethics I carry out the
> will of the universal will-to-live which reveals itself in me. I live my
> life in God, in the mysterious divine personality which I . . . experi-
> ence as mysterious Will within myself.[28]

That is what Goethe meant when he wrote his famous lines, "If
into the Infinite thou wouldst stride, just turn to the finite on
every side." [29]

Schweitzer concludes: ". . . the basic principle of ethics
. . . is: Devotion to life resulting from reverence for life." [30]
But he acknowledges that the ethical man who desires solidarity
with other wills-to-live must not expect to achieve this goal
completely—for no man can extricate himself entirely from
subjection to "the puzzling and horrible law of being obliged
to live at the cost of other life." He can not exist without in-

curring again and again "the guilt of destroying and injuring life." [31]

Struggle and guilt being inescapable in life, how can Schweitzer attribute "peace" to mystical union? It seems that solidarity with the manifestations of universal will-to-live can only be realized in a fragmentary fashion which more approximates perpetual frustration than peace. Frustrated desires for peace in an actual world of competition for life would seem the lot of the ethical mystic who seeks union with God through devotion of himself to the wills-to-live about him. It is the resignation consequent upon mystical relatedness which makes possible valuable peacefulness, though absolute tranquility is impossible. When Schweitzer speaks of peace, or quiescent being in will-to-love, he means a state very similar to the resignation which is an element of self-perfection.[32] He means in part the joy and satisfaction that come from active self-devotion to other manifestations of will-to-live in an effort to put a stop to the division of life against itself.[33] He also means the inner detachment that lifts one above the pain involved in this disunion of the will-to-live.

Peace means being *in God;* therefore, it is more than detachment—it is *attachment to* Cosmic Reality. The participation of one's finite will in will-to-love would be illusory if no effort were made to express that love in devotion to other wills-to-live. But this union of finite will with Cosmic Will does not occur only through ethical *action*. It can also be realized in the *attitude* of compassion, when the genuineness of compassion is certified by active self-devotion to the extent that is possible for the particular person. Paradoxically, this is *suffering peace*. The heart which really cares enough to do all that it can in the way of active self-devotion does not cease to care when it can do no more: it cares all the more. This frustration would be unbearable and probably result in an attitude of bitter despair if there were no cosmic dimensions in ethics. But because the compassionate heart is mystically related to Cosmic Reality as will-to-love, its suffering is redeemed from despair and transmuted into peace.

It is critically significant to the interpretation of Schweit-

zer's ethics that his most impressive words about peace and
mystical participation in the infinite Will of God are not spoken
in the language of philosophy. They are spoken in the language
of religion. They are spoken in the language of the Christian
faith:

> Where the active, suffering will seeks peace with God, there heart
> and mind are preserved in Christ Jesus. . . . There is only one hap-
> piness in life: the peace of God, which passeth all understanding.[34]

These words, so much more religious than the terms Schweitzer
employs in developing the purely philosophical aspects of his
thought system, are representative of his ethical mysticism. The
philosophical aspects of the system would seem to be theistic,
even religious, in only a pantheistic, dualistic or agnostic sense.
But the system is more than philosophical. Schweitzer's mysticism is a *Christ*-mysticism.

9. Jesus as the Christ

Schweitzer presents his ethical mysticism as a necessity of thought entirely independent of religious revelation. From this, many of his readers have concluded that traditional Christian language in his writings is not intended seriously.

Rolffs' interesting analysis of Schweitzer's thought— Schweitzer himself declared he had never read "a more thorough analysis" [1]—is based upon the premise that

> We are dealing here with a purely philosophic ethic. Only in one respect does it have anything to do with religion; namely, in that it says thought must end in mysticism. Otherwise, this ethic does not stand under the domination of religion at all. [2]

Rolffs specifically asserts that Schweitzer's decision to go to Africa as a doctor could not have been based on Christian faith, but was the result of his natural compassion for other creatures and of his obsessive desire to "pay back" life for the blessings which it had bestowed upon him.

But Rolffs is in error. We know that this is the case because we have Schweitzer's own testimony in the matter. In the same letter praising Rolffs cited in the foregoing paragraph Schweitzer goes on to add that nevertheless his critic's analysis had too strongly de-emphasized the role of religion:

> The holy music of religion sounds softly but clearly! I am very reticent (probably too much so) about my religious feeling. But everything is in the conclusion to the *Geschichte der Leben-Jesu-Forschung*: Jesus the Lord! Peace in Christ! Jesus has simply taken me prisoner since my childhood. . . . My going to Africa was an act of obedience to Jesus. [3]

This direct rebuttal of Rolffs' view is supported by other indirect evidence from various books by and about Schweitzer. Pierhal reports a conversation between Schweitzer and his mother which took place just before his first departure for Africa. When the latter tried to dissuade him from his plans at the last minute, her son is said to have rebuked her with the saying of Jesus to the effect that "Whosoever putteth his hand to the plow and looketh back is not worthy of the Kingdom of Heaven." [4]

The opening pages of Schweitzer's first account of his experiences, On the Edge of the Primeval Forest, explain his decision to come to Africa as a response to the parable of Lazarus and Dives, which he saw represented by medically advanced Europe and wretched Africa.[5] The same book contains the stirring account of a surgical operation unmistakably representing his going to Africa as an act of obedience to Jesus:

> The operation is finished and in the hardly lighted dormitory I watch for the sick man's awakening. Scarcely has he recovered consciousness when he stares about him and ejaculates again and again: "I have no more pain! I have no more pain!" His hand feels for mine and will not let it go. Then I begin to tell him and the others who are in the room that it is the Lord Jesus who has told the doctor . . . to come to the Ogowe.[6]

Further evidence of his essential Christianity is to be found in the autobiography, where he describes the reaction of his friends to his discovery and choice of the specific opportunity to serve in Africa. The decisive missionary publication which first turned his thoughts to Africa as a field for his activity was a direct appeal for discipleship to Christ. After addressing itself to those "on whom the Master's eyes already rested," the article declared, "Men and women who can reply simply to the Master's call, 'Lord, I am coming,' those are the people whom the Church needs." [7]

Of the opposition he faced in offering his services to the Paris Missionary Society Schweitzer says:

> In the many verbal duels which I had to fight, as a weary opponent, with people who passed for Christians, it moved me strangely to see them so far from perceiving that the effort to serve the love preached by Jesus may sweep a man into a new course of life, although they read in the New Testament that it can do so, and found it there quite in order. I had assumed as a matter of course that familiarity with the sayings of Jesus would produce a much better

appreciation of what to popular logic is nonrational, than my own case allowed me to assert. Several times, indeed, it was my experience that my appeal to the act of obedience which Jesus' command of love may under special circumstances call for, brought upon me an accusation of conceit, although I had, in fact, been obliged to do violence to my feelings to employ this argument at all.[8]

It is impossible to doubt the accuracy of Schweitzer's self-knowledge when he exclaims, as he did in an article written as late as 1950:

To me, however, Jesus remains what he was. Not for a single moment have I had to struggle for my conviction that in him is the supreme spiritual and religious authority, though his expectation of the speedy advent of a supernatural Kingdom of God was not fulfilled, and we cannot make it our own.[9]

This last sentence discloses why Rolffs was so sure that Schweitzer's going to Africa could not have had anything to do with Christian faith and discloses why so many Christians are dubious of Schweitzer's claim that he stands within the circle of their faith.

In his monumental *The Quest of the Historical Jesus* (1906), Schweitzer portrays Jesus as having fully shared the imminent eschatological expectations of many of his contemporaries. This Jesus is strikingly different from both the liberal Jesus of the late nineteenth century and the Christ who "had been riveted for centuries to the stony rocks of ecclesiastical doctrine." [10] Many persons have found it difficult to understand how this Jesus could be a religious authority for anyone. Yet Schweitzer's decision to go to Africa was not made until after the visage of the enigmatic Jesus depicted in the *Quest* was already clearly before him.[11]

It is not difficult to comprehend why many Christians have found Schweitzer's Jesus strange and have been perplexed that this strange figure should claim anyone's allegiance today. That Schweitzer's "consistently eschatological" Jesus was incomparably heroic is not enough for those already deeply accustomed to a different Jesus. It is not enough that Jesus was "the one immeasurably great man who was strong enough to think of Himself as the spiritual ruler of mankind" and to hurl Himself against the wheel of history in an unsuccessful effort to "set it moving on its last revolution." [12] For many, even such heroism cannot replace a resurrection upon the third day, an event of traditional Christian history which is nowhere mentioned by Schweitzer. Further, he deprives Jesus' ministry of the universality traditionally attributed to it by interpreting the ministry in the context of Christ's mistaken apocalyptic expectations. In Schweitzer's view, Jesus intended His preaching to be understood by a small predestined elect and to be incomprehensible to all others.[13] Apocalyptic thought anticipated that the elect must undergo the "Woes of the Messiah" during the last days, and it was only the elect whom Jesus intended to benefit by His death, which He believed would save them from the necessity of undergoing those anticipated woes.[14]

In Schweitzer's view, Jesus' ethical sayings were hardly intended as a timeless codification of moral law for all subsequent history. They were rather an "ethic of the interim," the interim between His preaching and the coming of the apocalyptic Son of Man.[15] The Beatitudes were no more than predictive statements about who would be revealed as members of the elect when the Son of Man appeared.[16] Even the injunctions to repentance, such as that to the rich young ruler, are interpreted eschatologically rather than morally.[17] Schweitzer has declared that "it was not Jesus Himself who gave its perfect spiritual form to the truth which He brought into the world . . . it received this in the course of the working of His spirit" in subsequent history.[18] Should we wonder that pious Christians have been dismayed and offended by this depiction of their Lord?

Schweitzer himself, from the very moment he first discovered this historical Jesus, began to turn his gaze aside from a countenance so lacking in form and comeliness. His reluctance to face the implications of his historical studies is evident in his early sketch of the historical Jesus contained in *The Mystery of the Kingdom of God* (1901). In this book he uses a magnificent figure of speech—that of the sun, which looks altogether different at high noon than it did when rising yet is still the same sun—to deny that thoroughgoing eschatology has any revolutionary consequences for the church.[19]

This reluctance is rationalized and carried further in the *Quest*. Maintaining that "We are experiencing what Paul experienced" in knowing Christ after the flesh, then knowing Him in this fashion no more,[20] Schweitzer asserts:

The abiding and eternal *in* Jesus is absolutely independent of historical knowledge and can only be understood by contact with *His spirit* which is still at work in the world. In proportion as we have *the Spirit of Jesus* we have the true knowledge of Jesus [author's italics].[21]

Again:

But the truth is, it is not Jesus as historically known, but Jesus, as spiritually *arisen within men*, who is significant for our time and can help it. *Not the historical Jesus, but the spirit which goes forth from Him* and in the spirits of men strives for new influence and rule, is that which overcomes the world [author's italics].[22]

Again: "Jesus means something to our world because a mighty *spiritual force* streams forth from Him and flows through our time also " [23] [author's italics].

As the italicized words show, Schweitzer attempts to create the impression that knowledge of the historical Jesus need neither affect one's religious devotion nor offend one's religious sentiments. He tries to find a spiritual Jesus within the historical Jesus, while using the latter to criticize the shallowness of that liberal theology which had tried to make Jesus a contemporary teacher of morals and founder of the Kingdom of God on earth.[24] He uses the spiritual Jesus as the source of inspiration for those very ideals for which the historical Jesus could not serve as authority. In thus deriving ideals from the spiritual Jesus, Schweitzer, for all practical purposes, is committing the fallacy he detected in liberal theology and pronounced futile:

projecting our own thoughts back into history to speak to us out of the past, and "tuning His denial of the world to our acceptance of it." [25]

Jesus is altogether spiritualized in many passages of Schweitzer's later writings, especially in the preface to the third English edition of the *Quest* (p. xv), written in 1950:

> The Gospel of the Kingdom of God came into the world in its late-Jewish form, which it could not retain. The Kingdom, expected to come immediately in supernatural fashion, fails to appear. . . . The situation thus created compelled *believers* to take a more and more spiritual view of the Kingdom of God and the Messiahship of Jesus, the former becoming a spiritual and ethical ideal to be realized in the world, and Jesus the spiritual Messiah who laid its foundations through his ethical teaching [author's italics].

Another essay of 1950 further discloses Schweitzer's advocacy of "a more and more spiritual view of the Kingdom of God":

> Just as Luther substituted his non-eschatological view of baptism for that of the early Church, convinced that it *was the authentic teaching* of the Gospels, so modern Protestantism substitutes its views of the Kingdom of God, and its coming for the eschatological view which Jesus presented as if it really represented the original. Historically both are wrong; but religiously both are right[26] [author's italics].

Schweitzer had in 1931 said of New Testament eschatology and modern notions of progress that "we can only harmonize these two things by an act, for which we claim *the right of necessity*" [27] [author's italics]. In 1934 the same idea was expressed:

> Progress in religion consists in its being constantly internalized and spiritualized. In this process it can come to pass that an earlier conviction which was thought to be direct reality later comes to be regarded as truth not in its original sense, but in its spiritual sense. . . . Not with the letter but with the spirit ought our belief preserve a common bond with the past.[28]

Schweitzer does not hesitate to assert that later Christians have a right to do whatever is necessary with primitive notions.

It is *we* who decide that we must reject Jesus' "religion of love
. . . clothed in the ideas in which He announced it" and determine to "re-clothe it in those of our modern world-view." [29]

Schweitzer's willingness to spiritualize Jesus and his conception of the Kingdom explains many remarks about the
ethics of Jesus and the world-view of Jesus which appear in
writings later than the *Quest* and appear to contradict its picture
of the historical Jesus. The spiritualization of Jesus makes
credible Schweitzer's seemingly extravagant declaration that
"the ethic of reverence for life is the ethic of Jesus, now recognized as a necessity of thought." [30] It is the spiritualized Jesus
who is spoken of when Schweitzer calls Him "the ethical ruler
promised by the prophets." [31] His words in the Sermon on the
Mount express "the truth that the ethical is the essence of
religion." [32] With the spiritualized Jesus in mind, Schweitzer
can say of the Beatitudes that in these "deep-reaching moral
sayings . . . the basic principle of morality shines out." [33]

The mighty thought underlying the Beatitudes of the Sermon
on the Mount, that we come to know God and belong to Him
through love, Jesus introduces into the late-Jewish, Messianic expectation, without being in any way concerned to spiritualize those realistic
ideas of the Kingdom of God and of blessedness. But the spirituality
which lies in this religion of love must gradually, like a refiner's fire,
seize upon all ideas which come into communication with it. Thus
it is the destiny of Christianity to develop through a constant process
of spiritualization.[34]

The "preaching of Jesus" can now be regarded, not as a
fiercely dogmatic eschatological proclamation, but as the classical
manifestation of undogmatic religion, which "limits itself to
fundamental ethical verities," "remains on good terms with
thinking," and tries "to realize something of the kingdom of
God in the world." [35]

The call to repentance can now be transposed from the
other-worldly key in which the historical Jesus had issued it
into Schweitzer's exhortation to and for this world. Repentance
was for the historical Jesus a cry for *God* to bring in His Kingdom,[36] but repentance is for Schweitzer's spiritualized Jesus *our*

first step of preparation for the work which *we* will perform to bring about the Kingdom of God upon earth. "The miracle must happen in us before it can happen in the world. . . . But there can be no Kingdom of God in the world without the Kingdom of God in our hearts." [37] The Kingdom of God can be equated with an inward spiritual condition; repentance is no longer an *instrument* for bringing about the Kingdom, but *is* itself a spiritualized version of the Kingdom.

Schweitzer can now describe the world-view of Jesus, previously depicted as totally unconcerned with the ongoing history of this world (because there was to be no ongoing history of this world), as expressive of world and life affirmation. In *Indian Thought and Its Development,* where Schweitzer is at pains to criticize the world and life denial of the Eastern thinkers, he comments that "the form of world and life negation found in Jesus is different from that of India" because Jesus "only denies the evil, imperfect world in expectation of a good and perfect world which is to come." [38] Indian ethics aim no higher than inactive self-perfection, but Jesus' ethics involve "active, enthusiastic love of one's neighbor" and therefore have an affinity with world- and life-affirmation which Indian thought does not possess.[39] "Because . . . it upholds an ethic which, so far as it touches the relation of man to man, is activist," the "religion of Jesus" is optimistic and life-affirming.

Jesus' meaning of active self-devotion enables Christianity to blend with the climate of opinion current in the modern world and to "modulate from the pessimistic to the optimistic world-view." [40] Schweitzer acknowledges that the original apocalyptic viewpoint of the historical Jesus has been modified by historical Christianity just as it has been modified by his own spiritualization of Jesus; but he states with assurance that the radical re-interpretation is justified:

> Historically and in actual fact this is a wrong interpretation, for the world-view of Jesus is thoroughly pessimistic so far as concerns the future of the natural world. His religion is not a religion of world-transforming effect, but the religion of awaiting the end of the world. His ethic is characterized by activity only so far as it commands men to practice unbounded devotion to their fellow-men, if

they would attain to that inner perfection which is needed for entrance into the supernatural Kingdom of God. [Note the contradiction between this sentence and the original interpretation of the Beatitudes.] An ethic of enthusiasm, seemingly focused upon an optimistic world-view, forms part of a pessimistic world-view! That is the magnificent paradox in the teaching of Jesus.

But the modern age was right in overlooking this paradox, and assuming in Jesus an optimistic world-view which corresponded to an ethic of enthusiasm and met with a welcome the spirit of Late Stoicism and that of modern times. For the progress of the spiritual life of Europe this mistake was a necessity. What crises the latter must have gone through, if it had not been able without embarrassment to place the new outlook on the universe under the authority of the great personality of Jesus! [41]

Finally, Schweitzer can say, "The world-view of Jesus, because it is fundamentally optimistic, accepts the ends aimed at by outward civilization." [42]

Historical veracity has clearly been subordinated to a conception of spiritual truth. The conflict between the two has been noted and the latter chosen in preference to the former. This verdict is valid enough, so far as it goes, and many interpreters of Schweitzer never probe deeper than this.

Schweitzer's tendency to spiritualize the historical or quasi-historical, so evident and so essential in his treatment of Jesus, makes another appearance in his treatment of J. S. Bach. It is Schweitzer's opinion that art is essentially the "translation of aesthetic associations of ideas," and that these ideas are symbolically present in great music all of the time, whether or not listeners are able to detect them. [43] But the meaning of a musical composition is expressed in *whole phrases* of the music, [44] not in individual words of the text set to individual notes. Mozart covered up his second-rate libretti with pretty music, but Bach penetrated to the *essential meaning* which lay behind his frequently awkward religious texts, and attempted to communicate this meaning in his musical compositions. [45] Bach does not paint successive events (any more than he does individual words) but "seizes upon the pregnant moment that contains the whole event for him, and depicts this in music." [46]

"Often he [Bach] presents the text in a false light; but he always brings into the foreground the idea that lends itself to musical expression." [47] Content is of central importance; form is merely a means of conveying it.

Schweitzer's interpretation of Bach parallels his interpretation of Jesus: spiritual reality is the permanent and timeless element; the form in which this is embodied is a vehicle for conveying it at a particular time in history. And if Leo Schrade is correct in his appraisal of Schweitzer as an interpreter of Bach, the parallel is even more striking. Schrade maintains that Schweitzer tends to brush aside historical knowledge concerning the great composer whenever that knowledge threatens to interfere with his finding in Bach's music whatever aesthetic truth he wants to find there. Schweitzer neglects the specifically religious motivation of Bach, in his concern to show the continuity of Bach's aesthetic language.[48] Moreover, he overlooks the insights into Bach's style indicated by historical research in favor of his theory that Bach expressed the ideal form of Ideas (*Urbilder*) in his musical compositions.

Although devoted to history as a scholar, Schweitzer even speaks against it whenever it seems to put its rights above the work of art. This is perhaps the most courageous manifestation of pure aesthetics through a historical subject to be found in any work of musical criticism. For at the time when Schweitzer brought out his Bach, the turn he made in the manner of interpretation was a venture liable to stir up [controversy among music critics]. The frankness in which he called upon the friends of music to move toward aesthetics and away from history is an act of courage that finds scarcely any equal in the musical literature of our day. It may be that this frankness accounts in part for the effect the book produced. Through the emphasis on aesthetics and the artistic quality Schweitzer's interpretation has become a literary achievement. To be historically right or wrong must at times be irrelevant. It was so to Schweitzer. . . .

Schweitzer set out to bring the work of Bach to his time as a living force. If men will not accept it as an active power, there will be no meaning to any interpretation. The work of musical art must stand in life, and not in history. This enormous trust in the power of music marks Schweitzer's aesthetics. And here lies the issue. His aesthetics, as presented through Bach, are fundamentally ethical. They do not exist for their own sake. They carry an ethical message for mankind. *For the sake of the message it could be no other than Bach who must proclaim it.* When Schweitzer describes Bach's attitude toward the religious texts whose servant the composer is in that he submerges himself into their depths to fathom their ideal meanings, it is the necessity of man's devotion and subordination to an ideal that alone would bring forth the message of truth understandable to all [author's italics].[49]

In these selections from Schrade, we can substitute "Jesus" for "Bach" and "religious" for "aesthetic" to obtain passages that might have been written about Schweitzer as theological spokesman. The first italicized sentence has an almost exact analogue in the *Quest,* where Schweitzer remarks, 'Jesus means something for our time because a mighty spiritual force streams forth from him and flows through our time also." [50] And his commentary on that fact might have been applied to Bach: "This fact can neither be shaken nor confirmed by any historical discovery." [51] Schweitzer subordinates history to aesthetics in order to retain his beloved Bach as the messenger of the truth he wants aesthetics to convey. Similarly, he has felt that it was necessary to "place the new outlook on the universe under the authority of the great personality of Jesus." [52]

Schweitzer spiritualizes both Jesus and Bach. He also historicizes, to some extent, the spiritualized representation; although he varies the extent to which he originally *creates* the spiritualized representation and varies the extent to which he *historicizes* the resultant spiritual representation. It might seem that he historicizes an originally created spiritual representation of Jesus (the optimistic and life-affirming Jesus), but merely spiritualizes what was already historically present in Bach (the Ideal form of Ideas in his music). However, in the light of an important ontological doctrine held by Schweitzer, the life-affirming Jesus pictured by him was historically present in the actual Jesus from the first. This ontological doctrine is that "nothing can appear phenomenally (i.e., in an historical event) which is not in some sense ideally present from the first." [53] With this doctrine in mind, Schweitzer often speaks as though it is not we who spirtualize the truths taught by and manifested in Jesus: it was Jesus Himself (or the Gospel itself), who by the ideal essence of His being endorsed and initiated the process of spiritualization.

For example, Schweitzer affirms that present day Christians are "at liberty to *let* the religion of Jesus become a living force in our thoughts, *as its purely spiritual and ethical nature demands*" [author's italics].[54] Convinced that "liberal Christianity was not reduced to living on an historical illusion, but could equally appeal to the Jesus of history," [55] he professes to find in the historical Jesus himself the first spiritualizer of the historical Jesus.[56]

Jesus' spiritualization of His historical self is implied in those passages in which Schweitzer speaks of Jesus' "fitting His teaching into late Jewish Messianic dogma," and describes His "kindling the fire of an ethical faith within the Messianic hopes which His hearers carry in their hearts" (as though Jesus Himself did not really share these hopes).[57] Jesus' death is interpreted as the act by which Jesus Himself "destroyed the form of His world-view, rendering His own eschatology impossible." The crucial point is this:

> Thereby He gives to all peoples and to all times the right to apprehend Him in terms of their thoughts and conceptions, in order that His spirit may pervade their world-view as it quickened and transfigured the Jewish eschatology.[58]

> Jesus spiritualizes the conception of the Kingdom of God, in that He brings it into subjection to His ideal and ethic of love.[59]

Schweitzer's strongest insistence that Jesus spiritualized Himself, and thus provided us with justification for further spiritualizing the historical Jesus, is contained in his 1950 preface to the third English edition of the *Quest*:

> It was Jesus Who began to spiritualize the ideas of the Kingdom of God and the Messiah. He introduced into the late-Jewish conception of the Kingdom His strong ethical emphasis on love, making this, and the consistent practice of it, the indispensable condition of entrance. By so doing He charged the late-Jewish idea of the Kingdom of God with ethical forces, which transformed it into the spiritual

and ethical reality with which we are familiar. Since the faith clung firmly to the ethical note, so dominant in the teaching of Jesus, it was able to reconcile and identify the two, neglecting those utterances in which Jesus voices the older eschatology.

Jesus is already the spiritual Messiah, as opposed to the Messiah of late-Jewish eschatology, in that He has the Messianic consciousness while living a human life in this world, and feels Himself called to awaken in men the desire for the spiritual qualification for entrance into the Kingdom. . . . As the spiritual Lord of the spiritual Kingdom of God on earth, He is the Lord who will rule in our hearts.[60]

This assumption that it was Jesus Himself who was the first liberal Christian, who merely spoke in the *language* of late-Jewish apocalyptic thought, does not appear to be compatible with the earlier view of the historical Jesus which is found in the *Quest* as published in 1906. For there Schweitzer declared:

The Jesus of Nazareth . . . Who preached the ethic of the Kingdom of God, Who founded the Kingdom of Heaven upon earth, and died to give His work its final consecration, never had any existence. He is a figure designed by rationalism, endowed with life by liberalism, and clothed by modern theology in an historical garb.[61]

Schweitzer has convinced himself that modern Christians are *right* in interpreting the facts of history to avoid any conflict with eternal spiritual truth. So convinced is he, in fact, that on one occasion he attributes to God this spiritualizing intent: "Christianity cannot get away from the fact that God has laid upon it the task of spiritualizing its faith." [62] This last conviction, coupled with the belief which we have noted in earlier chapters that God manifests Himself in the heart of men as Will-to-Love, enables him to say of Jesus' revelation: "[Christianity] must not only appeal to the historical revelation but also to the inward one which corresponds with, and continually confirms, the historical revelation." [63]

Schweitzer has changed his ideas about Jesus since 1906, but the spiritualized Jesus of his later writings has significant, in Schweitzer's mind essential, kinship with the fallible eschatological prophet of the first edition of the *Quest*. This early portrait of Jesus presents several aspects of His being which remain permanent parts of Schweitzer's concept of Jesus as the Christ. The *historical* Jesus whose enigmatic presence caused Schweitzer to go forth upon his tasks in Africa has continued to be the Jesus whose fellowship sustained him during his toils, sufferings, conflicts and even his theological revisions. Schweitzer has never spiritualized Jesus to the extent that nineteenth-century liberal theologians spiritualized Him, and has never lost the historical Jesus of the 1906 *Quest*.

Before proceeding further in our discussion of Schweitzer's Christology, we ought to recall the meaning of the phrase "Jesus as the Christ." The Greek word *Christos* is a translation of the Hebrew word *māshīah*, which means "anointed." The literal meaning of the English terms "Christ" and "Messiah" is "the anointed (one)." But because "Christ" and "Jesus Christ" have through long usage taken on a particular metaphysical meaning which was given to them by the development of church dogma in the first four centuries, many theologians (notably Paul Tillich) have begun to say instead "Jesus as the Christ" or simply "Jesus the Christ" in order to remind their readers of the original meaning of the appellation which applied to Jesus, and also to facilitate a new metaphysical interpretation of traditional Christian symbolism. It is not at all inconceivable, then, that Schweitzer should in a very profound sense regard Jesus as the Christ, "the anointed of God," even though He was not infallible. Jesus is the Christ for Schweitzer, not only because of the eternal truth that lies "hidden in His words" [64] as teacher, but also because the very eschatological framework in which these words were spoken makes their truth compelling for us:

. . . affirmation of the world . . . , if it is to be Christian, must in the individual spirit be Christianized and transfigured by the personal rejection of the world which is preached in the sayings of Jesus. It is only by means of the tension thus set up that religious energy can be communicated to our time.[65]

Real appropriation of Jesus' power as teacher can be attained only if "the spirit of the individual man" faces "its appointed task of fighting its way through the world-negation of Jesus, of contending with Him at every step over the value of material and intellectual goods." [66]

The historical Jesus is our example. His lack of concern for this-worldly considerations should be a model of the inner detachment which ought to be a part of our perfected selves. This same trait of His being is a reminder of our need for inwardness as seekers of the Kingdom, and stands against the tendency within liberal theology which threatens to "unstring the bow and make Protestantism a mere sociological force instead of a religious force." [67] His heroic courage should inspire us to take up our Cross and follow Him. In the postscript to *The Mystery of the Kingdom of God* Schweitzer states that the whole purpose of the book has been "to depict the figure of Jesus in its overwhelming heroic greatness and to impress it upon the modern age and upon modern theology." [68] Following Jesus as example does not mean that we imagine we are great enough to turn the wheel of history as He did. Instead, it means that we understand that His singleness of heart in devoting Himself to the service of God was achieved only through heroic struggle against all the temptations that we face.

> Our Lord met His suffering as a free being. . . . He did not stand above suffering; on the contrary, He knew a moment when the intolerable burden of His suffering broke Him. In Gethsemane He implored His disciples to remain with Him and watch with Him. The last cry which came from His lips was a shriek of despair on the Cross. It had to come to pass in this way in order that we in our hour of fear might be able to look upon Him as being a man just as we are. . . .[69]

Moreover, the historical Jesus is our Redeemer. The Christian "finds redemption in the gift of the Spirit of God through Jesus, whereby we are taken out of this world and brought to God." [70] The meaning of redemption through Jesus is explained in a sermon which Schweitzer delivered to candidates for confirmation while serving as pastor of St. Nicholas Church of Strasbourg:

What is religion? The knowledge that the love of God is greater than His righteousness, and that through the power of this love the sinful man in us, at the moment when it gives itself to God, may begin a new life; that he finds peace which raises him above his past. . . . It remains a secret just what went on inside us, that our spirit was stirred by the divine Spirit.[71]

As he phrases it in *The Mysticism of Paul the Apostle*, the Christian "advances into an ever deeper consciousness of sin, and attains in the struggle to die to sin a quiet certitude of the forgiveness of sin." [72] Thus Jesus is "He who brings peace with God into the hearts of men and women"—and it is interesting that when Schweitzer describes Jesus in this way to the Africans, "they understand Him." [73] Thus it is that "in life the Christian stands over life." [74]

How does this redemptive process take place? It occurs as men participate in the suffering life of Jesus the Christ; or, to use the Pauline language which Schweitzer has explicated and charged with such extraordinary vividness in his work on Paul, it occurs as men "die and rise with Christ." Dying must be understood as detachment from the world and suffering self-devotion to others. That is why

The Cross of Jesus remains always right in the center of our religion. We gaze upon it with the same sense of being gripped by it as our fathers did. . . . Our thoughts turn to the word which Jesus spoke to his disciples on the way to Jerusalem: suffering is a baptism, a holy event.[75]

It was on the Cross that "Jesus, who suffered, became the Saviour of the world."

Everyone who is moved by His Spirit should become capable of helping in the world. Power to help slumbers in everyone, but it becomes fully unleashed only when we have tasted the cup of woe. To drink the cup of Jesus means: to suffer sorrow freely, without compulsion, as he did.[76]

We shy away from the imitation of Christ because "it is too uncomfortable for us to comply utterly with what He wishes us to do, if we are to yield ourselves up to Him completely." But complete submission is the price of the fruits of redemption, and our reluctance to yield ourselves wholly explains why "there is no real peace, no real happiness, no real serenity in us." [77]

In a sermon to the Africans, Schweitzer refers to Jesus as the giver of peace, and tells them that this gift can be possessed only if they "let Jesus have power in their hearts" and are ready to be "led captive by Christ," for this is the "innermost fact involved in becoming a Christian." [78] Schweitzer considers that Paul understood superbly the importance of captivity to Christ:

> In Paul's doctrine of dying and rising again with Christ the sayings live again in which Jesus adjures His followers to suffer and die with Him, to save their lives by losing them with Him. What else does Paul do than to give those sayings of Jesus the meaning which they bear for all those who have ever desired to belong to Him?
>
> How penetratingly true is the lesson he teaches, that we cannot possess the Spirit of Christ as mere natural men, but only in so far as the dying and rising with Christ has become reality in us! [79]

If participation in the detachment from the world and the suffering of Christ is the way through which redemption is made possible for us, then participation in the New Being manifested in Jesus as the Christ is the fruit of redemption for us. What does "rising with Christ" mean? Simply that His spirit must "be born in us and take form in us." This interpretation of Paul's message is in Schweitzer's opinion "the fundamental and highest truth of Christianity, in which all those who really want to be Christians can meet one another and be one.[80] "Paul leads us out upon that path of true redemption, and hands us over, prisoners, to Christ." [81]

Christianity is a *Christ-Mysticism*, that is to say, a *"belonging together" with Christ,* grasped in thought and realised in experience. By simply designating Jesus "our Lord" Paul raises Him above all the temporally conditioned conceptions in which the mystery of His personality might be grasped, and sets Him forth as the spiritual Being who transcends all human definitions, *to whom we have to surrender ourselves* in order to experience in Him the true law of our existence and our being [author's italics].[82]

What does Schweitzer conceive Pauline Christ-Mysticism to be? The italicized words in the above quotation, plus the "prisoners of Christ" metaphor employed in the sentence preceding it, indicate that Christ-Mysticism is not for Schweitzer an absorption into essence of the type which he considers impossible, fruitless and dead.[83] Yet it does not seem to be the "mystico-natural" process by which baptized believers are actually "grafted into the corporeity of Christ" in a monophysitical union of substance with substance, which is Schweitzer's interpretation of the doctrine of dying and rising with Christ as it is expressed in the earlier chapters of *The Mysticism of Paul the Apostle*.[84] Against all modern tendencies to spiritualize Paul's eschatologically conditioned doctrine of baptism into "an individual and subjective experience," Schweitzer had proclaimed that it constituted in Paul's mind "a collective and objective event," an "actual physical union between Christ and the Elect." [85] He had contended, "The phrase 'We are all baptized into one body' (I Cor. 12:13) is to be understood literally." [86]

Schweitzer's reluctance to accept a strange primitive notion as normative for present-day faith, which we noticed in his reaction to his discovery of the historical Jesus, manifests itself in his attitude toward Pauline mysticism. When he discusses "Permanent Elements" in Paul's thought, he is driven to qualify his earlier position in the direction of spiritualization. He claims "the right to conceive the idea of union with Jesus on the lines of our own world-view, making it our sole concern to reach the depth of the truly living and spiritual truth." [87] And again he finds evidence in the primitive view of elements which demand and therefore legitimatize, even already initiate, the process of spiritualizing. Schweitzer likens Paul's mystical doctrine to radium, which "by its very nature is in constant emanation," and remarks that the Apostle's "quasi-natural process takes on, as it were of itself, spiritual and ethical significance." This is proof that the naturalistic-eschatological element "constitutes only the outward character of his mysticism." [88] Its "inner essence," however, is the spiritual truth contained in the notion of letting one's selfish desires die so that one can live a life of love and service. And this truth is just as valid as ever.

The dynamic character of the experience of dying and rising with Christ relates the actual view of the historical Paul to our view:

> Whereas in the Greek Mystery-religions the dying and rising again is a single experience undergone in the act of initiation, or at most revived from time to time in repetition of the initiatory act, for Paul it is an experience which, from the moment of baptism, is constantly repeating itself on the believer. In the Hellenistic mysticism the believer lives on the store of experience which he acquired in the initiation. With Paul, his whole being, from his baptism onwards, is a constantly renewed experiencing of the dying and rising again which began in that act. [89]

This theory of the necessity for constant renewal of the mystical union through being "given up to death for Jesus' sake" enables Schweitzer to equate mystical union with inward renunciation from the world, and to equate rising with Christ with active, sometimes suffering, striving towards a half-ethical and half-spiritual Kingdom of God within history. This theory also enables Schweitzer to derive from the "mystico-natural" content of the Pauline concept a "spiritual and ethical" content. [90] His ethics retain the imprint of its Pauline source: "Ethics are . . . the necessary outward expressing of the translation from the earthly world to the super-earthly, which has already taken place in the being-in-Christ." [91] Consequently, "the man who has undergone this translation has placed himself under the direction of the Spirit of Christ." [92] Christ-mysticism is therefore an *ethical* mysticism.

"In Jesus Christ, God is manifested as Will of Love." [93] Thus, being "delivered a prisoner, to Christ," "surrendering ourselves" to Him, or being "placed under the direction of the Spirit of Christ" means being seized by the Will-to-Love that was manifested in the Christ. And since, as we have seen in the previous chapter, "all living knowledge of God" depends on our experiencing Him as Will-to-Love,[94] it can be affirmed that "In union with Christ, union with God is realised in the only form attainable by us." [95] As H. Beintker has so aptly explained, this "only form attainable by us" might be further specified by saying that "the right relationship to Jesus is being gripped by him as the Christ—and therefore: being gripped by God." [96]

Schweitzer's ethical Christ-mysticism depends upon the participation of the finite will of man in the infinite Will of Love of God through the heroic, thoroughly human incarnation of that Will in Jesus as the Christ. For if the "true relation to Him is to be taken possession of by Him," then the "true understanding of Jesus is the understanding of *will acting on will*." [97] As Schweitzer exclaims, "Christian piety of any and every sort is valuable only so far as it means the surrender of our will to His." [98] And here there is no need for spiritualizing; it is precisely the historical Jesus who "moves us deeply by His subordination to God." [99] His errors in the realm of knowledge "do not destroy his spiritual authority as Lord of the will," [100] since "Knowledge of spiritual truth is not called upon to prove its genuineness by showing further knowledge about the events of world history and matters of ordinary life." [101]

The fullest and finest expression of Schweitzer's understanding of Jesus as "Lord of the will" is to be found in the concluding paragraphs of the modified second edition of the work whose first edition was translated into English as *The Quest of the Historical Jesus*. But because the published English edition of the *Quest* is based on Schweitzer's first edition of this work, most English and American readers have been denied the opportunity to read this clearest exposition of his Christology. An English translation of these concluding passages is provided as Appendix II. The reader interested in Schweitzer's Christology should examine them thoughtfully.

The passage just described contains several salient points. It is terribly difficult to translate the content of Jesus' message into a message which is relevant for our time, since Jesus' worldview is set in the framework of a primitive apocalyptic metaphysic that cannot be taken seriously by modern men. This all-important task of translation into our conceptions cannot be

accomplished while we focus our attention upon the *details* of
His life and teaching, in an effort to separate the permanent from
the transitory elements. The all-important question is: if the
Will of Jesus became active in our world-view, what transformation would be wrought in all our willing and hoping? Schweitzer
submits that where Jesus is acknowledged as Lord of the will,
where our wills are united to His in a mystical relationship, a
far deeper transformation is wrought than any transformation
which could be effected by new knowledge about Jesus. It is
a narrow and peculiarly insipid interpretation of Jesus which
believes that His significance for us consists in His teachings
about the fatherhood of God, the brotherhood of man, or those
creedal affirmations and cultic practices which will insure the
salvation of the soul. "In reality, He is an authority for us,
not in the sphere of knowledge but only in the realm of the will,"
because "the last and deepest knowledge of things comes from
the will." If Jesus is to mean anything to us, we must enter
into mystical relationship with Him—and we do that by "experiencing a clarification, enrichment and quickening of our
will by His. Thus do we find ourselves again in Him." We
do that by answering His call to follow Him as Lord of the
will and by accepting the tasks which He has to fulfill in our
time:

> And to those who obey Him, whether they be wise or simple, He
> will reveal Himself in the toils, the conflicts, the sufferings which they
> shall pass through in His fellowship, and, as an ineffable mystery, they
> shall learn in their own experience Who He is.[102]

Albert Schweitzer's ethical mysticism is a Christ-mysticism
because the only form of union with God attainable by us is in
the realm of the will, and Jesus is our authority in the realm of
the will because He is the embodiment of God as Will of Love.
Furthermore, it is Jesus as the Christ who is the source of power
for ethical willing and doing: He quickens our willing and hoping to an intensity that it would have been impossible for us
to achieve without Him. As our spiritual Lord, Jesus forges
mighty bonds of fellowship among all those who acknowledge

Him as the Christ. Finally, "the very strangeness and unconditionedness in which He stands before us makes it easier for individuals to find their own personal standpoint in regard to Him" [103]—because He demands that we *make a decision,* whether we will acknowledge Him or not.

IV. The Significance of Ethical Mysticism for Civilization

Schweitzer conceived of his writings on the philosophy of civilization as a four-volume work. He has discussed in the two volumes already published the need for this philosophical undertaking and its theoretical bases. As yet the implications of his ethical mysticism for civilization are not clear, least of all in regard to the question of how organized social life among men can be improved. But though his conception of organized social action has not yet been fully clarified, fortunately his position is clear on several important issues, one theoretical and two political.

10. Are Civilization and Reverence for Life Compatible?

One of the gravest criticisms of Schweitzer's philosophy alleges that a philosophy of universal reverence for life annihilates value hierarchies, and particularly weakens the pre-eminence of civilized values, thus contributing to rather than halting the disintegration of civilization. The gist of the criticism is that reverence for *all* life is too inclusive.

Interestingly enough, Schweitzer's reverence for life has also been attacked for being insufficiently inclusive. H. Richard Niebuhr, in his recent book *Radical Monotheism and Western Culture*, accuses Schweitzer of setting forth a "henotheism of the community of the living" and claims that this falls short of the ideal ethic since it does not include reverence for the dead and "also reverence for beings, inorganic perhaps, perhaps ideal, that though not living claim the wondering and not exploitative attention of us other creatures that have the will-to-live." [1] But

Niebuhr is mistaken when he implies that Schweitzer does not include inorganic beings within the circle of those to whom reverence is due: Schweitzer views cells and crystals (and thus, by implication, *everything* which has being) as expressive of will-to-live.[2] And furthermore, it is difficult to understand how Niebuhr can believe that Schweitzer's ethical mysticism rules out reverence for the dead. The doctor's high esteem for many thinkers and artists of the past shows great reverence for men of earlier generations.

That Schweitzer's valuations are too inclusive is the more frequent and also the more serious criticism. Oskar Kraus has suggested that Schweitzer is not even aware of the issue at stake:

> It is obvious that the term "reverence for life" expresses much more than the mere literal meaning of the words implies. It includes the realization and enhancement of values. Thus it presupposes a knowledge of what is of value and what is most excellent: it postulates a hierarchy of values and preference, a code of values. If it is to be our task to "raise human life to its highest value," this task can only be fulfilled if we have a table of values by which we can, as it were, estimate their respective worth. Schweitzer does not seem to realize this.[3]

As another critic has pointed out, the very conception of civilization implies gradations of higher and lower forms of life; it implies further that the more civilized person has attained a higher level of life-realization and therefore a higher degree of worth than the less civilized.[4] How then does Schweitzer hope to have a philosophy of *civilization* based on the absolute, universal ethic of reverence for all life?

Perhaps the apparent contradiction is more verbal than real. As Murry has suggested, and as Schweitzer's own writings reveal, when Schweitzer confesses himself a "mass murderer of bacteria" he still knows that as such he is an ethical being.[5] When he speaks of "winning fields from the jungle," he speaks of the *joy* that he feels because of this triumph over nature in the raw.[6] He takes it for granted that a farmer who kills hundreds of wild flowers while mowing his field in preparation for sowing crops is justified in his actions.[7] In all of this it is clear that he is operating on the unacknowledged principle that human life is preferred in the value hierarchy of wills-to-live. While he questions the assumption that "man's life is more important than any other form of which we know," he very significantly adds, "We happen to believe [that this is so]." [8] He states that human life is morally higher than animal life because the altruistic impulses which are limited and sporadic in animals are capable of consistent cultivation in human beings.[9] He emphasizes the necessity for intellectual and esthetic development in self-perfection, thus evidencing a belief that the human will-to-live is qualitatively superior, since intellectual and esthetic potentialities are specifically human. His emphasis upon these potentialities in preference to other drives which men share with lower animals suggests quite strongly that the human potentialities are more worthy of realization.[10]

Schweitzer offers further indications of belief that there are values more important than mere "life," sheer continuation of existence. His unwillingness to declare himself unconditionally a pacifist is one such indication. Of still greater significance is his conviction that suffering is worse than death. He professes gratitude that as a physician he is privileged to save his fellow humans, not only from death, but especially from pain, which is "a more terrible lord of mankind than even death." [11] This awareness that death is not the ultimate evil of finite existence is made explicit in these words from *Indian Thought and Its Development:*

However seriously man undertakes to abstain from killing and damaging, he cannot entirely avoid it. He is under the law of necessity, which compels him to kill and to damage both with and without his knowledge. In many ways it may happen that by slavish adherence to the commandment not to kill compassion is less served than by breaking it. When the suffering of a living creature cannot be alleviated, it is more ethical to end its life by killing it mercifully than it is to stand aloof. It is more cruel to let domestic animals which one can no longer feed die a painful death by starvation than to give them a quick and painless end by violence. Again and again we see ourselves placed under the necessity of saving one living creature by destroying or damaging another.[12]

This passage is especially significant in allowing flexibility in the application of reverence for life, a flexibility potentially relevant to other ethical issues not dealt with by Schweitzer himself.

The close proximity of the words "ethical" and "necessity" in the last quoted passage gives us an all-important clue for the reconciliation of the apparent conflict between Schweitzer's concern for civilization and his insistence that reverence for life is absolute and universal. The tension between these two poles of his thought is produced chiefly by his definition of "ethics" in such an extremely idealistic sense that the realm of "ethics" is altogether separated from the realm of "necessity." In one passage reiterating the unsatisfactory character of that morality which seeks compromises—morality which is in fact "not ethical but a mixture of nonethical necessity and ethics"—Schweitzer emphasizes that "all destruction of and injury to life, under whatever circumstances they take place," is *evil* and brings *guilt* upon the perpetrator. He writes:

> In ethical conflicts man can arrive only at subjective decisions. No one can decide for him at what point, on each occasion, lies the extreme limit of possibility for this persistence in the preservation and furtherance of life. . . .
> We must never allow ourselves to become blunted. We are living in truth, when we experience these conflicts more profoundly. The good conscience is an invention of the devil.[13]

In this excerpt from *Civilization and Ethics,* all killing, no matter what the circumstances, is *evil,* and is therefore banished from the realm of the ethical into the realm of *guilt* and *necessity.* To be sure, one must inevitably venture into the ugly land of necessity and bear the burden of guilt that weighs upon one there—but he must always be clear in his mind that he has crossed a border between two areas, a border across which no agreement can take place.

Yet in the preceding excerpt from *Indian Thought,* it was declared more *ethical* under certain circumstances to submit to the necessity of killing. No guilt was attached: quite the contrary. Furthermore, in Schweitzer's own life as physician, he does not really have a bad conscience over the necessity of killing germs in order to save humans. In his autobiography, he describes the ethical dilemmas presented by his medical practice, stressing that he is *happy* in the privilege that is his of acting as an *ethical* being: "I rejoice over the new remedies for sleeping sickness, which enables me to preserve life, whereas previously I had to watch a painful disease." Yet he regrets the necessity of destroying life while healing: "But every time I have under the microscope the germs which cause the disease, I cannot but reflect that I have to sacrifice this life in order to save another." The border line has been crossed. Schweitzer should experience *guilt*. But instead he speaks of a feeling significantly different from guilt:

> To the man who is truly ethical all life is sacred, including that which from the human point of view seems lower in the scale. He makes distinctions only as each case comes before him, and under the pressure of necessity, as for example, when it falls to him to decide which of two lives he must sacrifice in order to preserve the other. But all through this series of decisions he is conscious of acting on subjective grounds and arbitrarily, and knows that he bears the *responsibility* for the life which is sacrificed [author's italics].[14]

In softening "guilt" to "responsibility," Schweitzer concedes that reverence for life does give its blessing to ethical activity which involves doing harm to "lower" forms of life. To be ethical, we *must* accept the responsibility of advancing some wills-to-live at the expense of others, and some elements of the will-to-live at the expense of others. Beyond doubt, Schweitzer recognizes this responsibility and lives his life accordingly, exhibiting the utmost integrity in the exercise of this responsibility.

Schweitzer is deliberate in speaking frequently of the absoluteness and universality of the ethics of reverence for life and equally frequently of the inevitability of the natural necessity for killing. He is keeping present to our minds the recognition that if we relax the tension between ethics and necessity, which we are meant to feel every time we are forced to destroy life, we "blunt ourselves." To ease our consciences by formulating a *system* of value-assessments for various forms of will-to-live, or by "keeping in store adjustments between ethics and necessity all ready for use" would be to surrender to evil. We must always be "concerned at heart with all the human destinies and all the other life-destinies" around us.[15] Even the pages from *Civilization and Ethics* quoted above to show the radical split between necessity and ethics contain the words "We are living in truth when we experience these conflicts more profoundly."[16] Though "in practice, we are forced to choose," it can still be said that "the principle of reverence for life is none the less universal."[17]

If the above analysis is correct, it can logically be said that reverence for life is not incompatible with civilization. The command to show reverence for all forms of life is intended to sensitize our hearts by giving us an *attitude* of universal compassion, not to paralyze our hands by laying down an impossible and inflexible *rule* for conduct. Interpreted in this way, reverence for life has great relevance for "the ethics of ethical personality," because universal compassion is a valuable component of self-perfection, and true civilization requires the perfection of individuals.

It is less easy to define the relevance of reverence for life to "the ethics of ethical society." It is clear enough that reverence for life dictates a more humane treatment of animals, but what does this ethic have to say about some of the weightier problems affecting civilized society not even mentioned by Schweitzer? Many areas of the world are faced with a "population explosion" of such proportions that they can never achieve a civilized standard of living without conscious control of the birth rate—what does the ethic of reverence for life have to say about birth control? Many older persons are faced with the agonizing prospect of intense suffering from incurable diseases— what does reverence for life have to say about voluntary euthanasia? Many individuals, in this age of concentration camps and brainwashing, are faced with torture or a loss of self-identity far worse than physical death—what does reverence for life have to say about the legitimacy of suicide under certain conditions?

Schweitzer has not yet given us an analysis of such problems. Henri Babel, whose *La pensée d'Albert Schweitzer* is undoubtedly the finest work on Schweitzer in French and one of the most scholarly treatments of his thought in any language, attempts to deal with these problems in a manner faithful to Schweitzer, but his answers are inconclusive. He conjectures that suicide would be inadmissable under any circumstances. He is willing to grant that euthanasia is sometimes a tempting option; however, he warns that it would be "a grave violation of the reverence which we owe to life so long as it is given to us, even when distorted by pointless suffering." He implies that birth control would be permissible, since "Venus is inevitably followed by Mars"; i.e., since war is likely to result from overpopulation.[18]

Answers to these questions cannot be anything more than conjectures, no matter how well grounded in a study of Schweitzer's thought. He has not been silent, however, on two of the most pressing problems confronting civilization today. An analysis of his answers to these problems follows in the next chapter.

11. Political Problems

Schweitzer does not count it a part of his vocation as moral philosopher to speak out on concrete political issues. In the main, he is preoccupied with the type of motivation which should determine moral choice, the spirit which should pervade ethical action—and not with recommending which specific actions ought to be taken in this or that particular instance. But on two extremely important matters, perhaps the two most pressing matters that confront the people of the world and their political representatives today, he has expressed his views in some detail. These two issues are: atomic weapons (i.e., the need for a cessation of testing and for disarmament) and colonialism (i.e., the problems presented by the desire of former colonial peoples for political self-determination).

ATOMIC TESTING

To speak to this problem, Schweitzer has departed from his usual posture of "simply living and working" without speaking publicly. He has made public his protests against the peril of atomic testing. But for a long time he hesitated. As early as 1954 he was being urged to issue a statement on atomic warfare and testing, but at that time he limited himself to a letter in the London *Daily Herald* in which he reiterated his individualistic sentiments:

> What the world should do is to listen to the warnings of individual scientists who understand this terrible problem. This is what would impress people and give them understanding and make them realize the danger in which we find ourselves. . . .
>
> If they [the scientists] all raised their voices, each one feeling himself impelled to tell the truth, they would be listened to, for then humanity would understand that the issues were grave.[1]

His fullest statement on the issue reflects these sentiments again; indeed, the following excerpt from a conversation with Schweitzer reported by Norman Cousins presents our best evidence of his rationale for silence:

"All my life," he said, "I have carefully stayed away from making pronouncements on public matters. Groups would come to me for statements or I would be asked to sign joint letters or the press would ask for my views on certain political questions. And always I would feel forced to say no.

"It was not because I had no interest in world affairs or politics. It was just that I felt that my connection with the outside world should grow out of my work or thought in the fields of theology or philosophy or music. I have tried to relate myself to the problems of all mankind rather than to become involved in disputes between this or that group. I wanted to be one man speaking to another man about the lasting problems inside men and between them." [2]

Another probable reason for Schweitzer's hesitancy is the fact that he has never declared himself a complete pacifist, and does not appear to be really clear in his own mind how to answer the question of whether or not war is sometimes justified.[3] Like any civilized man, he is against war. He condemns not only its physical atrocities (he indicts the use of flame throwers in World War II specifically) but also the callousness which familiarity with such horrors breeds within human hearts.[4] Moreover, he shows an awareness of the collective nature of sin in regard to war, for he asserts: "The important thing is that we should one and all acknowledge that we have been guilty of this inhumanity." [5] He is even opposed to armed revolution, as his very interesting comments on Rosa Luxemburg demonstrate: he cites the sympathy for animals which she exhibited in prison as proof of the basic goodness of her heart and bewails the fact that she did not have enough faith in the power of the heart's ideals, but turned to violence.[6]

The very notion of resistance, even apart from violence, is abhorrent to Schweitzer. He states while discussing Gandhi:

The important thing is not that only nonviolent force should be employed, but that all world purposive action should be undertaken with the greatest possible avoidance of violence, and that ethical considerations should so dominate ourselves as to influence also the hearts of our opponents.[7]

Yet he cannot be strictly termed a pacifist. The evasiveness of a letter written in 1939 to an admirer who challenged him on this very point is revealing. He answered, "Naturally I am against war. War means brutality and stupidity. That I am against war is shown in my idea of reverence for life. While I spread that idea, I fight war in the deepest way." [8] Even more revealing is a statement in which he suggests an approach to recalcitrance which upholds the separation between the worldly and the spiritual, and therefore does not fall into the danger of "mixing up what is different in essence":

> The method is as follows. In combination with the ethical and spiritual means, recourse will be had to worldly purposive procedure. But when the use of force seems unavoidable, then as little force as possible will be employed. And it will be used in such a way that it is regarded only as a last expedient, and will be exercised, not in a worldly, but in an ethical spirit.[9]

That Schweitzer is not a pacifist is further evidenced in his choice of a particular criticism of the Jainist doctrine of *Ahimsa* (i.e., purity through inactivity and absolute refusal to kill). He states that the principle of not-killing and not-harming must not be autonomous, but subordinate to compassion. "It must therefore enter into practical discussion with reality. True reverence for morality is shown by readiness to face the difficulties contained in [morality]." [10]

But the drastically new situation created by atomic weapons finally persuaded Schweitzer to throw the weight of his moral influence behind an effort to awaken humanity to the risks involved in atomic testing. And when he finally spoke, he produced an admirably balanced and carefully reasoned appeal.[11] He has spoken three times over international radio about the problem, and the three speeches have been assembled into one publication, *Peace or Atom War?* In this little booklet, he points out the utter futility of atomic warfare, contending that limited atomic weapons and a limited atomic war are figments of the wishful imagination that no realistic person could seriously hope for. Among the new dangers which make the present situation unprecedented he lists genetic effects, the possibility of total destruction in a matter of minutes because of the unprecedented speed of rockets, and the related possibility that a mistake of human or electronic judgment might touch off a wholly unprovoked and unnecessary war.

Schweitzer fears that human judgment could easily be led astray by the pressure of constant anxiety that accompanies our mood of alertness against attack; he fears that entrusting human welfare to electronic brains is even more hazardous. He notes that the danger will only grow more acute if more nations come into possession of the weapons, and uses this as a major argument for immediate action to control the terrible instruments of destruction while only a few nations have them and control is still feasible.

He recommends that testing be stopped at once and that the highest officials of the atomic powers hold a conference in a neutral country, the purpose of which should be to reach agreement upon an open-skies inspection plan to insure atomic disarmament. The closing words of Schweitzer's appeal for a termination of nuclear tests deserve to be quoted in full:

> We cannot continue in a situation of paralyzing mistrust. If we want to work our way out of the desperate situation in which we find ourselves another spirit must enter into the people. It can only come if the awareness of its necessity suffices to give us strength to believe in its coming. We must presuppose the awareness of this need in all the peoples who have suffered along with us. We must approach them in the spirit that we are human beings, all of us, and that we feel ourselves fitted to feel with each other; to think and to will together in the same way.[12]

This appeal is significant for the appraisal of Schweitzer's social ethics, since it provides some important indications that his prejudice against collective activity for ethical ends is not so strong as his tendencies towards individualism and idealism might indicate. The later broadcasts contain a demand that

national *governments* have a responsibility to act ethically, im-
plying that he has finally acknowledged the importance of the
political structures of collective man in the struggle for peace
and justice. But this recognition of political organizations is
weakened by his indictment of international law for its failure
to "assert *itself*" [13]—as though "law" can assert itself apart from
the political institutions which formulate and enforce it.

That Schweitzer did not intend to violate his policy of
individualism by making his appeals for an end to nuclear
testing has been indicated by a close personal friend of his.
This friend maintains that in making the appeals Schweitzer
thought of himself as speaking in his role as the Nobel Prize
Laureate, and therefore as an individual. He would not have
spoken through the United Nations, since to do so it would have
been necessary for him to go there as the representative of some
large collectivity of men with national interests at stake.[14]

COLONIALISM

It cannot be denied that Schweitzer's attitude toward the
relationship between the white men of Europe and the black
men of Africa is paternalistic. He once remarked that "A
civilization which does not recognize its great task in the
world [*i.e.*, to make civilized human beings of the natives in
uncivilized regions] is no civilization.[15]

He believes that all men are entitled to seven fundamental
rights: to habitation; to free movement; to free use of soil and
subsoil; to freedom of labor and of exchange; to justice; to
live "within a natural, national organization"; and to education.[16] The benevolent colonial government must respect these
rights so far as possible, since they are indeed rights which belong equally to all human beings, regardless of race. Schweitzer
is no racist and has condemned racism with hot indignation.[17]
But it is inevitable and tolerable that these rights be abridged
to some extent during the period of colonial adjustment, since
the "normal" cycle of development among colonial peoples has
been broken by contact with technologically, scientifically and
commercially sophisticated Europeans.[18] "In the interest of

the development of the country" it may be necessary to take certain temporary measures that will in the long run be to the benefit of the natives.

Some enforced transplanting of colonial populations may be necessary, but this should only be done with "the future development of the good of the people" in mind, and always with "long foresight, careful planning and adequate warning." [19] The right to circulate freely is hindered by the necessity to maintain a labor supply in each territory and to insure the collection of colonial taxes.[20] Forced labor may sometimes be essential to provide a future in which labor will be less arduous, as when highways are built in order to facilitate transport and to do away with the frightful practice of long porterage by human carriers. But forced labor should be employed only where absolutely necessary, only for *public* services, and then only under the following supplementary conditions:

(2) That the sharing of women in such labor should only be (a) when it is near their own village to which they can return to sleep; (b) when plantation work is not needed (this time is in practice quite clear and sharply defined); (c) when they are not nursing a child. (3) That no children should be allowed to work. (4) That where the men live while working away from their villages, proper preparation shall be made in the way of sanitation, food, habitation; and (5) That the pace of the labour shall never be forced.[21]

The right to "natural, national organization" is given hardly a third of a page by Schweitzer; about all he has to say on this score is that it depends on a proper exercise of the educational mission of the colonial authorities, which should aim as much as possible at the training of skilled artisans. The development of craftsmen takes precedence over the creation of intellectually developed citizens:

Intellectual learning should in every colonial school be accompanied by the acquisition of every kind of manual skill; for their civilization it is more important that the natives should learn to burn bricks, to build, to saw logs into planks, to be ready with hammer, plane and chisel, than they should be brilliant at reading and writing, and even be able to calculate with $a + b$ and $x + y$. . . .

The native is in danger of cutting out the stage between primitive life and professional. That is, he tends to eliminate the stages of agriculture and handicraft. He has a certain antagonism to the use of tools, and a desire to sit in an office with a cigarette in his mouth and a pen in his hand. I am constantly hearing the phrase "I want to be a writer." At my hospital, recently, I was helping to carry things to the garden, partly in order to create this impression of the dignity of labour. I saw a native in white clothes standing by the fence, and asked him to join in and help. His reply was—"No, I am an intellectual; a brain-worker." [22]

Schweitzer notes that the educated native may have difficulty in finding a suitable wife; that is, one who suits him. [23]

Development should proceed at a pace geared to the maximum health and welfare of the people, not the quickest expansion of trade; it is better to leave certain areas altogether untapped "rather than develop along abnormal lines and with injustice." [24] The advantage in allowing one commercial company a trading monopoly in an area is that this will insure that the natives get good quality merchandise and are protected from harmful products; the disadvantage is that monopolies tend to produce exorbitant prices. [25] Africans should be protected from the ravages of alcohol, which has a devastating effect on both their health and their culture in general. [26] Needless to say, the benefits of modern medicine should be made available. [27]

The native should be taught the civilized virtues. They need to learn the art of hard work, says Schweitzer, especially the habit of avoiding famine by clearing more land for planting even though they have to go to the additional trouble of cutting down trees instead of burning them down. [28] They must be taught hygiene and freedom from superstition (Schweitzer considers deliverance from animistic fears as one of the greatest blessings Europe has bestowed upon the Dark Continent). [29] They should learn gratitude—or, at any rate, the habit of showing it tangibly! [30]

In bearing the white man's burden among the Africans, Schweitzer often maintains a wise relativism. He feels that the native law and judiciary proceedings can be applied more reliably than can European standards and procedures to situations in which native precedent is definite and accepted.[31] Although he once said that monogamy is "what Christianity demands," he is not in favor of abolishing polygamy where this would work a hardship upon the people.[32] He is of the opinion that justice in the colonies depends more upon the type of personnel who fill administrative posts than upon the policies set by ruling nations. To him, it is of supreme importance that governments and commercial enterprise put a stop to their practice of sending out "young, untested, inexperienced men of inadequate moral calibre into the interior to difficult posts": they must "send out as administrators tested men of humane feeling and goodwill . . . skilled, experienced men." [33] Schweitzer would allow tremendous latitude of action to the white administrator who combines good will with some pragmatic experience of native ways. He himself has felt no scruples against manipulating the natives by blackmail, bribery and great white lies. He has employed such measures when they were necessary to coerce the relatives of patients into contributing some work or payment to the hospital, when necessary to maintain the good will of witch doctors so that they would bring to the hospital the cases they could not cure, or when necessary to encourage helpfulness in the natives, lest it "disappear like an expiring flame." [34]

The justification given for colonial control rather than self-determination is that enlightened imperialistic rule is much to be preferred to the capricious rule of native chiefs which would result from Africa's contact with commercial Europe without colonial government.[35] The chiefs already have unlimited power, and as their appetites are broadened by contacts with traders who offer them undreamed of personal advantages in exchange for native labor they are tempted to use that power tyrannically.[36] To be sure, "imperialism" has in the past committed grievous crimes against the natives, and continues to do so; these facts must not be "suppressed or whitewashed." Yet

willingness to give these primitive and semiprimitive people of our colonies an independence which would inevitably end in enslavement to their fellows, is no way of making up for our failure to treat them properly. Our only possible course is to exercise for the benefit of the natives the power we actually possess, and thus provide a moral justification for it. Even the hitherto prevailing "imperialism" can plead that it has some qualities of ethical value. It has put an end to the slave trade; it has stopped the perpetual wars which the primitive people wage with one another, and has thus given a lasting peace to large portions of the world; it endeavors in many ways to produce in the colonies conditions which shall render more difficult the exploitation of the population by world trade. I dare not picture what the lot of the native lumbermen in the forests of the Ogowe district would be if the government authorities which at the present time preserve their rights for them in opposition to the merchants, both white and black, should be withdrawn.[37]

Further evidence of Schweitzer's conservatism in regard to self-determination for the natives is found in conversations with him reported by Grabs and Siebert. In a discussion with Grabs concerning nationalism, Schweitzer is reported to have said disapprovingly, "Even the natives, whose members can neither read nor write, are becoming nationalistic." [38] Siebert quotes him as having concluded a conversation on the unreadiness of the natives for independence with the remark, "Higher than freedom is virtue." [39]

How do Schweitzer's opinions regarding colonialism express themselves in his administration of the hospital at Lambarene? Most visitors have been taken aback by the lack of modernity. The very hygienic standards of the establishment have been called into question: Gunther called Lambarene "the most unkempt place of its kind I saw in all Africa." [40] The facilities for mental patients have been termed "horrible." [41] The privileged status of white patients is expressed in the privileged treatment accorded to them.[42]

The theory that lies behind privilege and segregation has been clearly expressed by Schweitzer:

The negro [sic] is a child and with children nothing can be done without authority. We must, therefore, so arrange the circumstances of daily life that my natural authority can find expression. With regard to the negroes, then, I have coined the formula: "I am your brother, it is true, but your elder brother." [43]

Schweitzer relates the sad experience of a missionary who "left the staff some years ago to live among the Negroes as their brother absolutely." His abandonment of "the social interval between white and black" caused him to "lose all influence," for "his word was no longer taken as the 'white man's word,' but he had to argue every point with them as if he were merely their equal." [44] The moral of the story: a European must "maintain the authoritative position of the white man"; he must see to "the prevention of unsuitable freedom"; he must uphold his "mental and spiritual superiority"; indeed, he should even preserve an element of fear in the feeling of the natives towards him. [45] In short, paternalism is the best arrangement in the colonies. [46]

Schweitzer feels that he must treat the natives like little brothers because his experience with them has apparently led him to conclude that they are lazy, irresponsible and unintelligent when faced with the task of building an adequately civilized life for themselves. [47] Black men simply cannot be counted on to do any work unless supervised constantly by a white man or a "relatively reliable Negro." [48] They have no foresight—that is why they allow famine to plague them and why they are reluctant to spend their energy in building permanent structures for the benefit of other patients who will follow later when they have gone. [49] Although the natives are capable of learning humanitarian sentiments and although they are patient in suffering, "kind-hearted," "good-natured and loyal," still they are naturally callous towards other men who do not belong to their in-group. When asked to help another patient who is not of their tribe, the natives murmur, "This not brother for me." [50]

How accurate is Schweitzer's theory of paternalism in describing the actual conditions and how appropriate is it in meeting the actual needs of the natives? And is the policy of paternalism appropriate today, even if it were appropriate when Schweitzer formulated it, thirty years ago? Does his authoritarian approach alleviate native irresponsibility—or does this approach in large measure encourage and perpetuate irresponsibility?

Lambarene and Schweitzer's policies there have been seen in different lights by different visitors. Marcus Bach, one of the more favorably impressed visitors, reports:

> The natives trust Schweitzer as no white man in Africa has ever been trusted. They love him, but what is more important is their conviction that he loves them. He loves them even when they abuse him, when they forget to thank him, when they insult him, when they steal from him.[51]

Fritz Buri applauds Schweitzer's "realism" on the entire question of colonialism.[52] McGregor sees his authoritarianism in a gentle light, for after describing Schweitzer's simplicity, his geniality at table and the way his staff hangs on his words, he declares:

> although there is much activity, there is no haste; although there is purpose, there is no grimness; although there are different races, there is none of that contrast one meets with in the other Africas; there is no obsequious deference by black to white; there is instead trust, faith and naturalness.[53]

Yet even McGregor qualifies his remarks by observing, "I heard it said that the doctor is an authoritarian who exercises strict discipline, and that his staff is in awe of him. This is partially true and noticeable in little things." [54]

Hunter admits that Schweitzer's ". . . Friends in France even intimate that at times some of his colleagues in Africa have found him a little arbitrary, a little dictatorial." [55] A young American who visited Lambarene recently is said to have come away with the impression that the staff there was "divided between those in more or less permanent, if private, revolt and those who thought of themselves as administering a sort of benevolent concentration camp." [56] Gunther is equally critical: he interprets Schweitzer's insistence that every white person wear a sun helmet as the perpetuation of a colonial symbol. In addition, he mentions cases in which Schweitzer used sarcasm to get work out of the natives. Gunther claims that "many African workers seemed unhappy and somewhat unfriendly—even surly." [57]

Yet Schweitzer's patriarchalism seems to be undiminished, according to an interesting report given by Gell. He quotes a recent guest at Lambarene to the effect that Schweitzer still considers Africans incapable of using a wheelbarrow! Moreover:

> On another occasion [the visitor] instructed a gang of laborers at the hospital to put a window-frame in upside down. Schweitzer arrived in time to hear him apologizing for this inexplicable mistake and having it put right. Whereupon the doctor took him aside, thrust an arm around his shoulders and explained patiently that a white man must never, *never* admit error to an African. [58]

Such opinions and reports about Schweitzer's administration of the hospital at Lambarene provide insights into the meaning and the applications of his ethical philosophy. If the hospital is really, as Gunther has suggested, nothing more than an exercise in penance, [59] then the conclusion might be drawn that his fundamental conception of ethics is that of an ethic of personal purification. Schweitzer's emphasis on self-devotion as a subsidiary form of self-perfecting does lend some credence to that interpretation. However, if his interest in providing a "witness to the power of the spiritual over the temporal" is so great that it causes him to neglect the care of sick bodies, [60] then his piety appears to be not only irrelevant but actually insidious in its concern for "the spirit."

But if his policy and actions may be interpreted as simply the tactical program of a practical man, whose primary concern is to accomplish a worthwhile task as easily and thoroughly as possible, then his theory is redeemed from the reproaches that it is egocentric or irrelevant. We might in that case strongly disagree with the methods chosen. We might consider his basic orientation obsolete since there are in many parts of Africa today enough "civilized" natives to provide capable self-government. But still we could interpret these erroneous methods as the expression of a pragmatic compassion which seeks simply the most direct way of providing medical care to persons who have none.

Cecil Northcott has posed the significant question. He reports that Schweitzer has refused proffered financial aid to the hospital because he feels that "the old rough beds, the sheets split down the middle, the corrugated iron buildings" are "sufficient witness to the power of the spiritual over the temporal." [61] He might also have called additional attention to the inadequate drug supply and the meager refrigeration space, or to the lack (until very recently) of X-ray equipment.[62] If, as Northcott believes, Schweitzer is only giving up modernity, that is one thing—but if he is giving up cleanliness, progress, efficiency and stable expansion as well, that is quite a different matter.

Schweitzer has a number of defenders. Many of them agree with Homer Jack, who insists, "But he never economizes with medicines, and despite his many old-fashioned ways he believes in making use of the very latest medical discoveries." [63] Even Gunther admits that the actual medical work is conducted in adequately antiseptic fashion.[64] Furthermore, the benefits of the hospital are extended to all; Schweitzer does not even charge full price on the bills to be paid by white employers for native employees, for fear that natives needing treatment will be kept away until seriously ill.[65]

The hospital grounds' appearance is similar to that of an unkempt native village. Homer Jack and Norman Cousins explain that this is by design: Schweitzer tries to "simulate as much as possible the conditions of the native village. The people flock to his Hospital because they feel at home there." [66] The argument is that if conditions were not typically African many natives simply would not come to receive the attention they need.[67] But this argument has been challenged. Gell speaks of another hospital in the Congo, founded two years before that at Lambarene, operating in very similar circumstances, and "no less popular with no less primitive people for being run on thoroughly modern, hygienic lines." [68]

Schweitzer's authoritarianism has also received many justifications. It is probably true that most natives do not have any sense of the value of "making improvements" and are therefore, by Western standards, exasperatingly lazy and in need of steady supervision.[69] Even Gunther, who is generally hostile to Schweitzer's methods, admits that the workmen he observed at Lambarene were

the worst workmen I have ever seen. They used their spades . . . with about as much animation as corpses. If they had spines, they were made of blotting paper. They were not too ill to work, but just plain lazy, as well as numb with boredom and indifference. . . . Schweitzer strode among them with explosive and hortatory grunts. He argued, threatened, cajoled. He took a spade himself.[70]

Cousins attempts to explain Schweitzer's "gruffiness" by pointing out that: (1) the doctor is very pressed for time; (2) he feels personally responsible for everything that goes on at Lambarene; and (3) experience has taught him that a "take-my-word-for-it" approach is best.[71] He also stresses that Schweitzer drives himself harder than anyone else. He would probably never ask another man eighty years of age to take up a spade. His gruffness does not necessarily connote disapproval to the natives, because they have become accustomed to the pattern and feel at home in it.[72] One is quoted as saying, "We do not become angry. How could we? Could a man be angry with his own father for telling him what to do?" [73] Final judgment upon Schweitzer's policies toward natives should not be made without taking into account a complaint voiced recently by Schweitzer: "Only those who have been through it themselves can imagine how exasperating, discouraging and depressing it is to deal with [the natives] on the building site." [74]

V. A Critical Appraisal of Schweitzer's Ethical Mysticism

12. Recapitulation

The final chapters of this book contain a critique of the various dimensions of Schweitzer's thought and an appraisal of his contribution to moral philosophy. Before evaluating the ethical mysticism of Schweitzer in our own terms, though, it would be well to assess the merits of his system on its own terms.

Schweitzer's overriding problem was the task of providing a foundation in thought for the world-view of ethical world- and life-affirmation. If only this foundation could be established, then the "noble and enthusiastic but not deep" will-to-civilization of the Enlightenment would be safe from the erosions of materialism and of speculative doubts about the goodness of life.[1] This task was accomplished to Schweitzer's satisfaction by his discovery of the ethic of reverence for life, an ethic which he regards as rational, absolute and universal. For Schweitzer, the very phrase "reverence for life" was characterized by a self-authenticating validity from the moment when he intuited it, as his description of that moment reveals:

> The iron door had yielded: the path in the thicket had become visible. Now I had found my way to the idea in which affirmation of the world and ethics are contained side by side! Now I knew that the ethical acceptance of the world and of life, together with the ideals of civilization contained in this concept, has a foundation in thought.[2]

Reverence for life, because it is an ethic which is rational in a direct and elemental, not a speculative, sense, is a necessity of thought for anyone who will only "reflect upon the first, the most immediate, and the continually given fact of his own consciousness": his will-to-live.[3] This ethic possesses the chief strength of the Kantian system in that it has compelling authority for all rational beings, and the chief legitimacy of the subjectivist ethical systems in that it springs from profound personal reflection rather than from external circumstances.

Reverence for life commands an altruistic self-devotion to all other forms of life. This command escapes the Kantian defect of formalism, since it has "an absolute and completely universal content"[4] which is theoretically the same in all situations, regardless of practicability. The command avoids the arbitrariness which was the chief defect of Schopenhauer's and Nietzsche's ethics since it defines the sphere of ethics in terms of a higher life-affirmation which includes a measure of life-negation (self-denial) with a benevolent purpose.

Since reverence for life relates one to the infinite will-to-live which is active in all beings, it brings one into a mystical relationship with the ultimate cosmic reality. But it is not a dead "Being-mysticism," for it demands a union with other beings which grows out of active self-devotion to their welfare.

Schweitzer has not so clearly made his case that reverence for life is relevant and adequate to the practical advancement of civilization. His contention is that the man who really reflects seriously upon his will-to-live, who allows his thought to "think itself to a conclusion," will arrive at an ethical mysticism capable, by its very inner nature, of settling all soluble practical problems. He claims that reverence for life puts an end to the superficiality and the dehumanization of modern life. It mitigates the estrangement from nature which is central to our sickness. It overcomes cynicism, pessimism and brutality. And Schweitzer can maintain that his philosophy has cleared the way for the rejuvenation of the church as an ethical force in society, since he has shown that dogmatic accretions obscure the real ethic of Jesus, which was essentially reverence for life.

But Albert Schweitzer would be the last to suggest that we accept his philosophy on his terms without examining it carefully on ours. He admonishes his readers to subject his thought, or that of any other thinker, to ruthless criticism.[5] We now address ourselves to that task.

13. Critique of the Ethic of Self-Perfection

Schweitzer intends his ethic of self-perfecting to develop the dimension of the human self which is most thwarted by material progress: the dimension of depth. His remarks concerning our "need for roots" have been reiterated so frequently by critics of contemporary technological society that they might seem trite, were it not for the extreme gravity of the peril. The need for "inwardness" is pressing if we are to avoid losing our souls in the plethora of commodities which are being thrust upon us from all sides by manufacturers, who often stimulate artificial needs in order to sell useless products.

Lewis Mumford has written that Schweitzer's life, as well as his thought, sets forth an admirable ideal of balanced *wholeness* which perhaps ought to be an important criterion of authentic existence as a truly human being.[1] Even though it seems logical that one should be able to render more service to others and achieve greater self-fulfillment by concentrating on the one single exercise of his talents in which he is most proficient or most needed by others, this may not be true. Lack of wholeness may not only jeopardize the emotional health of a person and therefore rob him of fulfilment, it may also infect all of his relationships with others, even without his being aware of it, and turn his efforts to serve others into a subtle discharge of hostilities. Single-minded devotion to the duties of one's vocation may be self-defeating if it leads to onesidedness. Anyone whose zeal for his vocation prompts him to feel that every moment of time and every drop of energy must be rationalized into a pattern of unceasing toil might do well to remember the figure of the old doctor, bent over his piano at Lambarene, alone with Bach in "honorable and profound" leisure. Schweitzer defines such leisure as "the hours of a man's life that he employs for himself and himself alone."[2] His stress on deep, honest meditation on the elemental realities of the universe is a message of wisdom.

The point of departure for a proper assessment of Schweitzer's doctrine of self-perfection is a phenomenological analysis of selfhood that distinguishes three different aspects of the self: the *existing* or *empirical* self (what the self is now, at this particular moment in its development); the *self-image* (what the self actually aspires to be and to appear in the eyes of others); and the *essential* self (what the self ideally ought to be in order to fulfil its highest potentialities).[3] For example, a man of frail physique and mediocre intellectual ability, meekly submissive in his contacts with other men and agonizingly shy in his contacts with women, may yet in his dreams picture himself as an aggressive hero who dominates other men and captivates women. Such a man may suffer acute guilt feelings because he does not live up to his self-image; or, on the other hand, he may make himself obnoxious to his associates by overcompensating for these guilt feelings through overly aggressive behavior. Both his behavior and his image of himself may violate a deeper conception of essential manhood which elemental thought could arouse in his self-awareness.

The life-negation which is demanded by higher life-affirmation is this: the self-image should be redefined in such a way as not to conflict with the essential self, and the existing self should move steadily toward as close an approximation of essential manhood as possible. Now, if Schweitzer is right in holding that compassionate self-devotion to other life is the most crucial factor in essential humanity, then unlimited affirmation of raw will-to-live would be illegitimate, for it would entail a gratification of the existing self, and of a perverted self-image, at the expense of the essential self. The man who chose to ratify his potential status as a truly *human* being would indeed regard it as a matter of course that "we should all take our share of the burden of pain that lies upon the world."[4] And certainly the common virtues of patience, self-control, humility, honesty and gratitude are elements of higher self-affirmation which oftentimes require negation of the existing self and its egocentric self-image.

There are many dangers to be avoided here. One is the danger that the definition of essential selfhood will be made identical with one's self-image. This can happen because one is unreflective, or it can happen because one confuses external personality with character, conventions with morality. No one has the right to require that all human beings, to qualify as human, should aspire to the same kind of personality he aspires to; nor has anyone the right to insist that all men should conform to the behavioral patterns that are found in his particular society. One's understanding of essential selfhood must be confined to qualities of character that are really essential to men who are in process of fulfilling their potential nature as children of God. The second formidable danger is that one fail to *accept* his existing self (which is what it is largely because of factors over which he had no control) and therefore demand that the existing self move too rapidly or too completely in the direction of essential selfhood.

Schweitzer's route to self-perfection admirably avoids the first danger, that of egocentrism and ethnocentrism. He maintains a wise relativism toward the African cultural patterns which surround him. His attitude of openness toward differences in taste is illustrated in a charming story told by Robert Minder, a former piano pupil of Schweitzer. Minder relates how Schweitzer insisted upon teaching him a number of simple, sweet melodies of obviously mediocre artistic quality. Schweitzer did this so that his student would always have in his repertoire a tune that would be congenial to the unsophisticated taste of elderly relatives whose opportunities in life had not been sufficient to give them an appreciation for the music of Bach or Beethoven! [5]

Schweitzer is more vulnerable to criticism as regards his involvement in the second great danger threatening a sound ethic of self-perfection, the danger that the empirical self will be rejected. The very term "self-perfection," which connotes static purity, a *condition* of flawlessness rather than a *direction* of development, raises the question as to whether Schweitzer appreciates adequately the depths of irrationality, selfishness and sheer evil which are built so stubbornly into the finite will-to-live. That he does not have an adequate appreciation of the depths of human sinfulness is suggested by his reference to "the sinful self *in* me" in one of his sermons.[6] This manner of speaking implies that the empirical self is something alien to one's being, something to be repressed rather than acknowledged and accepted.

Theologians and psychologists agree in asserting that self-rejection is likely to have perilous consequences. On the one hand, it results in pride, the desperate pride of the person who attempts to run away from his sense of guilt by denying that his empirical self is really a part of his total self. On the other hand, it results in despair, the bitter despair of the man who realizes that he can never fulfill completely either his self-image or his vision of essential selfhood. This problem is exemplified in Schweitzer's neglect of the Christian doctrine of grace. As one theological student at the University of Berne put it, "What has Albert Schweitzer got to say to the man who has failed?" [7] Schweitzer's exhortations to detachment and untiring self-devotion may be worse than irrelevant to such a man, especially if he has failed precisely because he has made impossible or badly chosen demands upon himself and has already extended himself to the limit in striving to fulfill these unrealistic demands.

Related to this tendency toward a lack of acceptance of the empirical self in Schweitzer's thought is his extreme faith in reason. A more sober estimate of the empirical self and a more open acceptance of its relation to the total self would have enabled him to see the fallacy of his claim that reverence for life is a necessity of thought. This claim is both unnecessary and unjustified. It is unnecessary since one's renunciation of certain knowledge about the world should leave him free from the necessity of requiring *certainty* about the rightness of the life-view to be chosen. For the sake of consistency, Schweitzer ought not to demand certainty regarding *human* nature any more than he demands certainty about nature in general. Werner has observed that just as (in the words of Schweitzer) one trusts that "the love of God is greater than His righteousness," so one need not *know* that his self-understanding is indisputably "right," one need only *decide* to understand himself as a creature meant to love rather than to hate or ignore other creatures. [8]

The claim that reverence for life is a necessity of thought is unjustified because Schweitzer's "proof" of reverence for life is a very tenuous one. There is a certain nobility in this claim, and in the line of reasoning which Schweitzer employs in an effort to establish it, that moves the sympathetic reader to exclaim, "Yes! It is so!" Even the skeptical reader, when he considers this line of reasoning in conjunction with the nobility of Schweitzer's life, is moved to sigh, "Would that it were so!" But the logic of Schweitzer's argumentation is defective.

The first logical fallacy of Schweitzer's approach is that it rests on the assumption that "rational thought" is the same in all thinking beings. This assumption has the corollary that reason is the ruling faculty in man, and that therefore to know the good is to do it. These assumptions were accepted widely during the Enlightenment, and those of us who live in the twentieth century may regard these suppositions with considerable nostalgia. But empirical psychology and sociology have given us valid knowledge about the formation of personality and the conditioning of thought processes by unconscious and cultural forces. Political history has taught us much about the utter unpredictability, irrationality and evil of human nature. We dare not assume that man is ruled by a universal reason, the same at all times in all minds and all cultures.

The second logical fallacy in Schweitzer's approach is that, as Hogg has pointed out in his perceptive articles, "will-to-live" may be postulated as the primary datum of self-knowledge only in the sense of "will-to-survive." [9] Human will-to-live may potentially contain will-to-love, but when will-to-love does become actualized in higher life-affirmation, this development represents a level of self-awareness far beyond the initial act of self-consciousness. Even in humans, the initial datum of self-awareness is the brute instinct of self-preservation, and it is misleading to speak of this instinct as containing "reverence." Will-to-live can reach quite a robust stage of development without ever being touched significantly by will-to-love; indeed, common experience suggests that this sort of development is more the rule than the exception. Such a development of will-to-live contains no special reverence for the higher values of the spirit which are so essential to Schweitzer's notion of self-perfection. [10]

Will-to-live which "thinks itself to conclusion" without actualizing will-to-love is apt to be ruthless in its suppression of other beings, for these other beings may be regarded as a threat to its own unfettered development. Far more persons adopt an attitude of ruthlessness or indifference toward life outside their own circle of family and friends than adopt an attitude approximating reverence for life. To say that their devotion to their in-group is a manifestation of ethical self-devotion is only half true, for the whole task of ethics is to widen the circle of those for whom ethical concern is felt and to whom service is rendered. To say, as Schweitzer does, that men who do not develop an attitude of reverence for life are "pathological phenomena," [11] or to say that such men have not thought elementally enough, is to beg the question.

Nothing inherent in the raw will-to-live guarantees that thought will lead to ethical self-devotion. Rational thought reaches ethical conclusions only when it works from a prior commitment to will-to-love, a commitment nurtured and enhanced by many civilizing influences which have their origin outside the self. These influences include, in addition to those cultural factors which can be empirically verified, certain others which we term spiritual. Ethics are a "natural" outgrowth of thought only in the sense that they are the product of a higher conception of the nature of human selfhood and human destiny, a higher conception which is itself the product of centuries of civilization. For ethics, what needs to be emphasized is not the solitary *thought* of the human animal become conscious of his will-to-live, but rather the *commitment* of the human self-in-society to a will-to-love which is different from and higher than raw will-to-live.

Schweitzer's own life is powerful testimony to the priority of a commitment to will-to-love over rational thought based on raw will-to-live. His prior commitment to will-to-love may be obscured by his well-intentioned but misplaced emphasis upon the role of ratiocination in ethics, but a careful examination of key passages in his argument for reverence for life as a necessity of thought shows the primacy of this commitment:

What shall be my attitude toward this other life which I see around me? It can only be of a piece with my attitude toward my own life. If I am a thinking being, I must regard other life than my own with equal reverence. For I know that it longs for fullness and deepness of development as do I myself.[12]

It is apparent here that Schweitzer's thought leaps directly from an attitude of reverence for one's own desires for fullness and deepness of development to a like attitude toward corresponding desires in others. But is this a purely *rational* step, one that any "thinking being," any being who calculates how to affirm his own will-to-live, *must* take? Schweitzer's strong commitment to will-to-love prevents his conceiving of any other step, but it is a movement of the mind which is obvious and unavoidable only to those who think within the context already established by their previous decision to honor the desires of others equally with their own.

The argument rests on the premise that it would be *inconsistent* for a thinking being not to accord other wills-to-live the same "reverence" which, on Schweitzer's view, is accorded to one's own will-to-live. But the definition of "consistency" depends again upon a prior moral decision. It can as logically be argued that the man who is "consistent" in affirming his will-to-live develops a fierce will-to-power that has no concern whatsoever for the well-being of other wills-to-live. Such consistency can only be avoided by a moral decision to incorporate a measure of ethical life-negation into the *higher* life-affirmation that includes self-devotion.

The priority of commitment for Schweitzer is even more evident from the many passages in which he speaks of the *mysterious* character of the impulse toward reverence for life, the "otherness" of this impulse:

The essential nature of the will-to-live is determination to live itself to the full . . . , to realize itself in the highest possible perfection. . . . [And] everywhere it strives to reach the perfection with which it is endowed. . . .

How this striving originated within us, and how it developed, we do not know, but it is given with our existence. We must act upon it if we would not be unfaithful to the mysterious will-to-live which is within us.[13]

This passage exhibits the role of commitment, the mystery of will-to-love and the nonempirical character of the "essential" self, all of which are hidden presuppositions in Schweitzer's thought. We are "endowed" with a potential fullness of being which we are intended to actualize. This potentiality is "given" to us in a mysterious way that we cannot comprehend fully. But it is clear that this "essential nature of the will-to-live" cannot be actualized without a decision on our part to be *faithful* to our destiny as higher beings in whom will-to-live is guided by will-to-love. And the motif of "faithfulness" is expressed again and again in Schweitzer's testimony concerning the influence of Jesus as the Christ on his life and thought.

14. Critique of Social Ethics

To assess the validity and merits of Schweitzer's social ethics, we must first disentangle the essential from the nonessential in his teachings and his life. This has seldom been done, either by his critics or his supporters. It is not that his teachings must be separated from his life, for there is a vital connection between the two. But that which is trivial or incidental in both life and philosophy must be differentiated from that which is central in his life- and world-view.

Most of the observers who have attempted to evaluate Schweitzer's social ethics have called into testimony his administration of the Lambarene hospital. Few of these discussions, however, have distinguished his central social goals from his incidental social practices and preferences. Analytical flaws of this kind are apparent in Norman Cousins' article, "The Point About Schweitzer." [1] In it, Cousins defends the doctor against the critics of his policies at the hospital, but without making those distinctions between the essential and the incidental implied in the article's title:

> The point about Schweitzer is not whether he brought a gleaming modern hospital to Lambarene. The point about Schweitzer is that he brought the kind of spirit to Africa that the dark man hardly knew existed in the white man. . . . If Schweitzer had done nothing else in this life than to accept the pain of these people as his own he would have achieved eminence. And his place in history will rest on something more substantial than an argument over an unswept floor. It will rest on the spotless nature of his vision and the clean sweep of his nobility.

Cousins is correct in arguing that the moral brilliance of Schweitzer cannot be extinguished by trivial departures from modern standards of order and cleanliness. He may be right in calling attention to Schweitzer's emphasis on the importance of the spirit of self-devotion, for Schweitzer does believe that any manifestation of this spirit is intrinsically valuable, regardless of whether or not its practical consequences are great. But

Cousins goes too far when he implies that a spectacular demonstration of self-sacrifice is all that matters. If a demonstration of the spirit of self-sacrifice had been all that mattered to Schweitzer, he could have remained in Europe after World War I had put an end to his original hospital at Lambarene, since the dark man had already been given a chance to see the spirit of benevolence in the white man. But Schweitzer cared about the pain-stricken bodies of the Africans, not just about the spirit of self-sacrifice, so he refused a chair at the University of Zurich to return to Africa and take up once again his work of healing.[2]

But Schweitzer himself bears partial responsibility for the excesses and misplaced emphases apparent in so many of his admirers. Schweitzer, in subsuming self-devotion under the category of self-perfecting, places severe limits on the effective practice of self-devotion.[3] If his care of patients in the Lambarene hospital is indeed less than satisfactory, the cause can be traced back to his suspicion of impersonal techniques, material comforts and the effect of these upon men's souls. If he has failed to train successors who can continue and expand the work which he has so nobly begun, then the fault is in a substantial degree attributable to his excessive individualism. The really central point about him is this: a man's nobility and vision are woefully restricted in scope if excessive preoccupation with his own "self-perfecting" distracts his attention from the needs of the fellow creatures to whom he is devoting himself. Since no man's life and vision are spotless, an exaggerated concern for spotlessness is apt to cause lessened effectiveness in the service of others.

True ethics must be *goal-directed*. The goal of helping the needy neighbor in the ditch must always be the primary consideration, not the effect that helping him will or will not have on the Samaritan who is presented with an opportunity to help. Schweitzer's administration of the hospital is goal-directed in the sense that his paternalistic treatment of the natives is a means that is dictated by his primary end, providing them with medical care. He is probably indifferent to any need for greater modernity for similar reasons: the actual medical instruments and treatment rooms are all that need to be rigorously antiseptic, and fussiness about the modernity of the entire hospital would constitute a distraction from the weightier matters at hand. In a larger sense, however, the goal-directedness of his social ethics may be doubted, for he has failed to perceive the obsolescence of paternalism and the enormous advantages to be derived from improved hospital facilities.

The best defense of Schweitzer's opposition to the modernizing of his hospital is the contention that he has seen in the modernizing process a danger of financial dependence. One of his close associates states that the doctor has refused financial help in acquiring more up-to-date hospital equipment only when he feared that the proffered aid would be conditional upon policy changes in the giving of medical care. But most of the critics who demand that Schweitzer modernize his technical equipment also demand that he change his policies, especially his policy of paternalism. This demand has been cogently expressed by C. W. M. Gell:

> His belief in the European's civilizing mission has strengthened with the years and now, in the evening of his life, it seems to obscure from him the perils and evils which may flow from withholding independence too long.[4]

Gell also deplores Schweitzer's defense of the political status quo in his Nobel Prize Address in 1954. In this address, he opposed agitation on behalf of independence for the former colonial countries on the ground that such agitation endangers "a long history of peace in many regions." Gell denounces Schweitzer's "obtuse inability to see that the period of colonial rule in Asia can hardly appear as 'a long history of peace' to the recently subjected peoples."[5]

Schweitzer's blindness on this issue is all the more surprising when we consider that the same Nobel Prize Address contains a trenchant plea on behalf of uprooted persons who have been deported or imprisoned as a result of the war and the postwar adjustments of borders. Schweitzer termed it "the most flagrant violation of the rights of man" that a people should be deprived of the land on which it has lived and be forced to move elsewhere. He even added a warning that "the realities of economics" must be observed in fixing new frontiers.[6] It is inconsistent to acknowledge the right of a people to occupancy and use of resources, to say nothing of self-determination, in some areas but not in others.

Some observers of African affairs point to the state of chaos which has existed in the former Belgian Congo since its independence as a vindication of Schweitzer's conservatism on the issue of colonialism. One may deplore the violence and disorder which characterized the first year of Congo independence, however, without concluding thereby that the "wind of change" which is blowing through Africa should be held back as long as possible, or forced to blow only along one given course. Other observers take the position that the major error which precipitated the woes of the Congo was not the haste with which Belgium withdrew once she had finally decided to do so, but rather the reluctance of the Belgian authorities to recognize the rights of the Congolese to proper education, economic opportunity, freedom of movement and self-determination. The eruption of violence on the part of the Congolese army in July 1960 can be explained and mitigated by a number of factors: the deep-seated resentment against the oppressive aspects of Belgian rule, the newer resentment of the soldiers against the rapid rise to power of the civil servant class, bad pay and the lack of any provisions for the military personnel to have adequate time off to celebrate independence.[7] Furthermore, "the extent of Congolese atrocity was nothing like what the horror headlines had implied," and "the Belgians' conduct actually contributed to the tension and added to the list of Congolese atrocities scores more brought about by their own men."[8] But the violence does not have to be condoned in order for the main lesson of the Congo to be appreciated; namely, that paternalism is obsolete in a world where "the revolution of rising expectations" teaches the poor and oppressed of every land that there is no moral justification for colonial rule.

As a former missionary with twenty-five years experience in the Congo asserts, "sober reflection suggests that the fault in the Congo was not on the side of haste but of tardiness":

There was time to get ready, but it was wasted. Great popular movements are like the tides of the ocean—they move at their own inexorable pace. Human power cannot hold them back, but human wisdom can make ready for their coming. African nationalism is such a force. If Belgium's wisest leaders had been given a free hand to do that which they knew must be done, beginning at the time when they knew they should begin, the present crisis would have been avoided. If their failures had not built up frustration and fear and distrust in the hearts of the Congolese, the seeds of Communist malice could not have taken root and grown. These are the real lessons of the Congo situation. May they be heeded in those places where there is yet time.[9]

The fundamental flaw in Schweitzer's social ethics is his notion that "the ethics of ethical society" are qualitatively inferior to "the ethics of ethical personality." To the Socratic fallacy that to know the good is to do it Schweitzer adds another fallacy: he believes that visualizing the good in the form of noble ethical ideals will insure a knowledge of how to do the good and the power necessary to "overcome reality" and actualize those ideals in society. His usual reluctance to make aggressive protest against specific social injustices is a case in point.

Another illustration of the confusion between the good and the practical attainment of the good in society is Schweitzer's resistance to governmental programs to improve the common life. Even while wishing man to commune with nature and declaring the importance of leisure and quiet, he has opposed the construction of public parks and reservations by government action.[10] Despite his awareness of the abuses of a laissez faire economic policy in the colonies, he does not even discuss the need for laws and regulatory agencies designed to mitigate these abuses, much less the practical details which ought to be provided for by such laws and agencies.[11]

Schweitzer is, in brief, a living embodiment of the extreme individualism which Max Weber and R. H. Tawney have analyzed in their well-known diagnosis of the "Protestant ethic" and the "spirit of capitalism." [12] He displays a most distressing complacency on the subject of colonial trade, which he assumes to be a necessity regardless of its effects upon human beings. He is suspicious of non-essential items of consumption, items consumed purely for enjoyment. He registers disdain for those who are unwilling to pour out their energies unremittingly in hard work.[13] And Schweitzer's embodiment of the Protestant-capitalist mentality is supremely expressed in his naive assumption that individual piety can be trusted to bring about a more tolerable degree of justice in the distribution of wealth.[14] The naivete of this assumption is recognized by all modern governments which employ a graduated income tax!

What Murry calls Schweitzer's "congenital individualism" is also expressed in his implied faith that the complex dilemmas of world politics in the nuclear age can best be solved by the simple expedient of the summit conference. Such conferences may result in temporarily eased tensions, but most experts in the field of international affairs are exceedingly pessimistic about the advantages that may accrue from "summitry." [15] What Schweitzer overlooks is that tensions between opposing political blocs are not caused primarily by lack of understanding, and that highly publicized conferences of national leaders may become nothing more than vehicles for propaganda. By creating false hopes among the people of the world, summit conferences may render a serious disservice to the cause of peace.[16]

Schweitzer's individualism rests on the erroneous belief that love in its pure form can be expressed in the institutions of society. He does not realize that love is an ethical ideal which is appropriate to relations between individuals or small groups of men, whereas justice is the more relevant ideal for large collectivities, especially civilized society as a whole. He does not realize that "justice is the institutionalized form of love." [17]

The first important negative consequence of Schweitzer's failure to recognize justice as the highest relevant ideal for social ethics is his underestimation of the importance of organized groups such as political parties and labor unions in the struggle for social justice. Such organizations are admittedly tainted with self-interest, and Schweitzer is undeniably right in regarding the activities of these groups as a form of compromise of the pure ideal of self-perfection. But the ethical personality who wants to be really effective in promoting the welfare of the weak and oppressed elements of society—the goal-directed ethical personality—must be willing to "compromise," for most of the social goals that are dictated by a concern for justice can only be achieved through the agency of organizations which are large enough and strong enough to exert significant social power.[18]

Another consequence of Schweitzer's unrealistic stress on ideal ends and pure means is his lack of concern for technical wisdom, i.e., wisdom regarding matters of strategy and tactics in the pursuit of ethical objectives. Had Schweitzer been more receptive in his reading of Aristotle and more judicious in his appraisal of utilitarianism, he might have avoided this neglect of the indispensable role of "practical reason" in social ethics. As Kraus points out in connection with his criticism of Schweitzer's estimate of utilitarianism, an awareness of the shortcomings of a purely scientific method in the *selection* of ethical ends does not require a rejection of scientific methods of *achieving* those ends.[19]

Schweitzer's individualism leads him not only to disdain political realism and underestimate technical wisdom, it leads him also to minimize men's need for corporate unity as a source of mutual enlightenment, inspiration and personal fulfilment. Every individual needs to have his insights sharpened and refined by dialogue with others. Every individual needs to have his resources revitalized and reinforced by contact with others who are working toward the same goals he is. Schweitzer, perhaps because of the extraordinary resources with which he is gifted, does not appreciate the intensity of these needs in most men and the importance of the social institutions which are designed to meet these needs. His lack of interest in the church is a symptom of this weakness in his thought.

It is ironic that all of these shortcomings in the social ethics of Schweitzer should be combined with his steadfast faith in the possibility of progress. The irony is that progress cannot be attained without political realism and technical wisdom. It cannot be attained in society as a whole by individualists who subordinate "the ethics of ethical society" to "the ethics of ethical personality." The irony is compounded by the fact that scorn for Schweitzer's individualistic idealism prevents many political realists from appreciating the worthwhileness of his sober "willing and hoping" for progress. That is unfortunate, for sober optimism is a valuable part of the world-view of world- and life-affirmation. Without at least a "will to believe" in the possibility of achieving a more tolerable justice in society, how can one unrestrainedly and consistently devote himself to the discouraging task of working for a more just social order? Is it not probable that much of the normlessness that characterizes modern society is rooted in the demoralization of fearing that there can be no hope for a better world in the future? If we are to be saved from the anxiety of meaninglessness, and from passage over into nihilism, we must be able to feel that life holds enough promise to justify the effort required simply to stay alive. We must be able to feel that in producing children we are doing more than perpetuating an absurd cosmic mistake that might as well be obliterated in nuclear warfare as not.

The critique of Schweitzer's social ethics must culminate by returning to the question concerning the relationship between reverence for life and civilization. Is the extension of ethical responsibility to all forms of life, even as an attitude which cannot be fully carried out in practice, a positive contribution to social philosophy?

In answering this question it is of prime importance to separate the essential from the trivial or the incidental in Schweitzer's life and thought. A fair answer is rendered all the more difficult by the numerous popular stories about reverence for life which lend themselves to caricature. It is hard to appreciate the ethical relevance of Schweitzer's insistence that it is morally wrong to swat a mosquito. It is even harder to find anything edifying in the story of his setting free some troublesome rats which his wife had succeeded in trapping.[20]

Yet even when one manages to disentangle Schweitzer's personal eccentricities from his ethical theory, serious objections must be raised. How could one live a meaningful existence if he were forced to feel at every moment a sense of guilt over his involvement in the natural necessity of living at the expense of other life? The experience of living would dissolve into a maddening chaos of unbearable tragedy. Universal reverence for life taken too seriously as a principle of ethical conduct would lead us to waste our energies in sentimental attention to forms of life less worthy of care than is human life, or in undue deliberation about which wills-to-live should be sacrificed in the interest of other life. As Bertrand Russell has remarked, the wasting of moral energy in protracted deliberation may in some cases be the most unethical option available.[21] Even as an attitude of mind, universal reverence for life would so paralyze us with the consciousness of ambiguity that we might be inclined to withdraw altogether from involvement in the ordinary responsibilities of daily life. I am persuaded that finally even the stringency of reverence for life as a spiritual attitude must be relaxed somewhat. I agree with Messer that the humane furtherance of higher life through the use of animal and vegetable life need not be termed a "necessity" and saddled with the charge of immorality. The furtherance of human life, even at the expense of other forms of life, is not merely "necessary," it is *good*, and there is no harm in calling it that.[22]

But despite its drawbacks, reverence for life ought not to be ridiculed as it has been by some of Schweitzer's critics.[23] Karl Barth is right in his assertion that one of the typical manifestations of man's sinful self-centeredness is his unreflecting supposition that his status as lord of creation gives him the right to kill animals indiscriminately and take enjoyment in cruel sports.[24] Barth interprets Gen. 9:2 as proof that men have a responsibility to take care of animals.[25] He praises the value of Schweitzer's "outcry" against the inclination of humans to be so "indifferent and thoughtless" in their treatment of animals.[26] As long as men remain as insensitive to the suffering of the lower creatures as their present treatment of them in bull rings, slaughterhouses, laboratories and kitchens reveals them to be, man's inhumanity to man will probably not diminish appreciably. In Boris Pasternak's words, there is something morally repugnant about "the elevation of man above the rest of nature, the modern coddling and worshipping of man." [27] Schweitzer's ethic of reverence for life, as a part of his critique of Western culture, is a reminder that this aberration is not confined to the Communist ideology.

15. Critique of the Cosmic Dimension

The cosmic dimension of Schweitzer's ethical mysticism is undoubtedly the most perplexing part of his thought system. It is also one of the most rewarding parts of his philosophy, for there is great profundity in the ambiguities that one finds here. Moreover, there is a challenge to the reader to develop further some of the fruitful insights that remain implicit rather than explicit in Schweitzer's world-view.

His renunciation of all attempts to "understand the meaning of the whole" has met with a wide range of reactions. Many sense a contradiction in his denial of meaning to the universe and his attribution of meaning to personal existence. Barthel charges that this separation between world-view and life-view implies an unacceptable dualism in the thought of Schweitzer, and contends that intelligence and will must be held together if a coherent life- or world-view is to be constructed.[1] Sawicky protests that man will fall into the anxiety of meaninglessness "if he sees himself placed in a senseless chaos without any way out."[2] Steinbuchel argues that if the world is a closed book, then so is the God who created it: consequently, one can hardly affirm the will-to-love which he may or may not feel in his heart as God.[3] On the other hand, P. Jeschke, H. Wegmann and Fritz Buri have agreed with Schweitzer that the beginning of wisdom lies in abandoning all hope that an optimistic-ethical life-view can be grounded in knowledge of the world.[4]

Reinhold Niebuhr has sensed merit in both sides of this controversy over knowledge of the universe, declaring his sympathy for the "naive dualism of prophetic religion" which in his estimation Schweitzer represents, but opposing the implication that man can or ought to be so satisfied with this picture of the universe that he abandons all endeavors to find a fuller and more consistent outlook.[5] Niebuhr believes that Schweitzer's dualism of will and reason leads to a "resulting picture of the world" in which "personality is in conflict with nature, divine and human personality sharing the conflict." No one can reasonably quarrel with Schweitzer's conclusion that man can never attain *certainty* about the working of the cosmos, or with his conclusion that, as Niebuhr has phrased it, "All life is a conflict of the soul with the inertia and the blindness of nature." Schweitzer is right to frankly disavow the pretentiousness which many metaphysicians have exhibited in claiming to establish a definitive total world-view.

But confusion arises from Schweitzer's tendency to write as though no coherent rational *hypothesis* about the whole were possible, while at the same time writing as though the elaborate world-view which he develops from his life-view were a "necessity of thought." This confusion hinges on the question of whether or not the "knowledge" that arises from inner experience is of the same order as the knowledge that arises from empirical investigation of external phenomena. Schweitzer is a man who believes so earnestly in the testimony of inner experience that he will not admit that his ethical world-view is merely a hypothesis. On the other hand, he is so suspicious of traditional metaphysics that he will not admit how far beyond a simple decision concerning one's life-view his theory of the universe extends.

The crux of the matter is that Schweitzer is a man of *rational faith.* He is a man of faith because he does acknowledge the world to be *"inexplicably* mysterious and full of suffering" [6] [author's italics]—yet he stakes his life on the belief that Cosmic Reality is nevertheless on the side of harmony rather than conflict, of meaning rather than meaninglessness. He believes, furthermore, that there is an objective "oughtness" in the world which, even though it cannot be demonstrated by observing the world, lays compelling claims upon man's existence. His belief in objective values becomes very evident when one compares Schweitzer with existentialist thinkers. There is an apparent parallel between his reliance on inner experience as opposed to outer knowledge and Sartre's dictum that *"l'existence précède l'essence"* or Camus' emphasis on the principle of justice that one feels within himself as opposed to the injustice that he sees operating in the world.[7] But there is a vast difference between existentialism and the subjective idealism of Schweitzer, because for him essence precedes existence.

Schweitzer absorbed from Georg Simmel a conviction that the potential "oughtness" of the essential self is just as real as the actual "is-ness" of the existing self—thus he came to attach great significance to his Berlin professor's dictum "Become what you are!" [8] For Schweitzer, then, the finite will-to-live already has a built-in definition of what self-perfection involves, and the whole point of elemental thinking is to clarify the vision of the essential self so that it may become ever more closely approximated in existence. Part of the definition of the essential self, moreover, is that in it the finite will is meant to have metaphysical union with Cosmic Reality. In contrast to most existentialists, Schweitzer is no metaphysical rebel. God is not dead and man is not God. But the point which must be emphasized, the point on which Schweitzer's rationalism goes too far, and might well need the corrective of existentialism's stress on *decision,* is that even a perfectly clarified vision of the essential self will not insure striving towards it. *This* vision must be selected from all the other perhaps more plausible, perhaps more enticing self-images that clamor for recognition; a man must say "Yes!" to just this vision and the life-view implied by it. It is a commitment of *will,* an act of *faith.*

But Schweitzer's is a *rational* faith because, again in contrast to existentialism, it is a complicated hypothesis about what is objectively real and good in the cosmos. It is more than an arbitrary leap into the darkness of a senseless existence, in which any view of one's self is as valid and as absurd as any other. Schweitzer's philosophy is a carefully thought out attempt to piece together those facts and experiences which seem to be authentic into an ordered pattern of meaning which is held to be valid for all men. In short, Schweitzer proclaims what Hogg has termed a "cosmic motive" for the ethical life:

If we are to be not only deeply in earnest about our ideals, but also nobly (instead of pig-headedly) enthusiastic in their service in face of every obstacle, we need to feel certain that they are no mere private dreams of our own, nor even merely ideals characteristic of the human species, but that they are somehow rooted in the universal nature of things. We need to be supported by a conviction that service of these ideals is precisely what the whole cosmic scheme demands of us, and that our loyalty or disloyalty to them is a matter of moment not to ourselves alone, nor to the community, nor to the human race, but to the universe.[9]

Although Schweitzer does not work out a *total* world-view based on metaphysical speculation, he certainly does emerge with a more rational hypothesis about "the whole" than many of his antimetaphysical comments might imply. May it not also be inferred that his world-view lends itself to further elaboration on the basis of certain provocative ideas that are implicit in his thinking? I am convinced that this is the case, and in the next-to-last chapter of this book I shall ask the reader to explore with me some possible elaborations of Schweitzer's world-view along the lines suggested by dominant motifs in his ethical mysticism.

VI. Schweitzer's Contribution to Ethical Philosophy

16. Ethical Norms Without Authoritarian Compulsion

We live in a time of tremendous moral confusion. Our age displays both a widespread flight from norms and widespread submission to authoritarian sources of norms. As a result, contemporary civilization suffers from a scarcity of true ethical norms, norms which are held to be valid apart from their source or the sanctions by means of which they are enforced.

Various schools of empiricism and existentialism attempt to dispense with traditional moral philosophy altogether, on the grounds that a search for objective standards of ethical conduct is a futile enterprise. Logical positivism, which seeks to apply the canons of pure empiricism in the analysis of ethical discourse, regards statements about the right and the good as nothing more than descriptive, emotive or persuasive statements. From the viewpoint of logical positivism, the ethical command, "Thou shalt not commit murder," is either meaningless or else reducible to one of the following equivalents: "We disapprove of murder in our society"; "You are likely to be punished if you commit murder"; "I don't like murder!" or "Please consider seriously the arguments which I shall advance as to why you should not commit murder." [1] Cultural relativists deny the existence of any universal patterns of human relations that can be designated as proper for man as such. [2] According to the popular interpretation of Freud, all normative theories of politics, religion, economics and art are based upon illusion: the only trustworthy reality in human experience is the libido, and the only sensible way to get along in this inevitably frustrating world is to

maximize pleasure and minimize frustration by prudently bal-
ancing the claims of the pleasure principle against those of the
reality principle.[3]

Some schools of existentialist thought are equally suspicious
of norms. Sartre and his followers deny any dimension of
oughtness in human existence. Neither God (He is dead) nor
society (it has no authority) has any binding claim upon the
individual, who is free to determine his essence as a man by
his existence, not vice versa. Any attempt to discover a doctrine
of essential selfhood would be absurd, for there are no regulative
a priori principles by which the existing self may be judged.[4]

This widespread normlessness has called forth a reaction in
the form of attempted escape from freedom into various kinds
of legalism. Legalism may be defined as a pattern of social
behavior which derives from inertia or authoritarian compulsion
rather than from whole-hearted affirmation on the part of the
person concerned. Secular legalism manifests itself in the
spineless "other-directedness" which prompts many persons to
submerge their individuality in the "togetherness" and "belong-
ingness" that is so highly prized in modern society.[5] Religious
legalism is to be found in Roman Catholicism's inflexible attitude
toward birth control and divorce, or in moralistic Protestantism's
condemnation of certain forms of amusement and certain
patterns of consumption. The "Protestant ethic" of the hard-
driving American businessman is another variant of legalism
which stands midway between secularism and religiosity. The
unrelenting frugality, diligence and acquisitiveness of this way
of life may have lost its religious roots in Judaism and Calvinism,
but its compulsiveness still persists in the new social ethic of
the organization man.[6]

Normlessness and authoritarianism are combined in a unique
way in contemporary European neo-orthodox theology. On the
one hand, theologians of this school contend that the reason
and will of fallen mankind have been so crippled by original sin
that men have no adequate way of knowing or doing the good
apart from Christian revelation. They regard the very attempt
to formulate moral philosophy as impious, since such an attempt

constitutes arrogant rebellion against man's rightful Ruler. In the words of Martin Luther, one of the greatest heroes of neo-orthodoxy:

> Were all men to concentrate their united efforts to attain wisdom and virtue by their natural reason, knowledge and free will . . . yet such wisdom and virtue are in the sight of God nothing but sin and altogether reprehensible. The reason is, they are not attained in the grace of God.[7]

On the other hand, these "crisis theologians," as they are called, are obsessed with the idea of the authority of the Bible and the idea that "pure doctrine" is the necessary and virtually all-sufficient source from which ethics flow.

It is in the context of the normlessness and authoritarianism of present-day thought that Schweitzer's contribution to ethical philosophy must be evaluated. It is especially in the light of the contemporary theological situation that his work can best be appreciated, for his contribution to ethics is inextricably bound up with his contribution to theology. Because he conceives of God as "Ethical Personality" as well as cosmic Will-to-Live, his thought is capable of furnishing ethical norms. Because God as Ethical Personality is conceived of as pure Will-to-Love, lacking the jealousness and vindictiveness so often attributed to deity by traditional theology, Schweitzer's ethics avoid the coerciveness of both moralistic and theological legalism. The purity of his understanding of God is particularly striking when we consider the history of man's vision of God in orthodox Christianity, and when we consider the ethical teachings propounded by today's theologians.

No single unambiguously defined conception of God can be attributed to Christianity, for it is a religion which has endured for many centuries and been spread abroad into many cultures. Even when church councils agree on certain religious terminology there can be many different interpretations of that terminology. That which is condemned as heresy in one century may be accepted as valid in another; that which was central at one point in the development of doctrine may be forgotten or denied in another age or another culture. One of the most interesting alternations of emphasis in the history of Jewish-Christian thought is that between the themes of God's holiness and God's love.

This alternation of emphasis is explained by Carl Jung as a gradual struggle for recognition of the "female-principle"—of tenderness, acceptance, unconditional love—in Western man's God-consciousness.[8] The book of Job is regarded by Jung as a challenge to the dominance of the "masculine-principle," the arbitrariness of a God who does not scruple to allow his faithful subjects to be tortured by Satan. The coming of the Christ a few centuries later is God's answer to Job's justifiable complaint, and the exaltation of the Virgin Mary in subsequent Christian thought represents an achievement of greater balance between "masculine" holiness and "feminine" love in God. On the whole, however, orthodox Christianity has portrayed God in authoritarian terms.

The dominant image of God in Christianity is that of a heavenly King to whom unquestioning obedience is due. Even the image of God as Father has usually carried the connotation of an Oriental Patriarch whose awesome righteousness looms larger than His love. The love of this Patriarch has been restricted, for the most part, to those of His own household: those chosen to be His children by royal election, or those who become His servants by paying Him the homage required by His venerable authority. The doctrine of blood atonement, which holds that God's honor must be upheld by the payment of a fitting ransom for man's unpardonable sin; the odious doctrine of predestination, which proclaims that "By the decree of God, for the manifestation of His glory, some men and angels are predestined unto everlasting life, and others foreordained to everlasting death"[9]; the fundamentalist's frenetic attempt to pressure everyone he meets into a "decision for Christ"; Roman Catholicism's insistence that there is no salvation outside the Church—these notions result from traditional theology's determination that the sovereignty of God must not be compromised by an unseemly degree of magnanimity in His love. Small wonder that Feuerbach saw a contradiction between authentic love and traditional Christian faith.[10] Small wonder that until such doctrines are unambiguously repudiated by official church spokesmen, the gracious love of God which they proclaim can scarcely be trusted.

The psychological implications of an authoritarian concept of God are skillfully outlined by Erich Fromm in *Man for Himself*. His analysis of the authoritarian conscience is of enormous relevance for ethics.[11] The basic drive of such a conscience, argues Fromm, is *fear*. Fear makes a person feel good when he has pleased whatever authority holds him in submission. Fear goads him whenever he has been disobedient to the authority. The prime offense against this kind of conscience is rebellion, and as the story of Adam and Eve illustrates, the worst form of rebellion is the desire to be like the authority.[12] As the legend of the Tower of Babel and the myth of Prometheus indicate, "The supremacy of the authority is questioned by the attempt of the creature to cease being a *thing* and to become a creator." [13]

The first effect of the authoritarian conscience upon the person afflicted with it is a sense of guilt concerning creative activity. This feeling of guilt, rooted as it is in the sense of absolute dependence upon the authority, is itself the finest sacrifice that can be offered up as a sign of submission.

> Paradoxically, the authoritarian *guilty* conscience is a result of the feeling of strength, independence, productiveness and pride, while the authoritarian *good* conscience springs from the feeling of obedience, powerlessness, and sinfulness.[14]

In this symbiotic relationship "even punishment is better than rejection," for the victim feels that he could not even exist apart from his reliance on the authority.

The second effect of the authoritarian conscience is that the victim "takes over the role of the authority by treating himself with the same strictness and cruelty." [15] Thus masochistic tendencies are "permitted to operate under the disguise of virtue," and the lingering hatred of the authority is turned against oneself. [16]

The authority of the lawgiver makes its subjects feel guilty for their many and unavoidable transgressions. The guilt of unavoidable transgressions before authority and the need for its forgiveness thus create an endless chain of offense, guilt feeling, and the need for absolution which keeps the subject in bondage and grateful for forgiveness rather than critical of the authority's demands.[17]

The final insulation against liberation from this vicious circle is the fact that unsuccessful attempts to break out of it constitute, in the mind of the subject, "proof of guilt, and only by renewed submission can the good conscience be regained." [18]

The most important ethical effect of the authoritarian conscience is that it causes its victims to channel their unconscious resentment toward the authority (against whom they cannot express hostility) into aggressive hostility toward those from whom they do not fear retaliation. Fromm contrasts this unhappy conscience with the "humanistic conscience," which is "the voice of our true selves" summoning us "to live productively, to develop fully and harmoniously—that is, to become what we potentially are." This non-authoritarian conscience is "the voice of our loving care for ourselves," for our essential selfhood. Such a conscience frees the person for creative self-realization and ethical self-devotion to others, because when one truly loves himself he is able to love others more freely and fully. Ethical self-devotion is a "phenomenon of abundance" in the self.[19]

The significance of Schweitzer's non-authoritarian conception of God is magnified when one analyzes in detail the bad effects of theological absolutism. In the first place, an authoritarian conception of God has a negative rather than a positive effect on the vertical dimension on one's life, on one's relationship to God. Instead of fostering love for God and an affirmative attitude toward the world which God has given us to live in, the authoritarian pattern arouses resentment and suppressed hatred against Him. Worship may become nothing more than an effort to propitiate the arbitrary deity for the hostility toward Him which cannot be admitted, either to Him or to oneself. Obedience to His commands may become nothing more than a form of other-worldly hedonism in which virtue is the price that is paid for an expected future reward. The moral failings which inevitably occur may be frantically denied or agonized over in orgies of repentance. The child of God cannot hope to develop maturity in creative self-reliance, for he thinks that God wants him to remain weak, insecure and utterly dependent.

The traditional authoritarian conception of God has a second deleterious effect upon ethics. It tends to cause a preponderance of disvalue in the horizontal dimension of life, the area of one's relationships with his fellow creatures. A syndrome of fear, resentment, hostility and aggression perverts one's interpersonal activities. In the imagery of the parable of the Good Samaritan, the victim of the authoritarian conscience will be inclined to take out his hostilities on weaker neighbors by kicking them into the ditch instead of caring for them lovingly. If his creative energies have been merely sapped instead of perverted by his symbiotic relationship to God, he may simply lack the will or the vitality to bind up the wounds of his injured neighbors. Or, as in the case of a fundamentalist, the "help" he gives may be to drag them off to the court of the petty tyrant who holds him in thrall.

The sophisticated theological world flatters itself that its conceptions of God are above these criticisms. In many ways this is true, for recent Christian theology can hardly be charged with a *manifest* emphasis upon the arbitrary authoritarianism of God. Sophisticated theologians are certainly not biblical literalists, and they agree that fundamentalism is a plague upon Christendom. They seek to reinterpret predestination in such a way as to obviate "the moral argument against Calvinism," [20] and they maintain that hell, although it may have been an "ultimate sanction" in Christian thought, has not been the "ultimate motivation." [21] They contend that the authoritarian theme in the church's witness to God is subordinate to the theme which pictures Him as generous Creator and loving Redeemer, and they assert that the good news of God's redemptive action in Christ has unique power to make ethics truly a "phenomenon of abundance" wherein "we love, because He first loved us." [22] They argue that the surest remedy for normlessness and legalism is the Pauline doctrine of justification by faith. And they do not object to the conception of God as a Monarch, for they consider His reign to be ultimately benevolent. Not only do they find God's commands entirely just; they praise Him for supplying the grace needed to obey these commands. They declare that the Divine King has a *right* to command what He will, for it is His will which defines goodness, not goodness that sets limits to His will.[23] Thus they do not regard sinful man as having any rights before God. Man really ought to be "grateful for forgiveness rather than critical of the authority's demands."[24]

The sophisticated Protestant theologians of this century deserve to be commended for their zeal in combatting moralistic legalism wherever they find it. They deserve to be praised for their attempt to make real in contemporary Christianity what one writer has termed "the triumph of grace." But they have not gone far enough. The criticism that has been lodged against the nature and effects of the authoritarian conscience are more relevant to crisis theology than its adherents care to admit, for there is a *latent* emphasis on authoritarianism in their conception of God which vitiates their work. By their continued emphasis on dogma, on correct belief, they fail to escape from theological absolutism. By laying such stress on right doctrine they imply that God's love is conditional upon man's acceptance of certain ideas about His nature and work, and in so doing they perpetuate a theological legalism that is inimical to both religion and ethics. So long as God's love for man is pronounced limited by *any* condition which must be satisfied before man can be encompassed in that love, the authoritarian conscience will be prevalent among those who take God seriously. Accustomed as they are to theories of politics which condemn absolutism and theories of parental care which condemn possessiveness, the majority of modern men will rebel against a patriarchal God and many of this number will end by drifting into relativism or nihilism. And many of those who submit to the authority of this Patriarch will suffer a tragic warping of their spiritual nature and a crippling loss of ethical vitality.

The ethical thinking of contemporary European theologians

gives ample evidence of the continuing dominance of the authoritarian conscience in continental theology. All attempts to construct an ethical theory by inquiring into the nature of the right and the good are denounced as illegitimate. Karl Barth declares, "If man has the right to question, God does not have the right to command." [25] Emil Brunner maintains that only the love which is supernaturally revealed in Christ can be a genuine principle for ethics. [26] Equally illegitimate is all moral *action* not rooted in the soil of Christian doctrine. Following Augustine's dictum that the virtues of pagans are nothing more than "splendid vices" and Luther's assertion that "all the good works of the Gentiles and all natural works are evil," Barth admonishes that "all direct and particular brotherhood . . . which forgets that men can be brothers only in God [is] grossly immoral." [27] Barth believes that "love of men is in itself trivial." [28] This view is shared by a clergyman of Barthian persuasion who writes, "A good deed which is non-religious is not good but evil. . . . A good deed, when done apart from God, becomes a blasphemy, for the doer is pretending to be God." [29]

Such views do have an inner logic. Since natural man is corrupted in all his faculties and all his ways, he cannot possibly think really good thoughts or perform really good actions. Even man's creative abilities work to his disadvantage, for they tempt him to fall into pride.[30] It follows that only God Himself can be the agent of really good thoughts and actions, and that man can do no more than be a conduit through which the energy of God pours.[31] For Barth, repentance is "the primary ethical act," all other aspects of the moral life being of secondary importance.[32] Proper motivation is a weightier concern than the achievement of the social goals sought by ethical action; indeed, the significance of ethical actions lies not in the increased welfare of the neighbor who is served but in the fact that such actions are gestures of religious fidelity, "tokens" of inward grace.[33] And since the central purpose of ethics, as of life as a whole, is "solely to glorify God," [34] the essence of proper motivation is not love but obedience. The most shocking statement of the primacy of obedience is found in Kierkegaard's principle of "the teleological suspension of the ethical." In *Fear and Trembling*, Kierkegaard interprets the biblical story of the sacrifice of Isaac as a parable which teaches that because man's duty to God is absolute "the ethical is reduced to a position of relativity." [35] Just as Abraham was called upon to sacrifice his only son to God, so the man of thoroughly obedient faith may be directed "to give his love to his neighbor the opposite expression to that which, ethically speaking, is required by duty." [36]

Continental crisis theology is incapable of providing ethical norms, because all specific ethical norms are subordinated to authority and obedience. The very thought of "Christian virtues" or an "ideal Christian character" makes Barth, Brunner and Bultmann cringe: God is the great "minus sign" which nullifies man's definitions of right conduct.[37] The quest for general ethical principles is wrong because such principles tend to destroy the freedom of the Christian man and because they tend to place man in the position of judging God.[38]

In justice to these continental theologians, I must point out that they are motivated in large measure by a concern for the decay of Western civilization similar to Schweitzer's. They believe that true civilization can be built only upon the theological foundations they are endeavoring to repair. They believe that the man who truly loves God-in-Christ, as they understand Him, cannot help loving his neighbor as himself. They believe, with Luther, that direct concern about "good works" is of little avail, whereas humble faith in God will surely produce ethical fruits.[39] They believe, with Calvin, that "without the fear of God, men do not even observe justice and charity among themselves." [40] Above all, they and their followers believe that love for the neighbor will be refined in quality if it grows out of Christian faith:

Love that seeks merely to pursue the claims of the neighbor and the self impartially out of a sense of obligation to do so ends up being calculating and prudential; it remains essentially self-centered still. Hence, the only genuine answer to the perversion of man's natural will is to be found by first loving God with heart, soul, mind and strength and by discovering in that act how God loves the neighbor.[41]

But even a sympathetic appraisal of the intention of the crisis theologians cannot conceal the perils to ethics inherent in their theocentric approach. Faced with this blind theocentrism, Schweitzer and many other moral philosophers have been compelled to retreat to the position which is the point of departure for Schweitzer's philosophy of civilization, a position which has been forthrightly articulated by Nicolai Hartmann:

Ethics with its cluster of problems is the natural advocate of man in the realm of metaphysics. It defends him against being degraded by high-flying speculation, against the surrender of his special rights to the Creator or to the world. It rehabilitates him cosmically and metaphysically. For this it needs no speculative device. It can simply hold fast to its own phenomena. It stands nearer to the facts than general metaphysics. Metaphysics must heed ethics; not ethics, metaphysics. The position of ethics is the stronger.[42]

-    A retreat from blind theocentrism need not be a retreat from a valid metaphysical world-view, a world-view that recognizes its limitations and the primacy of life-view. Furthermore, a retreat from theological absolutism need not be a renunciation of the Christian faith, as Schweitzer demonstrates. Indeed, Schweitzer himself is a perfect illustration of the fact that Christian thinkers who possess a lively sense of the nature of God as Will-to-Love ought to resist the authoritarianism of European crisis theology more strongly than anyone else. And he is not alone in his opposition to this form of Christianity precisely on the grounds that it is a perversion of authentic Christian faith. Nels Ferre and H. Richard Niebuhr, who labels Barth's theology "Christomonism," have attacked the tendency to eclipse God behind elaborate theological doctrines concerning Christ.[43] Paul Tillich issues an injunction against the worship of God as *a* being, even the Supreme Being, contending that any theology which does not penetrate to the "God beyond God," to "Being itself," is idolatrous.[44] Reinhold Niebuhr pleads with the Barthians to remember that "There is no substitute for common sense, even for theologians."[45]

Reinhold Niebuhr has demonstrated his own good sense by pointing out that "if the sense of the absolute and transcendent becomes so complete an obsession as it is in Barthian theology all moral striving on the level of history is reduced to insignificance." [46] His essay "The Relations of Christians and Jews in Western Civilization" [47] is a milestone on the road leading away from theological absolutism. In this essay Niebuhr praises the ethical vigor of Judaism and urges the Christian church not to attempt to press its particular understanding of the Jewish-Christian tradition on men and women of the Jewish faith. While arguing that in theory Christianity has greater resources for sound ethics than Judaism, he acknowledges that in practice Jews have often demonstrated superior moral wisdom and vigor. (The inescapable implication—that the widespread "evangelization of the Jews" is a dead issue for the Christian church—occasioned no little consternation among some European churchmen!)

As Roger Shinn has observed, ". . . just as Christian ethics has rediscovered its theological foundations, theology [must] rediscover its ethical foundations." [48] The irony of theological absolutism can be illustrated by reference to the parable of the sons and the vineyard. [49] Theological absolutists may be likened to the second son of this parable, the one who said "Yes!" to his father's request that he do some work in the vineyard—but never fulfilled his promise. By devoting virtually all of their energy to the praise of God's sovereignty and by insisting that no one can do acceptable work in the vineyard until he has said "Yes!" to God by affirming His *name*, the continental theologians may be guilty of thwarting His *will* for life in the vineyard. But if God is Will-to-Love and if His purposes in the world are benevolent, surely He is more concerned about justice, freedom and equality in the world than He is about our obeisance to His name. Surely, His holiness must be defined in terms of love, not vice versa.

The irony of theological absolutism is compounded by its pretensions to a standpoint above all merely human ideologies. [50] Reinhold Niebuhr's criticism of such pretensions is annihilating:

There is a special pathos in the fact that so many of the Christian leaders of Germany are inclined to follow this form of flight from daily responsibilities and decisions, because they are trying to extend the virtue of yesterday to cover the problems of today. Yesterday they discovered that the church may be an ark in which to survive a flood. Today they seem so enamored of this special function of the church that they have decided to turn the ark into a home on Mount Ararat and live in it perpetually. . . .

We seem always to be God rather than men in this theology, viewing the world not from the standpoint of the special perplexities and problems of given periods but *sub specie aeternitatis.*[51]

Sometimes the "flight from daily responsibilities and decisions" to which Niebuhr refers takes the form of religious estheticism. According to Kierkegaard, who is the father of present-day religious existentialism, there are three "stages on life's way." [52] The lowest stage is the esthetic stage, in which a person drifts aimlessly from one hollow pleasure to another. Next comes the ethical stage, in which he finds meaning in life by devoting himself to the performance of ethical duties. Highest of all is the religious stage, in which a richer spiritual meaning is added to the person's life, but without sapping his ethical vitality. Religious estheticism results from a failure to retain ethical vitality or to gain a true understanding of what the religious stage means:

> Religion becomes a matter of . . . exciting intellectual and artistic enjoyment. . . . Religious life becomes stimulating, emotionally right to the point of surfeit, a cult of in-groups who know how to savor their anxiety and their pleasure—all these, but never an inconvenience.
>
> [Religious estheticism] promotes exquisite skill in penitence, but does not repent—does not repent of anything in particular. It adopts from the existentialists the vocabulary of the concrete, but rarely rights concrete wrongs. It is skillful in defining [Christian love], careless of the needs of God's children. It adores the Christ who died for men; it neglects the Christ who said, "Why do you call me Lord, Lord and not do the things that I say?" [53]

Theological absolutism may serve as a lens through which some Christians see a God of genuine love to whom they are moved to respond gratefully and energetically. But it is of the

utmost importance that adherents of this viewpoint realize how
impossible it is for many millions of people today to see through
that lens. Let the theological absolutists realize that the "scandal
of particularity," the notion that God plays favorites in revealing Himself, is for many men an insurmountable barrier
to religious faith.[54] Let them consider how blasphemous it is to
declare that God's mysterious love can only be experienced fully
in one particular religion that is based upon one particular revelation at one particular moment in history. Let them consider how
grievously they are defeating the purposes of God in human
society by refusing to acknowledge that the son who cannot
bring himself to say "Yes!" to the image of the Father in traditional Christianity may still be a legitimate heir to the Father's
love, and may still do good work in the vineyard. Let them consider how *unnecessary* theological absolutism is, since whenever
God's will is done in the vineyard, his glory is upheld in the most
significant way. And if they want modern man to trust the
graciousness of God, let them repudiate unambiguously and un-
equivocally such reprehensible relics of traditional theology as
the doctrines of blood atonement, predestination and hell.

An awareness of the perils of theological absolutism, and of
the incompleteness of the triumph of grace in contemporary
Christian theology, highlights the significance of Schweitzer's
triumph over authoritarian compulsion. His supposed agnos-
ticism is an important part of this contribution to both ethics
and theology. Schweitzer pronounces neither a final "Yes!" nor
a final "No!" to the name—the existence—of a personal deity.
He merely works in the vineyard, confident that if there is a
God worthy of worship and service, His will is love. If a choice
had to be made between God's holiness and His love, Schweitzer
would choose the latter. But he has wisely decided to bypass the
question of God's sovereignty, choosing rather to assume that
God's love is His holiness, and committing himself so unre-
servedly to the service of Will-to-Love that the speculative question about God's omnipotence simply does not arise.[55] And by
ignoring the monarchical attributes of deity, Schweitzer does
away with the necessity for man to sink into self-preoccupation,

waiting for more grace than he has been given or bemoaning his guilt, paralyzed by a sterile determination to purge his motivation of the last vestige of pride.

Schweitzer also meets the problem of authoritarian compulsion with his doctrine of higher life-affirmation, which insures that compassionate self-devotion to others will not be conceived of legalistically. Within the context of Schweitzer's notion of essential selfhood, self-devotion is seen as the highest mode of self-fulfilment, a form of self-expansion.[56]

Schweitzer's triumph over normlessness is related to the positive emphasis in his theology, his affirmation of the moral aspect of Cosmic Reality as Will-to-Love or as "Ethical Personality." His establishment of love as the supreme ethical norm is related specifically to his understanding of Jesus as the Christ, for Jesus is the perfect example of love as compassionate self-devotion. In theological terms, Jesus is the New Man who gives us a new vision of our essential nature as men. In philosophical terms, the doctrine of essential selfhood declares compassionate self-devotion to be the law of man's essential nature, whether it conveniently expresses his empirical nature or not. In either case, the meaning is the same: love is a norm that is applicable to every man, regardless of whether he finds it easy to devote himself to other beings. Thus Schweitzer restores the concept of *duty* to its rightful place of honor as one of the fundamental categories of moral philosophy. He safeguards this norm from irrelevance by insisting that the only way to relate ourselves to the infinite Will-to-Live is by serving individual finite wills-to-live in the world.

The ethical mysticism of Schweitzer succeeds in avoiding both legalism and normlessness. It is a philosophy that provides ethical norms without authoritarian compulsion.

17. Schweitzer's Reinterpretation of Jesus as the Christ

Schweitzer offers us not only a purified concept of God, but also a fresh and vital understanding of Jesus as the Christ. His Christology is his chief inspiration and the chief inspiration he offers to other Christians; furthermore, it is an indispensable aspect of his ethic of reverence for life.

Schweitzer's direct inference of universal reverence for life from the sole premise of one's awareness of his own will-to-survive is comprehensible and valid only upon the supposition that some living will intervenes between one's own and other wills-to-live, and also between one's empirical self and one's understanding of essential selfhood. Jesus as the Christ manifests will-to-love raised to the highest peak of intensity, and this revelation enables the existing self to redefine both its self-image and its essential self-understanding. Having experienced Jesus' manifestation of will-to-love, the will-to-live perceives the meaning of human existence in terms of the New Adam, the New Man, who is defined in the Suffering Servant of God, Jesus the Anointed One. Will-to-love is interposed between the will-to-live and its perception of other wills-to-live, and the natural struggle of creature against creature is transcended, because a heightened ethical concern for other wills-to-live becomes possible for the self that has been touched by God as Will-to-Love in Jesus as the Christ. Schweitzer's own decisions and reflections were influenced by Him for many decades before his philosophy received systematic formulation, and the unacknowledged but decisive link in his philosophic logic is his encounter with the New Man.

Schweitzer's conception of revelation resembles Rudolph Otto's notion of an inner "faculty of receptivity and a principle of judgment and acknowledgement" which enables a person to recognize the true definition of his essential self when it is revealed to him.[1] But just as Otto emphasizes that this "universal 'predisposition' is merely a faculty of receptivity . . . not a capacity to produce the cognitions in question for oneself independently," so Schweitzer confesses that it is from the revelation of God as Will-to-Love in Jesus as the Christ that man can best gain an understanding of his essential self.[2]

The impact of the Christ on the receptive self is a uniquely intense form of the influence of friends on the development of any person, which Schweitzer describes by speaking of the "tinder" inside everyone which "catches fire successfully only when it meets some flame or spark from outside, i.e., from some other person." [3] This distinction between the potentiality that is a part of the empirical self and the enlightening and empowering actuality that is in Jesus as the Christ is the key to an understanding of the problem of immanence. The Holy Spirit is outside us, but we become truly ourselves and realize the potential that is within us only through becoming another kind of being under the power of the Spirit. Schweitzer states that the spark from outside comes to us from some other *person,* and the appropriation of Jesus as the Christ is faithful to this idea, since it is the historical Jesus—who is fully man as well as New Man—whom we acknowledge as Lord.

To be sure, there are a number of inconsistencies in Schweitzer's Christology. His 1906 depiction of the historical Jesus cannot be completely harmonized with his spiritualized and spiritualizing Jesus of 1950. The residue of validity in the largely discredited findings of the "realized eschatology" school of New Testament interpretation complements rather than negates Schweitzer's "thoroughgoing eschatology[4]; however, it still cannot be said that the historical Jesus' expectation of an immediate end to earthly history is compatible with the spiritualized Jesus' optimistic, world-affirming outlook. Schweitzer's suggestion that the historical Jesus' eschatological ethics are universally valid is inconsistent with his characterization of Jesus' teachings as an interim ethic which had no real concern for questions of "mine and thine," much less any consciousness of the complex problems of would-be moral men in the immoral societies of subsequent centuries, especially our own. Finally, it is difficult to reconcile the narrow predestinarian views of the historical Jesus with the belief that He is the incarnation of God as *universal Will-to-Love.*

Twentieth-century New Testament scholarship has raised a larger issue than any of these specific questions about the accuracy of Schweitzer's delineation of Jesus. Scholars have been compelled by their findings to ask whether it is possible for any researcher to discover the Jesus of history "as he really was in His life on earth, which includes, of course, what He did, and said, what He intended, and what He taught." [5] This larger question grew out of the discovery that the Biblical accounts of the life of Jesus are not disinterested records of exactly what was said and done at given times and given places. The Gospel accounts are now known to be collections made by various interested editors of stories, sayings and catechetical materials which were preserved in oral or written form by various groups of early Christians. [6] Therefore, what we have in the four Gospels is not a *photograph* of Jesus of Nazareth, but rather four differing *portraits* of the man whom the four evangelists considered to be the "Anointed One" of God. And of course each portrait is rendered in such a way as to present him as they saw him and wanted the church to see him. For example, the writer of the Gospel of Matthew understood Jesus as the New Moses, the giver of the New Law, and he relates a number of stories about Jesus which are not mentioned in the other gospels—stories designed to fortify the parallel between Jesus and Moses. [7]

The first fact concerning the Gospels established by recent New Testament research is their unreliability as chronological accounts:

> Karl Ludwig Schmidt demonstrated that the order of events in the Gospels is not based upon a memory of the order of Jesus' public ministry inherent in the material, but rather is largely the contribution of the redactional process, which assembled unrelated stories, sayings, and small individual collections for devotional purposes, and then arranged them topically or theologically without any serious interest in chronology or geography. [8]

A second fact recently established is that the Gospels cannot be trusted as impartial reports of "what really happened" in the life and after the death of Jesus, for they are "editorials" rather than "news dispatches" concerning the events reported. Important evidence to substantiate this fact was accumulated by the form critics, who classified individual *pericopae* (groups of verses that originally formed one "unit" of church tradition about Jesus) according to "the function in the Church's life responsible for the rise of each identified form." [9] Thus certain passages were identified as cultic hymns for use in worship services, others were seen to be codifications of moral teachings or theological doctrines for the instruction of converts, etc.[10] These discoveries indicate that the New Testament is essentially the preserved *kerygma* (literally, "preaching": the proclamation of the early Christians about their faith) of the early church. The Jesus of the Gospels is "Jesus *as known in the church* both before his death and afterwards." [11] The "history" of the Gospels is "kerygmatized history (in secular language: history presented in a biased way under the authority of the *kerygma*)." [12]

The details of Schweitzer's reconstruction of Jesus' life are placed in doubt by form criticism. The tenth chapter of Matthew (to cite one passage on which Schweitzer leans very heavily) is now thought to be an idealized account of a missionary venture of the Palestinian Church which probably occurred about A.D. 70, with the "charge" to the missionaries having been put back into the mouth of Jesus in order to give it greater urgency.[13] The transfiguration, which Schweitzer interprets as an ecstatic vision experienced by Jesus and the three disciples who are mentioned in the account, and which Schweitzer is forced to suppose misplaced from proper chronological sequence, is now regarded by many scholars as an episode created by the early Christians out of their experience of Jesus' presence with them even after His death.[14] Recent study raises objections to numerous other details of Schweitzer's thesis. But his most important finding, that Jesus and the earliest circle of His followers expected the imminent coming of the Son of Man, has been accepted by virtually all scholars. At least one form critic has used this central tenet of Schweitzer's "thoroughgoing eschatology" to explain the development of the various later theologies that can be discerned in the New Testament.[15]

The realization that a successful quest for the historical Jesus is *impossible*, in the nineteenth-century sense of the quest, has led a number of today's prominent theologians to contend that such a quest is also theologically *illegitimate*. They maintain that an attempt to formulate a "scholarly reconstruction of Jesus' biography by means of objective historical method" is really a new kind of Pharisaism. They reject objective historical quests as attempts to "avoid the risk of faith by supplying objectively verified *proof*" of the divinity of Christ and of the rightness of faith in him.[16] The bold affirmation is now being made that the authoritativeness of the Christian religion rests solely on the *kerygma,* and that anyone who asks for something more objectively certain is a skeptic who simply fails to understand the nature of religious faith.[17]

But what is the primitive church's *kerygma* to modern man? What to him are the New Testament myths about the victory of Christ over the demons and death, or about the coming of the Son of Man in glory? He knows that sickness, sin and death are still very much with us, and that the Son of Man has not come as predicted. The incredibility of the New Testament's "three-story universe" prompted Rudolph Bultmann to lead the way in a new endeavor to demythologize the *kerygma.* Demythologizing is the term applied to the effort of scholars and theologians to strip away the mythological framework in which the early Christians expressed their faith concerning the person and work of Jesus, in order to reveal the essential message of the New Testament in a form which can be apprehended by modern people. In Bultmann, this message seems to become a religious version of the understanding of authentic human existence articulated by existentialists such as Martin Heidegger: it is a message about the "eschatological" character of man's life; i.e., about the way in which man is called upon by God to *decide, now,* for or against Him. Just as Jesus called upon the men of His time to "repent, for the Kingdom of Heaven is at hand," so the preaching of the *kerygma* about Him calls men today to an imperative decision regarding a mode of self-understanding which is the spiritual analogue of the Kingdom.[18]

Many theologians protest, however, that "demythologizing" really means "dekerygmatizing," and that the resultant viewpoint is unsatisfactory for Christianity. It is charged that in the process of demythologizing, the Christian gospel is reduced to a timeless truth, a "symbolized principle" that is not really related to or dependent upon historical revelation.[19] This position is regarded as a logical absurdity because the unique content of the *kerygma* is precisely its assertion that the transcendent has entered history in the form of a *person* and in certain *events* centering in this person. Therefore, unless the kerygma confronts us with the concrete persons and events in question, unless it provides an encounter with the *historical* Jesus, it is not the true *kerygma* at all.

The changed theological situation created by form criticism and demythologizing has given rise to a new kind of quest of the historical Jesus. The new quest does not seek to uncover the factually historical Jesus, who remains forever inaccessible behind the veil of the early church's preaching; it seeks instead the "interpreted historical" Jesus whom the *kerygma* proclaims. This new quest is possible because twentieth-century historiography has learned that the writing of history is not possible without interpretation. Even a photograph or a news dispatch exhibits the selectivity of the reporter; "fact" and "interpretation" are so closely intertwined that they cannot be separated in the writing or the reading of history. James M. Robinson, a leading student of the new quest, believes that "the historian's task is increasingly seen in the identification of the meaning of *historical* event, rather than merely in the establishment of chronological and causal sequence." [20] History is now concerned with

the dimension in which man actually exists, his "world," the stance or outlook from which he acts, his understanding of his existence behind what he does, the way he meets his basic problems and the answer his life implies to the human dilemma, the significance he had as the environment of those who knew him, the continuing history his life produces, the possibility of existence which his life presents to me as an alternative. . . .[21]

The method of the new quest consists in "moving below the surface of terms and even concepts to the level of theological meaning and existential significance." [22] It seeks to understand "the act of intention, the commitment, the meaning for the participants, behind the external occurrence[s]" of the New Testament. For "in such intention and commitment the self of the participant actualizes itself, and in this act of self-actualization the self is revealed." [23] The possible and relevant way to know Jesus, then, is to apprehend His "understanding of His existence, His selfhood, and thus in the higher sense his life."[24]

There are two significant relationships between this new quest for the historical Jesus and Schweitzer's quest of almost sixty years ago. The first is that Schweitzer anticipated the later approach in his understanding of Jesus as Lord of the will and in his idea that our relationship to Him must be one of will to will. The parallel between Schweitzer's concept of Jesus as our authority in the realm of the will and Robinson's focus on commitment as the determinative element in selfhood is striking. When Robinson states that "selfhood results from implicit or explicit commitment to a kind of existence, and is to be understood only in terms of that commitment," [25] he echoes Schweitzer's declaration that "The last and deepest knowledge of things comes from the will . . . , which constitutes the primary and ultimate essence of the persons [of the New Testament]." [26] Jesus can be the Christ for us because He defined His essential selfhood as compassionate suffering service and He actualized this self-understanding by a commitment to God as Will-to-Love—a commitment so strong that it did not dissolve even when challenged by the prospect of death on the Cross. The parallels between the two quests can also be seen in Schweitzer's assertion that "we have the true knowledge of Jesus in proportion as we have the spirit of Jesus," [27] and in his conviction that it is "Jesus as spiritually arisen within men who is significant for our time and can help it." [28] Schweitzer was thinking of the necessity for interpretation of the historical Jesus when he wrote that his understanding of Jesus as Lord of the will was "historically wrong but religiously right." [29]

The second significant relationship between the new quest and that of Schweitzer is that Schweitzer's interpretation retains a fidelity to factual history that the former is not even interested in retaining. Schweitzer's historical Jesus is not merely an "interpreted historical" Jesus; He is also, in fundamental respects if not in detail, a *factually* historical Jesus. As a result, Schweitzer's Christology is far more able to elicit response and command respect from contemporary Christians who believe that their faith cannot claim to be historical unless it has a reasonable basis in "what really happened" in Palestine nineteen centuries ago. Many modern people cannot accept the interpreted historical Jesus as the Christ if He is too closely bound to an insufficiently demythologized *kerygma* or if His life and person are insufficiently grounded in what can be reasonably known of the factually historical Jesus. It is for this reason that the new quest is rejected by so many scholars and laymen as incomplete.[30] In the new quest, interpretation so overwhelms fact and the *content* of the interpretation of Jesus is so largely determined by the primitive *kerygma* that genuine historicity evaporates. Moreover, believers are asked to accept a number of doctrines about Jesus and God that are either unnecessary or illegitimate from the standpoint of a morally sensitive modern man. Schweitzer's Jesus, on the other hand, does not demand a belief that God acted in history through Him in a fashion any different from that in which He always has been and always will be eager to act in the lives of men who submit their will to Him as Will-to-Love. The only new discovery which might unsettle Schweitzer's interpretation of Jesus is Bornkamm's conjecture that Jesus did not go to Jerusalem *seeking* vicarious death.[31] But even a negative answer here would not alter the fact that Jesus was willing to undergo death in order to do what he conceived as the will of the Father for the good of His children.

The Jesus portrayed by Schweitzer is able to "move us deeply by His subordination to God." [32] Even the supposition that He thought of His death as efficacious only for the elect would not affect His authority in the realm of the *will*, for He did give Himself for the purpose of saving God's own from suffering—and although today we may have an expanded conception of the scope of God's love, we cannot find a more superb demonstration of right commitment of will than we find in Jesus. Schweitzer's portrait presents Jesus as a man who was completely human in His susceptibility to temptation, weariness, faintness of heart and even despair. Yet His will was so perfectly united with God's that He suffered death in order to carry out His understanding of what God's love demanded. This Jesus is our authority, our Lord, in the realm of the will. And as Schweitzer declares, this Jesus stands before us in all His "unconditionedness," calling upon us to decide whether or not we will follow Him and come into mystical fellowship with Him as we go about the tasks which He has for us today.

The thesis that Albert Schweitzer is a legitimate, indeed, a brilliant interpreter of Christian faith will cause surprise, dismay or disgust in various admirers of Schweitzer. To those who regard him as "the greatest living Christian" but have no substantial knowledge of his writings, it will doubtless come as a shock to realize how unorthodox he is. To those who hail him as a great debunker of Christianity, the prophet of a new naturalistic philosophy which is destined to replace an obsolete religion, it will be a source of irritation to discover that his feet are firmly planted in the Christian tradition. The former group will think him guilty of heresy; the latter group will attempt to deny that he takes Christianity seriously, on the assumption that any attempt at a thoughtful reinterpretation of Christian faith can be nothing more than a futile attempt to pour new wine into a worn-out wineskin.

The charge that Schweitzer is heretical is less formidable than the contention that his reinterpretation of Christianity is futile, which implies the irrelevance of Christianity for intelligent persons of today. The charge of futility further implies that theologians and ministers who no longer accept the orthodox formulations of Christian faith ought to make a clean break with Christianity, rather than deceive gullible parishioners, students and followers by changing the meanings of traditional symbols behind their backs. Clergymen who continue to use traditional religious language without believing what this language means to their congregations are accused of disingenuousness, if not actual hypocrisy.[33]

This is a serious charge, and it deserves to be answered with greater seriousness than most theologians exhibit when faced with it.[34] The charge may be answered, first, by pointing out that every religion is always apprehended on a number of different levels by different sorts and conditions of men.[35] It is unrealistic and narrow-minded to demand that Christianity must mean one thing and one thing only to all believers. Secondly, there are no prima facie grounds for questioning the integrity of those who seek to express their deepest convictions about human existence through a reinterpretation of Christian faith. Nothing is more evident from an examination of the history of Christian thought and art than the necessity for, and the ubiquity of, the activity of reinterpretation. The biblical drama of the Christ is not a simple given which can be frozen into creedal affirmations and distributed uniformly to passive believers. As Schweitzer insists, every age and every individual must encounter Jesus directly and struggle to win from Him the truths which He embodies. Therefore the task of reinterpretation is both endless and personal.

Schweitzer's work as a reinterpreter of Christianity has been characterized by a wise avoidance of controversy over speculative and organizational issues. By holding himself aloof from disputes about doctrine and arguments about the relative merits of different denominations, Schweitzer has manifested his realization that it is the ultimate Cosmic Reality, not the terms men use to talk about it or the forms of worship they employ in regard to it, which is finally important. By refusing to declare himself a theist or a pantheist, Schweitzer gives forceful expression to his conviction that an ethical-mystical relationship with God is more important than recognition of His name and authority. And by giving Jesus a central place in his description of his own life and thought, Schweitzer gives ample proof of his belief that Christianity is still worthy of reinterpretation. His understanding of Jesus as the Christ may provide the basis for a new stage in the "continuing Reformation" which the Christian church must constantly undergo if its gospel is to be relevant for each succeeding generation.

Schweitzer's understanding of Christian faith is ideally qualified to be a basis for the continuing Reformation in our day because of the fact that it is not a closed system. It is an open-minded system in regard to both philosophy and theology, and also in regard to both the future and the past. Not only is there room for further elaboration of his world-view in philosophical terms, there is also room for a continued use of traditional Christian symbols in his reinterpreted theological position. Although Schweitzer's conscientious rationalism and his equally conscientious individualism have prevented him from appreciating the significance of the church and its heritage of religious symbolism, a reinterpreted appropriation of this symbolism is not in the least inconsistent with his thought. Once the mighty cosmic drama of the New Testament has been demythologized in our heads, we can allow it to be remythologized in our hearts. We can appreciate the essential meaning of the creeds, the liturgies and the art of the church, through which men of other centuries expressed their hope and trust about the meaning of human existence, because we participate in that same existence and may share essentially the same hope and trust. The biblical figure of the Suffering Servant whose stripes heal the wounds of his people, the Lamb of God whose flesh and blood make us whole, the Pauline *Christus Victor* who smashes the power of the demons and sets men free from sin and death— all of these can still be for us the images through which we express our faith that ultimate Cosmic Reality is infinite Will-to-Love as well as infinite Will-to-Live. Thus Schweitzer's Christology enables us to maintain genuine spiritual continuity with the community of the faithful who have in various ways at various times and in various places acknowledged Jesus as Lord. Thus the Christ of the church can still be acknowledged as the Anointed One in that He is the incarnation of our trust that God somehow stands beside us in our estrangement from Him and from each other, that He understands our suffering and bears it with us, and that we are meant to have fellowship with Him as we respond to the challenge of our destiny as co-creators of the world which He intends to see brought to fulfilment.

18. Ethical Mysticism as a World-View

Two cardinal concepts in Schweitzer's philosophy have significant parallels in other philosophies of the twentieth century and lend themselves to further elaboration. These concepts invite expansion into a richer world-view of world- and life-affirmation which, although nowhere explicit in Schweitzer's writings, is in no way inconsistent with the spirit of his ethical mysticism.

One of these concepts is that of Cosmic Reality as universal will-to-live divided against itself but seeking reunion with itself through will-to-love. The other concept is that of compassionate suffering as the highest dimension of the process in which will-to-live seeks reconciliation with other wills-to-live from which it is separated. From these two notions emerges a conception of ultimate Cosmic Reality as suffering love working to heal the division within itself, a conception which is the philosophical counterpart of the drama of redemption celebrated in Christian theology.

This conception of the cosmos as being seeking reunion with itself has deep historical roots in the metaphysics of Plato and Augustine, as well as contemporary parallels in the philosophy of Whitehead and the theology of Tillich. Paul Tillich himself confesses "the suspicion that Schweitzer and I have similar fathers in spirit." Tillich considers himself related to Schweitzer indirectly in that both he and Schweitzer stand "in the line of" Schelling, Goethe, Nietzsche, Bergson and Whitehead. Tillich further acknowledges a direct influence of Schweitzer's thought upon his own:

I feel now more than in earlier years the impact of Schweitzer's idea of the inviolability of life. I even have a large section in the forthcoming volume of my *Systematic Theology* under the title, "The Inviolability of Life." [1]

Even though Schweitzer avoids the term "Being," which is the central concept employed by Tillich, there is nonetheless a striking parallel between the two men's understanding of

Cosmic Reality. Schweitzer writes of the division within universal will-to-live and of the will-to-love that seeks to overcome this division; Tillich writes of the estrangement of being from Being itself and of a power of reconciliation that seeks to heal this estrangement.

In *Love, Power and Justice,* Tillich contends that a differentiation of Being itself into individual beings was necessary in order that love of the most profound sort might be experienced in the universe. This self-division of Being itself was necessary because love in its most profound dimension is a reconciling force which overcomes estrangement. Had there been no differentiation, there could have been no separate, separated manifestations of Being: the Creation would have been devoid of its most noble quality, profound love. Therefore God (Being itself) took upon Himself the estrangement involved in self-division. God's power now draws back together the estranged beings which fill the universe, those beings which are indeed restless until they find reconciliation once more in the Being itself from which they sprang.[2] When estranged beings—who were made free in the process of differentiation and therefore have some responsibility for initiative in the process of reconciliation—acknowledge their estrangement from God, when they face the despair of this estrangement, then they may be able to experience the reconciling power of God's grace. It is possible to assume that although the individual personality does not retain its physical body or its self-conscious identity after death, still the freedom and individuality of beings is preserved even when they have been drawn back into a reconciled relationship with Being itself. If this assumption be granted, profound love-overcoming-potential-estrangement would continue to exist in the universe even after the sting of separation had been overcome through the establishment of a relationship of reconciliation.

In the face of the mysterious division within the universal will-to-live, Schweitzer can only retire into a resigned renunciation of hope for knowledge about the world. But if one applies to Schweitzer's categories those of Tillich, it becomes possible to regard the very differentiation of the universal will-to-live into various free, and therefore conflicting, manifestations of the will-to-live as an act of God as Will-to-Love. The process of differentiation can be interpreted as the bringing about of the condition without which self-conscious awareness of will-to-love and participation in it would have been impossible. To be sure, this explanation does not abolish the burden of pain that mars finite existence and troubles the heart of Schweitzer and every other man. But it offers some clues to a meaningful interpretation of creation as a whole.

For as Tillich indicates, the ontological understanding of love implies that God Himself takes estrangement upon His own Being. It is God Himself whose Being undergoes differentiation in order that men might become self-conscious beings aware of reconciling love and capable of responding to it freely. It is the universal will-to-live which undergoes separation in order that individual wills-to-live might experience the reconciling power of will-to-love drawing them towards a relationship of restored wholeness and inviting them to take part in the process of reconciliation by tempering the existing will-to-live with will-to-love.[3]

If God Himself participates with man in the suffering of estrangement which He ordained and which He has the power to heal, the implications are stirring: first, our suffering because of the division within the universal will-to-live is not barren, since in it we have the fellowship of God, who also bears the same suffering in a measure infinitely greater than we; and second, our suffering is not devoid of hope, since we know that God's ultimate purpose is the achievement of a reconciliation deepened by profound love. We enjoy the fellowship of God in our experience of estrangement because we know that He would not bear the burden of estrangement with us unless He loved us. He might have remained aloof in the undifferentiated bliss of His Being, or He might conceivably have effected a token differentiation which did not allow us genuine freedom of genuine selfhood. In either case He might have saved Himself from the pain of self-division, pain which was not a one-time affair but which is a continuing Cross, because the conflicts involved are unceasing. Because He participates in the

same longing for reconciliation that we know, He stands beside
us in our suffering, thus giving powerful testimony that He
loves us and that He has chosen to give Himself to us and for
us. We enjoy the assurance of hope that will-to-love will ultimately heal the division within will-to-live, and that we shall
enjoy a restoration of harmony of Being, a harmony which is
more than sheer absorption.

Does the responsibility of man end when he acknowledges
his estrangement and accepts the offer of God's reconciling
grace? Schweitzer would say that the man who has experienced
will-to-love vitally and has become mystically related to God
as ethical personality will take an active part in the process of
reconciliation himself. Confronted with the dilemma of life
divided against itself, the ethical person seeks to "put a stop to
this disunion of the will-to-live so far as the influence of his own
existence reaches." [4]

I am convinced that Schweitzer's notion of reverence for
all forms of life has greatest significance in this ontological context, since the ontological approach views all beings as sharing
the same qualitative status as manifestations of Being itself.

But even more promising than Schweitzer's reverence for
life as a fruitful application of his call for self-devotion, and as
a corollary to Tillich's ontology of love, is the doctrine of co-
creatorship. The idea of co-creatorship is implicit in Schweitzer's
references to man's destiny as "an active, purposeful force in
the world," [5] and in his mention of "our cooperation with the
activity which the world-spirit wills for us." [6] Whitehead states
the doctrine explicitly:

> God is in the world . . . creating continually in us and around
> us. Insofar as man partakes of that creative process does he partake of
> the divine, of God. . . . His true destiny as co-creator in the
> universe is his dignity and his grandeur.[7]

God is creating the world in us as will-to-love which seeks to
minimize and make progressively less prevalent the clash of
will-to-live against will-to-live which characterizes the estrangement of existence. We participate in that creative process, and

therefore in God, insofar as we will and live love. The very attitude of compassion is intrinsically valuable, for there are many instances of will-to-live estranged from itself which we are powerless to prevent or heal, and in such cases all we can do is to feel the pain of the conflict, where not to do so would be to blunt ourselves.

Effective co-creatorship requires, however, that Schweitzer's social ethics be purged of its tendencies toward sentimentality and the irrelevant piety of "clean hands." Tillich's notion of justice as the "form of being" that gives adequate structure to the power encounters between being and being provides a valuable corrective to Schweitzer's idealism and a helpful definition of the framework in which co-creatorship must function in society.[8] As he says, "Love shows what is just in concrete situations,"[9] and it is love which reunites estranged beings—but it is justice which is required to "preserve that which is to be united."[10] The writings of Reinhold Niebuhr and John Bennett, among others, provide counsel concerning the strategies which co-creatorship must employ as it goes about its tasks in society, and suggests limits beyond which man's creative energies dare not venture, lest *hybris* turn noble rebellion into vicious oppression.[11]

Not only does the conception of co-creatorship correct Schweitzer's frequently naive and irrelevant individualism, but it also offers a richer interpretation of the meaning of the "cosmic motive" for ethics than his austere doctrine of agnostic renunciation of metaphysics. Co-creatorship based on ontology offers a possible answer to the desire of the soul for unity mentioned by Reinhold Niebuhr in his review of *Civilization and Ethics*:

> Ultimately, of course, the soul's desire for unity cannot be denied. We will explore until we find some unifying concept between various types of reality, such as nature and personality. . . . And it may be that such a search will be or has been crowned with more success than Schweitzer is willing to admit.[12]

Co-creatorship affords a possibility of affirming the world and life because it gives us a glimpse of new understandings of the

purpose of human ethical striving, of sin, of forgiveness and of
the relation of God to history.

Toynbee's concept of challenge and response further eluci-
dates the problem of purpose in human striving, when challenge
and response are interpreted in the light of co-creatorship. Just
as the challenge of a not-very-favorable environment is necessary to the development of a great civilization,[13] so the conditions of estrangement and freedom are necessary to the highest
development of man as a spiritual being. If God had placed us
in a perfect Eden where no suffering existed, then we could
never have known the depths of compassion that characterize
love in its richest dimension. Suffering is the category of experience in which we enjoy the most meaningful fellowship
with both God and man. To be sure, the challenge may sometimes be too great, and individuals no less than civilizations may
be crushed: this is the dysteleological surd which no explanation
of the universe can completely do away with, and to the extent
that this is true there is still a place for Schweitzer's notion of
inward detachment as a complement to outer activity. Yet the
reality of co-creatorship invites us to join in the process of
overcoming the challenge of evil less from a sense of duty than
from a positive awareness that in responding thus we fulfill
our nature as potential co-creators of the not-yet-finished world.

Since the destiny of man is to approach more nearly the
spiritual stature of co-creatorship which God intends for him,
sin is the failure to participate in co-creatorship—and this is a
fresh and far more constructive understanding of the meaning
of sin than traditional notions of sin as disobedience and self-
assertiveness. Sin is primarily a failure to respond to God's
challenge, a challenge which is at the same time an invitation
to realize our essential nature as his children. This conception
of sin does not make of it a legalistic, works-righteousness notion according to which sin is the failure to achieve some required condition of purity or self-abasement. Rather, sin is a
refusal to answer God's call at all. Sin is a refusal to turn one's
head, heart and hands in the direction which He has provided
for the fulfillment of essential selfhood. Sin is a refusal to

acknowledge the estrangement existing between one's own being and other beings, between oneself and Being itself.

On the ethical level, sin is the refusal to *care* about the burden of suffering and pain that limits the functioning and growth of the wills-to-live around one. More than that—since it is possible to acknowledge estrangement without participating in the process of reconciliation—sin also involves failure to express compassion in ethical activity. Although compassion has inherent value in regard to those manifestations of estrangement which cannot be alleviated by the person concerned, wherever the possibility for amelioration exists but is not carried out, there compassion loses its power-of-being and becomes a hollow or even hypocritical illusion. Sin, in brief, is "coming short of the glory of God": failing to participate in the glorious process of co-creatorship that He intends as the true destiny and grandeur of His children.

A corollary of the new understanding of sin is a new understanding of forgiveness. Forgiveness is not atonement in the sense of a one-time act at one point of history; it is a process aiming toward an eventually perfect at-one-ment of Being and a present at-one-ment among estranged beings, both in their relation to Being itself and in their relation to each other. It is the assurance that the privilege of participation *with God* in the process of co-creatorship is still and forever open to us, regardless of how many times in the past we have failed to respond to its challenge and will undoubtedly fail again in the future.

The anxiety of guilt which afflicts us is removed by our knowledge that God is continually with us in the process. Were He not "standing by man even when man is in the wrong" we would continually be prompted by frightful anxiety into the retreat of despair or the excesses of compulsive efforts to justify ourselves before God and men. "To stand by the wrongdoer and to suffer redemptively the consequences of his wrong is the meaning of forgiveness," [14] and that is just what God does. Nor does the assurance of forgiveness minimize for an instant the horror of sin. Whenever we fail to do what lies within our power to bring reconciliation in the place of estrangement, the pain of that estrangement continues to rest upon God, and we are guilty, in the words of Paul, of crucifying anew the King of Glory.

Finally, the notion of co-creatorship has implications for our conception of God and His relation to history. Since "God's own being is qualified by whatever of good or ill has taken place among His creatures," [15] the "enduring consequences" of human conduct within history are nothing less than awe-inspiring. The awareness that our fellowship with God is so real that what we do or fail to do within history affects the eternal Being of God is surely a more powerful stimulus to responsible use of our freedom than traditional theologies of an immutable, impassive deity. This awareness inspires us to respond joyfully to His challenge, knowing that "we are responsible for doing here and now in the situation in which we stand whatever will serve the work of God who is seeking to bring all life to fulfilment in that universal community of love which is the real good of every creature." [16]

19. The Challenge of Schweitzer

No assessment of Albert Schweitzer's contribution to moral philosophy would be complete without a final word concerning the influence of his life. Because he is the embodiment of his theory he compels us to remember that ethical thought has no value unless it is taken seriously. It is not a game, a matter of manipulating words and concepts until a pretty picture emerges. It is not a contest of wits, to determine which philosophers shall win a prize for the most nimble mind. Nor is it a balm for the conscience whereby one can reassure himself that he is a good person because he has let so many good thoughts pass through his mind.

With Schweitzer, ethical mysticism is a call to decision. His life reinforces the interpretation that he has given to Jesus, especially the eschatological element in his thought. As Rudolph Bultmann and his followers have emphasized, along with Schweitzer, the meaning of eschatology for contemporary man is the *urgency* of the call. One is faced with a choice between light and darkness now, and the decision for or against the forces of God has abiding consequences in terms of the kind of selfhood one will realize. Whether we admire Schweitzer or not, whether or not we accept his philosophizing and theologizing—this is not the point. The significance of his life consists in its powerful testimony to the claim which our understanding of good and evil lays upon us. And if we choose to commit ourselves to a self-understanding that includes compassionate self-devotion in its definition of essential manhood, then like Schweitzer we must take up our share of the burden of suffering that lies upon the world.

Appendix I

The Ethics of Reverence for Life*

ALBERT SCHWEITZER

In the history of world thought we seem to be met by a confusion of antagonistic systems. But if we look closely, we see that certain essential laws of thought are to be discerned. And as we trace them, we see a certain definite progress in this bewildering history. In fact, there emerge two main classes of problems. To begin with, we see certain facade problems, important looking, but not really connected with the main structure. Questions as to the reality of the world and the problem of knowledge belong here. Kant tried in vain to solve the essential questions by busying himself with these scientific, facade problems. Admittedly they are intriguing, but they are not the real, elementary matters.

We are concerned with the other problems, the essential ones. As we know life in ourselves, we want to understand life in the universe, in order to enter into harmony with it. Physically we are always trying to do this. But that is not the primary matter; for the great issue is that we shall achieve a spiritual harmony. Just to recognize this fact is to have begun to see a part of life clearly.

There is in each of us the will to live, which is based on the mystery of what we call "taking an interest." We cannot live alone. Though man is an egoist, he is never completely so. He *must* always have some interest in life about him. If for no other reason, he must do so in order to make his own life more perfect. Thus it happens that we want to devote ourselves; we want to take our part in perfecting our ideal of progress; we want to give meaning to the life in the world. This is the basis of our striving for harmony with the spiritual element.

* Reprinted from *Christendom*, I (Winter, 1936), no. 2, pp. 225-239.

The effort for harmony, however, never succeeds. Events cannot be harmonized with our activities. Working purposefully toward certain ends, we assume that the Creative Force in the world is doing likewise. Yet, when we try to define its goal, we can not do so. It tends toward developing a type of existence, but there is no coordinated, definite end to be observed, even though we think there should be. We like to imagine that Man is nature's goal; but facts do not support that belief.

Indeed, when we consider the immensity of the universe, we must confess that man is insignificant. The world began, as it were, yesterday. It may end tomorrow. Life has existed in the universe but a brief second. And certainly man's life can hardly be considered the goal of the universe. Its margin of existence is always precarious. Study of the geologic periods shows that. So does the battle against disease. When one has seen whole populations annihilated by sleeping sickness, as I have, one ceases to imagine that human life is nature's goal. In fact, the Creative Force does not concern itself about preserving life. It simultaneously creates and destroys. Therefore, the will-to-live is not to be understood within the circle of Creative Force. Philosophy and religion have repeatedly sought the solution by this road; they have projected our will to perfection into nature at large, expecting to see its counterpart there. But in all honesty we must confess that to cling to such a belief is to delude ourselves.

As a result of the failure to find ethics reflected in the natural order, the disillusioned cry has been raised that ethics can therefore have no ultimate validity. In the world of human thought and action today, humanitarianism is definitely on the wane. Brutality and trust in force are in the ascendant. What, then, is to become of that vigorous ethics which we inherited from our fathers?

Knowledge may have failed us; but we do not abandon the ideals. Though they are shaken, we do not turn from them to sheer scepticism. In spite of being unable to prove them by rational argumentation, we nevertheless believe that there is a proof and defense for them within themselves. We are, so to speak, immunized against scepticism. Indeed, the classical scepticisms were, after all, puerile. That a truth cannot be proved by argument is no reason why it should be utterly abandoned, so long as it is in itself possessed of value. Kant, trying to escape from scepticism, is a pre-indication of this immunity. In intent, his philosophy is great and eternal. He said that truth is of two kinds: scientific and spiritual. Let us look to the bottom of this; not by Kant's method, however, since he was often content with naive reflections on very deep questions. We shall avoid his way of seeking abstract solutions, and distinctions between material and immaterial. Instead, let us see that truths which are not provable in knowledge are given to us in our will-to-live.

Kant sought to give equal value to Practical and Theoretical Reason. More, he felt the demand for a more absolute ethic. It would, he thought, give new authority to spiritual and religious truth, thus making up for the loss involved in not being able to verify these truths by knowledge. This is the very heart of Kant's gospel, being much more important than anything he taught about space and time. But he did not know where to find the new ethic. He only gave a new, more handsome, and more impressive facade to the old. By his failure to point out the new ethic, he missed the new Rationalism. His thought was on too narrow a basis.

I

The essential thing to realize about ethics is that it is the very manifestation of our will-to-live. All our thoughts are given in that will-to-live, and we but give them expression and form in words. To analyze Reason fully would be to analyze the will-to-live. The philosophy that abandons the old Rationalism must begin be meditating on itself. Thus, if we ask, "What is the immediate fact of my consciousness? What do I self-consciously know of myself, making abstractions of all else, from childhood to old age? To what do I always return?" we find the simple fact of consciousness is this, *I will to live*. Through every stage of life, this is the one thing I know about myself. I do not say, "I am life"; for life continues to be a mystery too great to understand. I only know that I cling to it. I fear its cessation—death. I dread its diminution—pain. I seek its enlargement—joy.

Descartes started on this basis. But he built an artificial structure by presuming that man knows nothing, and doubts all, whether outside himself or within. And in order to end doubt, he fell back on the fact of consciousness: *I think.* Surely, however, that is the stupidest primary assumption in all philosophy! who can establish the fact that he thinks, except in relation to thinking *something?* And what that something is, is the important matter. When I seek the first fact of consciousness, it is not to know that I think, but to get hold of myself. Descartes would have a man think once, just long enough to establish the certainty of being, and then give over any further need of meditation. Yet meditation is the very thing I must not cease. I *must* ascertain whether my thoughts are in harmony with my will-to-live.

Bergson's admirable philosophy also starts from such a beginning. But he arrives at the sense of time. The fact of immediate consciousness, however, is much more important than the sense of time. So Bergson misses the real issue.

Instinct, thought, the capacity for divination, all these are fused with the will-to-live. And when it reflects upon itself, what path does it follow? When my will-to-live begins to think, it sees life as a mystery in which I remain by thought. I cling to life because of my reverence for life. For, when it begins to think, the will-to-live realizes that it is free. It is free to leave life. It is free to choose whether or not to live. This fact is of particular significance for us in this modern age, when there are abundant possibilities for abandoning life, painlessly and without agony.

Moreover, we are all closer to the possibility of this choice than we may guess of one another. The question which haunts men and women today is whether life is worth living. Perhaps each of us has had the experience of talking with a friend one day, finding that person bright, happy, apparently in the full joy of life; and then the next day we find that he has taken his own life! Stoicism has brought us to this point, by driving out the fear of death; for, by inference it suggests that we are free to choose whether to live or not. But if we entertain such a possibility, we do so by ignoring the melody of the will-to-live, which compels us to face the mystery, the value, the high trust committed to us in life. We may not understand it, but we begin to appreciate its great value. Therefore, when we find those who relinquish life, while we may not condemn them, we do pity them for having ceased to be in possession of themselves. Ultimately, the issue is not whether we do or do not fear death. The real issue is that of reverence for life.

Here, then, is the first spiritual act in man's experience: reverence for life. The consequence of it is that he comes to realize his dependence upon events quite beyond his control. Therefore he becomes resigned. And this is the second spiritual act: resignation.

What happens is that one realizes that he is but a speck of dust, a plaything of events outside his reach. Nevertheless, he may at the same time discover that he has a certain liberty, as long as he lives. Sometime or another all of us must have found that happy events have not been able to make us happy, nor unhappy events to make us unhappy. There is within each of us a modulation, an inner exaltation, which lifts us above dependence upon the gifts of events for our joy. Hence, our dependence upon events is not absolute; it is qualified by our spiritual freedom. Therefore, when we speak of resignation it is not sadness to which we refer, but the triumph of our will-to-live over whatever happens to us. And to become ourselves, to be spiritually alive, we must have passed beyond this point of resignation.

The great defect of modern philosophy is that it neglects this essential fact. It does not ask man to think deeply on himself. It hounds him into activity, bidding him find escape thus. In that respect it falls far below the philosophy of Greece, which taught men better the true depth of life.

I have said that resignation is the very basis of ethics. Starting from this position, the will-to-live comes first to veracity as the primary ground of virtue. If I am faithful to my will-to-live, I cannot disguise this fact, even though such disguise or evasion might seem to my advantage. Reverence for my will-to-live leads me to the necessity of being sincere with myself. And out of this fidelity to my own nature grows all my faithfulness. Thus, sincerity is the first ethical quality which appears. However lacking one may be in other respects, sincerity is the one thing which he must possess. Nor is this point of view to be found only among people of complex social life. Primitive cultures show the fact to be equally true there. Resignation to the will-to-live leads directly to this first virtue: sincerity.

II

Having reached this point, then, I am in a position to look at the world. I ask knowledge what it can tell me of life. Knowledge replies that what it can tell me is little, yet immense. Whence this universe came, or whither it is bound, or how it happens to be at all, knowledge cannot tell me. Only this: that the will-to-live is everywhere present, even as in me. I do not need science to tell me this; but it cannot tell me anything more essential. Profound and marvelous as chemistry is, for example, it is like all science in the fact that it can lead me only to the mystery of life, which is essentially in me, however near or far away it may be observed.

What shall be my attitude toward this other life? It can only be of a piece with my attitude towards my own life. If I am a thinking being, I must regard other life than my own with equal reverence. For I shall know that it longs for fulness and development as deeply as I do myself. Therefore, I see that evil is what annihilates, hampers, or hinders life. And this holds good whether I regard it physically or spiritually. Goodness, by the same token, is the saving or helping of life, the enabling of whatever life I can to attain its highest development.

This is the absolute and reasonable ethic. Whether such-and-such a man arrives at this principle, I may not know. But I know that it is given inherently in the will-to-live. Whatever is reasonable is good. This we have been told by all the great thinkers. But it reaches its best only in the light of this universal ethic, the ethic of reverence for life, to which we come as we meditate upon the will-to-live. And since it is important that we recognize to the best of our ability the full significance of this ethic, let us now devote our attention to some commentaries upon it.

Our first commentary: The primary characteristic of this ethic is that it is rational, having been developed as a result of thought upon life.

We may say that anyone who truly explores the depths of thought must arrive at this point. In other words, to be truly rational is to become ethical. (How pleased Socrates would be with us for saying this!) But if it is so simple a matter of rationality, why has it not long since been achieved? It has, indeed, been long on the way, while in every land thought has been seeking to deepen ethics. Actually, whenever love and devotion are glimpsed, reverence for life is not far off, since one grows from the other. But the truth of the matter is that thought fears such an ethic. What it wants is to impose regulations and order that can be duly systematized. This ethic is not subject to such bounding. Therefore, when modern thought considers such an ethic it fears it, and tries to discredit it, by calling it irrational. In this way its development has been long delayed.

Again, it may be asked if this sort of meditation is not definitely that of civilized rather than primitive men. The primitive man, it may be argued, knows no such reverence for life. To this I must agree, having associated with primitives in my work in Africa. Nevertheless, it remains true that the primitive who begins to meditate must proceed along the same path. He must start with his own will-to-live, and that is certain to bring him in this direction. If he does not reach a point as far along the way as we do, that is because we can profit by the meditations of our predecessors. There are many great souls who have blazed sections of the trail for us. Proceeding along that way, I have led you to this conclusion: that rational processes, properly pursued, must lead to the true ethic.

Another commentary: What of this ethic? Is it absolute? Kant defines absolute ethics as that which is not concerned with whether it can be achieved. The distinction is not one of *absolute* as opposed to *relative*, but *absolute* as distinct from *practicable* in the ethical field. An absolute ethic calls for the creating of perfection in this life. It cannot be completely achieved; but that fact does not really matter. In this sense, reverence for life is an absolute ethic. It does not lay down specific rules for each possible situation. It simply tells us that we are responsible for the lives about us. It does not set either maximum or minimum limits to what we must do.

In point of fact, every ethic has something of the absolute about it, just as soon as it ceases to be mere social law. It demands of one what is actually beyond his strength. Take the question of man's duty to his neighbor. The ethic cannot be fully carried out, without involving the possibility of complete sacrifice of self. Yet, philosophy has never bothered to take due notice of the distinction. It has simply tried to ignore absolute ethics, because such ethics cannot be fitted into tabulated rules and regulations. Indeed, the history of world teachings on the subject may be summarized in the motto: "Avoid absolute ethics, and thus keep within the realm of the possible."

We have already noted that Kant did postulate and demand an absolute ethics as the founadtion for a spiritual ethics. He knew it must be more profound than what is just and reasonable. But he did not succeed in establishing what it was. All he did was label ordinary ethics "absolute." Consequently, he ended in a muddle of abstraction. As Descartes said, "Think," without telling what to think, so Kant demanded, "Observe absolute ethics," without elucidating what the term involved. The ethics he proposed could not be called absolute in matter of content. His "Practical Ethics" proved to be simply the good old utilitarian ethics of his own day, adorned with the label, "absolute." He failed by not thinking far enough. To justify the name, absolute ethics must be so not only in authority, but in matter of content as well.

Another commentary: Reverence for life is a universal ethic.

We do not say this because of its absolute nature, but be-

cause of the boundlessness of its domain. Ordinary ethics seeks
to find limits within the sphere of human life and relationships.
But the absolute ethics of the will-to-live must reverence every
form of life, seeking so far as possible to refrain from destroying
any life, regardless of its particular type. It says of no instance
of life, "This has no value." It cannot make any such exceptions, for it is built upon reverence for life as such. It knows
that the mystery of life is always too profound for us, and
that its value is beyond our capacity to estimate. We happen to
believe that man's life is more important than any other form
of which we know. But we cannot prove any such comparison
of value from what we know of the world's development. True,
in practice we are forced to choose. At times we have to decide
arbitrarily which forms of life, and even which particular individuals, we shall save, and which we shall destroy. But the
principle of reverence for life is none the less universal.

Ordinary ethics has never known what to do with this
problem. Not realizing that the domain of ethics must be
boundless, it has tried to ignore any absolute ethic. But when
its boundlessness is realized, then its absoluteness is more plain.
Indian thought recognizes this, but it limits its effectiveness by
making ethics negative. The characteristic attitude of Indian
thought is less a positive reverence for life, than a negative duty
to refrain from destroying. This comes about through a failure
to appreciate the essentially illusory nature of an ethic of inac-
tion. Nor has European thought been free from that same illusion. The great works on philosophy and ethics in recent years
have all tried to avoid absolute ethics by concentrating on a
type which should apply only socially. But when reason travels
its proper course, it moves in the direction of a universally applicable ethic.

Another commentary: A universal ethic has great spiritual
significance.

Ordinary ethics is too narrow and shallow for spiritual
development. Our thought seeks ever to attain harmony with
the mysterious Spirit of the Universe. To be complete, such
harmony must be both active and passive. That is to say, we
seek harmony both in deed and in thought. I want to understand

my ethical activity as being at the service of the Universal Spirit.

Spinoza, Hegel, and the Stoics show us that the harmony of peace is a passive harmony, to which true philosophy leads us, and towards which religion tries to lead us. But this does not suffice, since we want to be at one in activity as well. Philosophy fails us here because of too narrow an ethical basis. It may seek to put me in relation to society, and even to humanity at large (although contemporary philosophies are in some instances directed only towards the relationship to a nation or a race). In any case, no philosophy puts me in relationship to the universe on an ethical basis. Instead, the attempt is made to take me there by knowledge, through understanding. Fichte and Hegel present such an intellectual philosophy. But it is an impossible path. Such philosophies are bankrupt. Ethics alone can put me in true relationship with the universe by my serving it, co-operating with it; not by trying to understand it. This is why Kant is so profound when he speaks of practical reason. Only by serving every kind of life do I enter the service of that Creative Will whence all life emanates. I do not understand it; but I do know (and it is sufficient to live by) that by serving life, I serve the Creative Will. It is through community of life, not community of thought, that I abide in harmony with that Will. This is the mystical significance of ethics.

Every philosophy has its mystical aspects, and every profound thought is mystical. But mysticism has always stopped with the passive, on an insufficient basis, as regards ethics. Indian, Stoical, mediaeval, all the great mysticisms, have aimed at achieving union through passivity. Yet every true mysticism has instincts of activity, aspiring to an ethical character. This fact explains the development of Indian mysticism from the detachment of Brahminism to modern Hindu mysticism. Mediaeval mysticism, in the same way, comes in its great exponent, Eckhardt, to the point where it longs to comprehend true ethics. Failing to find the universal ethic, it has commonly been content to exist with none. But in the universal ethic of reverence for life, mystical union with the Universal Spirit is actually and fully achieved. Thus it is proved to be indeed the true ethic. For it must be plain that an ethic which only commands is incomplete, while one which lets me live in communion with the Creative Will is a true and complete ethic.

III

In what sense is this a natural ethic; and how does it stand in relation to other explanations of the origin of ethics?

There have been three general classifications of ethical origins. The first is a spiritual interpretation. We find in Plato, Kant, and many others, the assertion that ethics comes out of an inherent, insubstantial, given, sense of duty, which has its source in our own power of reason. Through it, we are told, we see ourselves bound to the immaterial world. The exponents of this view believed that they had thus given great dignity to ethics. But there are difficulties in the way of accepting this view. It bears little resemblance to our own ethical sense; and we cannot see how it can be carried into our lives in this world in which we live.

The second classification comprises the intellectual theories of ethics. Here we find such philosophies as those of the Stoics, and Laotze. This group claim to see ethics in the natural world, and conclude thereby that whoever is in harmony with the universe is by that fact ethical. Now, this is a grand theory, and it is based on a profound realization that one who is truly in such harmony must be ethical. But the fact remains that we do not in deed [sic] understand the Spirit of the Universe. Therefore, we cannot draw any ethics from such an understanding. Consequently, these theories of ethics are pallid, and lacking in vigor. What they really amount to is a negative quietism, which has been tinged with ethics.

The third classification consists of three kinds of natural ethics. There is, to start with, the suggestion that ethics exists within our very natures, waiting to be developed. It is argued that we are primarily composed of egoism, but that we nevertheless have an inherent selflessness. Altruism, as we know it, is thus simply exalted egoism. Man is assumed to get his greatest fulfillment in society; wherefore, he must serve it, sacrificing his own wishes temporarily. But such an explanation is childish.

Next, comes the sort of natural ethics which is said to exist in man's nature, but is incapable of being developed by the individual himself. Society, so the theory runs, has worked out a system of ethics in order to subject the individual to its will. Centuries of such exalting of society have had beneficial results, but it is mere delusion to imagine that that is native to us which has actually been created by society. But observe how childish this is also. I grant that society has its place in ethics, but the fact remains that I have individual as well as social relationships, and society simply cannot be responsible for the ethic which determines my dealings in the individual sphere.

The third type of natural ethics was expounded by Hume. It admits that ethics is a matter of sentiment, but explains that it is given in the nature of man, for the sake of preserving his life. Thus, in the late eighteenth century, came Hume's teaching that ethics is natural, while in the same period came Kant's realization that it must be absolute.

To explain that ethics is a matter of feeling, prompted by our own hearts, Hume called it sympathy. The capacity to understand and live others' lives in our own is, he said, what makes us developed individuals. In this, he was joined by George Adam Smith. They were headed in the right direction, too. If they had properly explored sympathy, they would have reached the universal ethic of reverence for life. But they stopped on the very threshold of their great opportunity, because they were dominated by the contemporary dogma that ethics is concerned only with the relationship of man to man. Therefore, they twisted sympathy to mean only a relationship between like kinds. Spencer and Darwin did the same thing in their time, putting ethics on the basis of the herd. This brought them to the explanation of non-egoistic action as arising from herd instinct. What Darwin failed to see is that the herd relationship is more than this superficial sort of instinct. He did, it is true, catch a glimpse of the possibility of sympathy extending beyond the range of man and society. But he concluded that it was just a higher development of the herd instinct!

It is only when we break loose from such traditions that

we find sympathy to be natural for any type of life, without any restrictions, so long as we are capable of imagining in such life the characteristic which we find in our own. That is, dread of extinction, fear of pain, and the desire for happiness. In short, the adequate explanation of sympathy is to be found rooted back in reverence for life.

But let us inquire into this sympathy more closely. On what foundations does it exist? What is its natural explanation? To answer these questions, let us ask ourselves how we can live the life of another being in our own lives. In part, we depend upon the knowledge received through our senses. We see others; we hear them; we may touch them or be touched by them. And we may then engage in activities to help them. In other words, there is a natural, physical aspect to the matter which anyone must recognize. But what *compels* all this?

The important thing is that we are part of life. We are born of other lives; we possess the capacities to bring still other lives into existence. In the same way, if we look into a microscope we see cell producing cell. So nature compels us to recognize the fact of mutual dependence, each life necessarily helping the other lives which are linked to it. In the very fibers of our being, we bear within ourselves the fact of the solidarity of life. Our recognition of it expands with thought. Seeing its presence in ourselves, we realize how closely we are linked with others of our kind. We might like to stop here, but we cannot. Life demands that we see through to the solidarity of all life which we can in any degree recognize as having some similarity to the life that is in us.

No doubt you are beginning to ask whether we can seriously mean that such a privilege extends to other creatures besides man. Are they, too, compelled by ethics? I cannot say that the evidence is always as apparent as it may be in human instances. But this I can say, that wherever we find the love and sacrificial care of parents for offspring (for instance) we find this ethical power. Indeed, any instance of creatures giving aid to one another reveals it. Moreover, there are probably more proofs than we might at first think. Let me tell you of three instances which have been brought to my attention.

The first example was told me by someone from Scotland. It happened in a park where a flock of wild geese had settled to rest on a pond. One of the flock had been captured by a gardener, who had clipped its wings before releasing it. When the geese started to resume their flight, this one tried frantically, but vainly, to lift itself into the air. The others, observing his struggles, flew about in obvious efforts to encourage him; but it was no use. Thereupon, the entire flock settled back on the pond and waited, even though the urge to go on was strong within them. For several days they waited until the damaged feathers had grown sufficiently to permit the goose to fly. Meanwhile, the unethical gardener, having been converted by the ethical geese, gladly watched them as they finally rose together, and all resumed their long flight.

My second example is from my hospital in Lambarene. I have the virtue of caring for all stray monkeys that come to our gate. (If you have had any experience with large numbers of monkeys, you know why I say it is a virtue thus to take care of all comers until they are old enough or strong enough to be turned loose, several together, in the forest—a great occasion for them—and for me!) Sometimes there will come to our monkey colony a wee baby monkey whose mother has been killed, leaving this orphaned infant. I must find one of the older monkeys to adopt and care for the baby. I never have any difficulty about it, except to decide which candidate shall be given the responsibility. Many a time it happens that the seemingly worst-tempered monkeys are most insistent upon having this sudden burden of foster-parenthood given to them.

My third example was given me by a friend in Hanover, who owned a small cafe. He would daily throw out crumbs for the sparrows in the neighborhood. He noticed that one sparrow was injured, so that it had difficulty getting about. But he was interested to discover that the other sparrows, apparently by mutual agreement, would leave the crumbs which lay nearest to their crippled comrade, so that he could get his share, undisturbed.

So much, then, for this question of the natural origin of the ethic of reverence for life. It does not need to make any pretensions to high titles or noble-sounding theories to explain its existence. Quite simply, it has the courage to admit that it comes about through physiological make-up. It is given physically. But the point is that it arrives at the noblest spirituality. God does not rest content with commanding ethics. He gives it to us in our very hearts.

This, then, is the nature and origin of ethics. We have dared to say that it is born of physical life, out of the linking of life with life. It is therefore the result of our recognizing the solidarity of life which nature gives us. And as it grows more profound, it teaches us sympathy with *all* life. Yet, the extremes touch, for this material-born ethic becomes engraved upon our hearts, and culminates in spiritual union and harmony with the Creative Will which is in and through all.

Appendix II

Concluding Statement from Die Geschichte der Leben-Jesu-Forschung*

ALBERT SCHWEITZER

What is the historical Jesus to us when we preserve Him from any spurious admixture of the present with the past? We are struck by a direct awareness that His personality, despite all its strange and enigmatic qualities, has something great to say to all ages so long as the world shall last, no matter how much the knowledge and attitudes of men may change. We know that He can enrich our religion profoundly. We feel ourselves called upon to articulate clearly this elemental feeling, so that it does not soar away in dogmatic formulas nor lure historical research into the inevitably hopeless attempt to modernize Jesus by diluting or explaining away whatever is historically conditioned in His preaching—as though He would mean more to us thereby.

In the final analysis, the whole scientific quest for the historical Jesus has only this single aim: to set forth accurately the natural and unforced interpretation of the oldest accounts. To know Jesus and to understand Him requires no preliminary erudition. Nor is it necessary that we know the details of His public ministry or be able to reconstruct a "life of Jesus." His very being, that which He is and wills, manifests itself in a few of His lapidary sayings and thrusts itself upon us. We know Him without knowing much about Him, and we sense His eschatological significance even without having a scholarly knowledge of this concept. For the characteristic thing about

---

* This is an original translation, with two exceptions: I have retained a few phrases from Walter Lowrie's Introduction to *The Mystery of the Kingdom of God*, and I have preserved intact the magnificent closing of *The Quest of the Historical Jesus*.

Jesus is the way in which He looks beyond the perfection and blessedness of the individual to the perfection and blessedness of the world and of an elect humanity. His will and His hope are centered upon the Kingdom of God.

In every world-view historically conditioned elements are intertwined with timeless elements. The crucial factor is the *will* which penetrates and molds the conceptual materials out of which the world-view is made. Since these materials are subject to change, there is no world-view, regardless of how great and profound it may be, which does not contain some historically conditioned elements. But the will itself is timeless: it reveals the unfathomable and irreducible essence of a person and it also exercises a decisive influence on the ultimate development of the world-view held by that person. It makes no difference, however great a change may occur in conceptual materials or in the world-views to which they belong: the distance separating any two world-views will be only so great as the distance separating the direction of the wills that determine these world-views. Although the variations which result from differing conceptual materials may seem to be decisive, they are ultimately only of secondary importance. For the same will, regardless of the conceptual materials through which it manifests itself, always creates a world-view in which it can express itself.

Since the presuppositions of perception and cognition, which in our sense can be defined as a world-view, became set— that is, since the individual began to take into account the totality of being, the world as a whole, and to reflect on the changing relationships (both passive and active) between the All and himself as a knowing, willing subject—no further developments of far-reaching significance have taken place in the spiritual life of mankind. The problems which occupied the Greeks still concern the most modern philosophy, and contemporary scepticism is essentially the same as that which found a hearing in classical thought.

Because of the fact that Jesus expressed His world-view in the primitive metaphysics of late-Jewish apocalypticism, it is exceedingly difficult to translate His ideas into our modes of expression. The task is simply impossible so long as one tries to go about it by separating the permanent from the transitory in detail. This approach is so lacking in force and decisiveness that its apparent contributions to our religion are bound to be illusory.

Actually, there is no point in seeking to separate the permanent from the transitory. What is needed is a translation of the fundamental thought of that world-view into concepts which are familiar to us. What we need to know is this: how would the will of Jesus—grasped in all its directness and concreteness and comprehensiveness—how would it invigorate our conceptual material, and create from it a world-view of sufficient ethical vitality and power to be counted the modern equivalent of the world-view that He created in terms of late Jewish metaphysics and eschatology?

Up to now, those who have tried to reconcile Jesus' world-view with ours have weakened the distinctiveness of His thought. In so doing, they have also weakened the will which is expressed in this thought. It loses its originality and ceases to exert an elemental influence upon us. That is why the Jesus of modern theology is so remarkably lifeless. Jesus is greater, despite His strangeness, when allowed to remain in the eschatological world. And He affects us more deeply than the modern Jesus.

The work of Jesus was to fill the late-Jewish eschatology with His natural and profound morality, and thereby to express, in the conceptual materials of that age, a hope for ethical perfection of the world and a will dedicated to that end. All attempts to ignore His world-view as a totality, and to reduce His significance for us to nothing more than His revelation of the "fatherhood of God," "the brotherhood of man," and so forth, will inevitably lead to a narrow and peculiarly insipid interpretation of His religion. In reality He is an authority for us, not in the sphere of knowledge, but only in the realm of the will. It is His destiny to clarify and heighten the driving forces of hope and will that we and our fellow men bear within us, until they reach an intensity which would have been impossible without the impact of His personality. Thus it is that in spite of all differences in conceptual materials, He forms our world-view according to the essence of His and arouses in ours the energies that surge in His.

The last and deepest knowledge of things comes from the will. Hence thought which strives to frame a final synthesis of observation and knowledge in order to construct a world-view is directed by the will. For the primary and ultimate essence of the persons and ages in question is the will.

If our age and our religion have failed to apprehend the greatness of Jesus, if they have shied away from the eschatological coloring of His thought, the fault is not merely their inability to accommodate themselves to the strangeness of it. The crucial reason is to be found elsewhere. Their willing and hoping had not been stamped with the indelible mark of an intense yearning for the moral perfection of the world—and this is what was decisive for Jesus and His world-view. Eschatology, in the broadest and most general sense of the term, was missing. They found in themselves no equivalents for the thoughts of Jesus; consequently, they were in no position to transpose His world-view from the key in which late-Jewish apocalypticism was played into one that would be familiar to their ear.

There was no answering chord of sympathy between their world-view and that of Jesus. As a result, the historical Jesus remained a stranger to them, not only in His thought material but also in His very essence. His ethical enthusiasm and the directness and power of His thought remained inaccessible to them, because they knew nothing similar to this in their own thought and experience. So they continually endeavored to make of this "fanatic" a contemporary man and theologian, one who would be duly observant of the accepted rules of moderation and propriety in all that He did. Conservative theology, like the older orthodoxy to which it is akin, could not appropriate the historical Jesus, for it also neglected the great ethical ideals which were struggling for vital expression in His eschatology.

Our civilization and our religion have found it impossible to attain a real knowledge of the historical Jesus and a religious relationship with Him, because their willing and hoping and longing have not been tuned to the same pitch as His. There could be no vital fellowship between Him and a generation utterly devoid of all directness and all enthusiasm for the ultimate aims of humanity and existence. In spite of all its progress in historical perception, it really remained more foreign to Him than was the rationalism of the eighteenth or early nineteenth century, which was drawn close to Him by virtue of its enthusiastic faith in the advancing moral progress of mankind.

If we read through the expositions of Christian faith and Christian ethics which have appeared in recent decades, we are amazed to discover how feebly most of them set forth the elemental moral thought of the yet-to-be-achieved general perfection of mankind. These studies seem to have produced only a quavering tone that echoes as it fades away, whereas they ought to have resounded with the stirring basic theme of every true ethical world-view.

Thus the real essence of Jesus remains inoperative. He has been changed from a living man into an "Agent of Revelation" and a "Symbol." In Drews's interpretation of religion (an interpretation influenced by the period of Greek-Oriental decadence) the ethical and eschatological currents are so weak that there is no longer any place at all for the historical Jesus.

Only in so far as the conceptual materials of an age are charged with ethical-eschatological vitalities does that age have a real and living relationship to Jesus. This means that its world-view must exhibit the equivalent of the will and hope which were central for Him; that is, it must be dominated by the thoughts which are found in Jesus' concept of the Kingdom of God.

If the signs of the time do not mislead us, we are entering into an age that is drifting in precisely the opposite direction. All progress in knowledge notwithstanding, we have experienced in the past few decades a stagnation of our civilization which manifests itself in every area of life. There are even numerous signs of a genuine retrogression. The sickness displays manifold symptoms, but the root cause is to be found in this condition: nothing in our civilization, including religion, is providing enough ethical ideals and energies. It has lost the great aim

of the moral perfecton of all mankind, and it is hemmed in by
the walls of national and sectarian ideals instead of encompassing
the whole world in its vision. Its greatness and its goodness
pretend to be self-sufficient, whereas they ought to put themselves
at the service of that general ethical perfection which, in accordance with the preaching of Jesus, one may call the Kingdom of
God. These values of civilization only possess genuine ethical
worth to the extent that they do serve this end.

But the abandonment of the mighty striving for perfection
of the world, a striving which was so very passionately intent
upon achieving its goal, has brought about a weakening of our
religion and our ethics. As a result, our world-view is deficient
in judgment concerning events and relationships as well as in
devotion to the task it has of providing a great compass which
could point out to people the road ahead and show them their
highest duties at all times.

This abandonment of ethical eschatology is avenged. Instead of fighting for the triumph of the ethical spirit of God,
through which individuals, sectarian groups and people at large
might be filled with sustaining inspiration, mankind today is
on the verge of delivering itself into the hands of the spirits of
thoughtlessness and resigning itself to the stagnation and decline of civilization. And this means the repudiation of all
that lifts mankind to the heights of true humanity. Those who
see where we are headed and do not allow themselves to become
insensitive to the tragedy of our situation, but rather experience
again and again the woe that hangs over the future of the
world, are ready to encounter the historical Jesus and to understand what He has to say to us despite the strangeness of His
language. With Him (who also experienced a similar despair
in the terms of thought current in His day) they perceive that
we shall be saved from present conditions through a mighty
hope for the Kingdom of God and a will dedicated to it. With
Him they know that such a hoping and willing can afford to be
scornful of the circumstances as they appear. With Him they
perceive that we must find support, freedom and peace in our
faith in the invincible power of the moral spirit; that we must
spread this faith and the convictions concerning daily life which

it involves; that we must find the highest good in the Kingdom of God and live for it.

Of greatest importance in this world-view are its qualities of enthusiasm and heroism, which spring from the will and faith that are centered in the Kingdom of God and which are augmented rather than diminished by unfavorable conditions. A religion possesses just so much of an understanding of the historical Jesus as it possesses of a strong, passionate faith in the Kingdom of God. The other claims that religion might make concerning its bond with Him are unreal; they exist only in words and formulas. We possess only so much of Him as we permit Him to preach to us of the Kingdom of God. All lesser disputes over metaphysics and conceptual materials simply fall into the background. The only thing that matters is this: that the significance of the concept of the Kingdom of God for our world-view is the same as it was for Him, and that we experience in the same way that He did the urgency and the power of that concept.

The important thing is a *will to will understanding* of Jesus, for in this the essence of the world-view is communicated. An analysis of the details of His activities and His preaching, the intention of which is to distinguish between enduring and obsolete elements, is unnecessary. His words translate themselves as it were automatically in the idiom appropriate to our conceptual materials. Many of these words which at first strike us as strange become true in a profound and eternal sense even for us, when we accept with open minds the power of the spirit which speaks in Him. When confronted with the difficulties of making His message clear and alive for present-day hearers, one could almost call to mind His saying, "Seek ye first the Kingdom of God and His righteousness, and all these things shall be added unto you."

The change in conceptual material requires, of course, that the ultimate perfection which he expected as a supernatural event be expected by us only as the result of ethical endeavor. One ought not to employ violent exegesis to read into his words our concept of gradual development. What matters, though, is that our allegiance to the ideal of a kingdom created by ethical endeavor should be pursued with the same ardor which inflamed His devotion to the divine intervention that He awaited, and that we should be prepared to give up everything for it.

Even the part of His preaching which modern man normally regards as a stumbling block can no longer disturb us if He is known will to will. He saw no intrinsic value in work, property and many other things which we value as ethically good, because for Him these things were not included in the blueprint of the Kingdom. But for us the plans appear to have been redrawn, so that some things which were formerly excluded are now a prominent part of the building. At any rate, we work in the service of the Kingdom of God and thus maintain fellowship with Him, because we regard the Kingdom as the measure of all moral worth.

The late-Jewish thought material made it inevitable that He should think in predestinarian terms and accept nationalistic limitations on his ministry. Of this fact there can be no doubt. And there are many other aspects of His thought which must be acknowledged to be strange and offensive. But these are always historically conditioned elements, part of the conceptual material which simply fades from view as soon as the will of Jesus manifests itself to us.

So the eschatological interpretation of Jesus is not, as is so often supposed, something which makes his preaching more difficult for our age to comprehend. If we focus our attention upon all that is self-authenticating in His person and in His Sermon on the Mount, then all which is strange and offensive can be dealt with at our leisure. All that takes care of itself as soon as we recognize that He was conditioned by the conceptual materials with which He had to work. Neither long speeches nor great learning is required. In reality the true Jesus is easier to proclaim than the modernized Jesus, if only one lets that which is elemental in Him speak out, in order that He may really be for us, too, the one who preaches with authority and not as the Scribes.

Even the fact that the historical Jesus regarded the Kingdom of God as something transcending morality and thus proclaimed only an "ethic of the interim" does not affect what He has to say to us, because this drawback is removed if we translate His preaching into our metaphysics. His mighty personal ethic teaches us that whoever wishes to work for the Kingdom of God can only accomplish something if he continually purifies himself inwardly and makes himself free from the world.

Our relationship to the historical Jesus must be simultaneously truthful and free. We give history its due and then make ourselves free from its conceptual materials. But we bow before the mighty will that stands behind it, and we seek to serve this will in our time, that it may be born in us in new vitality and fruitfulness, and that it may work toward fulfillment in us and in the world.

But it is not true to say that we possess the idea of the moral perfection of the world and the ideas we have of what must be done in our time because we have obtained them through historical revelation. These ideas lie within us; they are given with the ethical will. Because Jesus, as one Who stood in the line of succession of the greatest among the prophets, summed up these ideas and taught them with the utmost thoroughness and directness, and because He embodied them in His own great personality, He helps us to be similarly dedicated and to become ethical forces in our own time.

This interpretation of religion and of the person Jesus is usually dismissed as one-sidedly moralistic and rationalistic. In order to overcome this reaction, we need only call to mind the fact that if this interpretation is really alive and potent, it encompasses religion in its totality. For all that man can really say about salvation boils down to this: it means being set free from the world and from ourselves through a fellowship of the will with Jesus, and being filled with power and peace and courage for life. Let no one forget that Jesus Himself was essentially a rationalist and a moralist. That He was conditioned by late-Jewish metaphysics is incidental.

In the final analysis, our relationship to Jesus is of a mystical sort. No personality of the past can be transported to the present by means of historical reflection or affirmations about His authoritative significance. We enter into relationship with Him only by being brought together in the recognition of a common will, and by experiencing a clarification, enrichment and quickening of our will through His. Thus do we find ourselves again in Him. In this sense every deeper relationship between men partakes of a mystical quality. So our religion, in so far as it is to be regarded as specifically Christian, is not so much a "Jesus-cult" as it is a Jesus-mysticism.

Only in this manner does Jesus also create fellowship among us. He does this, not by being a symbol or anything of that sort, but in the following way: to the extent that we, with one another and with Him, are of one will—to put the Kingdom of God above everything else, and to serve in behalf of this faith and hope—to this extent is there fellowship between Him and us and the men of all generations who have lived and do live in the same thought.

This is the touchstone by which all movements for religious unity must be evaluated. False compromises are of no avail. All concessions by means of which liberal religion seeks a rapprochement with dogmatic religion will only result in ambiguities and inconsistencies that weaken its own position. The differences are rooted in the conceptual materials presupposed by each side, and all efforts for agreement in this area are futile. These differences loom so large because there is a dearth of elemental, living religion. Two thin streams of water run side by side through the boulders and gravel of a great river bed. It really does not matter that here and there someone tries to clear away the piles of rock that separate them, in a vain effort to make them flow together. But when the water rises and overflows the boulders—then the two will become one. Thus dogmatic and liberal religion shall be united: when willing and hoping are once again directed towards the Kingdom of God, when the spirit of Jesus once again becomes something elemental and powerful in them. When this occurs, they shall be drawn together so closely in the essence of their world-view and religion that the differences of conceptual material, though not done away with, will sink beneath the surface, just as boulders are covered by a rising flood and finally cast only a faint glimmer out of the depths.

Jesus was hailed by men who thought of Him in terms of

the late-Jewish conceptual materials as Messiah, Son of Man, and Son of God—but for us these names have become historical parables. If He applied these titles to Himself, that was because they were historically conditioned expressions of his awareness that He was a master and a leader. We have no designation which defines what He is for us.

He comes to us as One unknown, without a name, as of old, by the lakeside, He came to those men who knew Him not. He speaks to us the same word: "Follow thou me!" and sets us to the tasks which He has to fulfill for our time. He commands. And to those who obey Him, whether they be wise or simple, He will reveal Himself in the toils, the conflicts, the sufferings which they shall pass through in His fellowship, and, as an ineffable mystery, they shall learn in their own experience Who He is.

Notes

For the sake of convenience, the following abbreviations will be used for sources cited repeatedly:

Books

Christianity and the Religions of the World (CRW)
Civilization and Ethics (CE)
The Decay and Restoration of Civilization (Decay)
Ehrfurcht vor dem Leben (Ehrfurcht)
Indian Thought and Its Development (Indian)
Memoirs of Childhood and Youth (Childhood)
More from the Primeval Forest (More)
The Mystery of the Kingdom of God (Mystery)
The Mysticism of Paul the Apostle (Paul)
On the Edge of the Primeval Forest (Edge)
Out of My Life and Thought (Out)
The Quest of the Historical Jesus (Quest)
The Theology of Albert Schweitzer (Theology)

Periodicals

The Christian Century (CC)
Evangelisch-Protestantischer Kirchenbote für Elsass und Lothringen (KEL)
Rundbrief für den Freundeskreis von Albert Schweitzer (Rundbrief)
The Saturday Review of Literature (SR)
Schweizerische Theologische Umschau (STU)

Articles from Periodicals

"Afrikanisches Tagebuch," *Universitas*, I, 8 (November, 1946)— *Tagebuch.*
"The Ethics of Reverence for Life," *Christendom*, Winter, 1936— *Reverence.*

I

CHAPTER I

1. John Gunther, *Inside Africa*, p. 712. The phrase quoted from Gunther in the following paragraph is also from this page.
2. Albert Einstein, "Schlichte Grösse," *Ehrfurcht*, p. 232.
3. Jacques Feschotte, *Albert Schweitzer: An Introduction*, p. 78.
4. Aurel Wolfram, *Albert Schweitzer und die Krise des Abendlandes*, p. 39.
5. An especially bad case of the former practice is to be found in A. Sorel-Nitzberg's article, "Reflexions sur l'Ethique d'Albert Schweitzer," *Hommage à Albert Schweitzer*, p. 97.
6. Cited by Norman Cousins from a letter to the editor, *SR*, XXXVII (October 23, 1954), 23.
7. George Seaver, *Albert Schweitzer: The Man and His Mind*, p. 305.
8. Magnus Ratter, *Albert Schweitzer*, p. 232.
9. Marcus Bach, *The Circle of Faith*, p. 168.
10. Jean Pierhal, *Albert Schweitzer*, p. 82 (quoting *More*, p. 102).

11. Hermann Hagedorn, *Prophet in the Wilderness*, pp. 53-54.

12. Clement C. Chesterman, "An Elephant in Ebony," *To Dr. Albert Schweitzer*, p. 28.

13. Bach, *op. cit.*, p. 150.

14. Lawson Hepher, cited in *ibid.*, p. 149.

15. Homer A. Jack, "Twenty Questions About Albert Schweitzer," *CC*, LXXV, 1243. Copyright 1958 Christian Century Foundation. Reprinted by permission.

16. From a personal conversation with a former teacher there.

17. Cousins, *Dr. Schweitzer of Lambarene*, pp. 219-220.

18. Quoted from a personal conversation with John Baillie held in November, 1956. Actually, Baillie misquoted Schweitzer, for he said "respect *pour* la vie"—so perhaps he did not hear the tiresome phrase too often, after all! Yet I must admit that his irritation was probably just as understandable as was mine over his flippant dismissal of my question.

19. Emil Brunner, *The Divine Imperative*, p. 195.

20. Peter Vogelsanger, "Albert Schweitzer als Theologe," *Reformatio*, IV (January, 1955), p. 13. The same article continues with a tirade against the followers of Schweitzer (Buri and Werner in particular), who in Vogelsanger's opinion have betrayed their master by drawing conclusions which he never intended (p. 18). This charge is answered by Ulrich Neuenschwander, one of the youngest members of the "Bern School" of liberal theologians, who quotes a letter from Schweitzer in which the doctor endorses the work of his followers in the following words: "I can only say that I agree with you in such remarkable fashion that it is almost uncanny (*unheimlich*)." (See "Auswirken der Gedanken Albert Schweitzers in der gegenwartigen Theologie," *STU*, XXV [February, 1955], 23.)

21. Oscar Cullmann, *Christ et le Temps*, p. 30, quoted by George Marchal, "Albert Schweitzer le Theologien," *Etudes et Témoignages*, p. 118.

22. Karl Barth, *Kirchliche Dogmatik*, III, 4, pp. 367, 397, and *Ibid.*, II, 1, pp. 636-637 (English translation).

23. *Ibid.*, p. 399.

24. *Ibid.*, pp. 398-399.

25. H. Beintker, "Albert Schweitzer's Theologische Bedeutung," *Wissenschaftliche Zeitschrift der Ernst-Moritz-Arndt Universität*, IV (1954-1955), 235-236, 242.

CHAPTER 2

1. Theodore Siebert, "Unerwartete Begegnung im Elsass," *Rundbrief*, IX (January, 1956), 48.

II

CHAPTER 3

1. *Out*, p. 116.

2. *Out*, p. 237.

3. *Decay*, p. 36.

4. *Ibid.*

5. *CE*, p. 2.

6. *Decay*, pp. 17-32.

7. *CE*, p. 268.

8. *Out*, pp. 116-117; *Decay*, pp. 29-32, 74-75.

9. *Decay*, p. 20.

10. *Out*, pp. 116-117.

11. *Out*, p. 117; *Decay*, pp. 33-52.

12. *Ibid.*

13. *CE*, p. 16.

14. Schweitzer, "Religion in Modern Civilization," *CC*, LI (November 21, 1934), p. 1483. Copyright 1934 Christian Century Foundation. Reprinted by permission.

15. *Out*, p. 276.

16. *Edge*, p. 166.

17. *Paul*, p. 384.

18. *Out*, p. 79.
19. *Out*, p. 73.
20. *Decay*, pp. 33-34, 45-59.
21. *Ibid.*, p. 52; *Out*, p. 117.
22. *Decay*, p. 55.
23. *Out*, p. 117.
24. Schweitzer, "Religion in Modern Civilization," p. 1519.
25. *Out*, p. 122.
26. *Ibid.*
27. Schweitzer, "Die Philosophie und die allgemeine Bildung im neunzehnten Jahrhundert," *Das Neunzehnte Jahrhundert, 24 Aufsätze zur Jahrhundertwende.* A translation of this essay is available from The Albert Schweitzer Education Foundation, Chicago, Illinois.
28. *Ibid.*, p. 68.
29. *Quest*, p. 153.
30. *Ibid.*, p. 1.
31. *Ibid.*, pp. 323-324.
32. *Ibid.*, p. 324.
33. *Ibid.*, p. 4.
34. *Ibid.*, p. 2.
35. *Ibid.*, p. 397.
36. *Ibid.*, p. 396.
37. *Ibid.*, p. 397.
38. "Die Philosophie und die allgemeine Bildung im neunzehnten Jahrhundert," pp. 66-67.

CHAPTER 4

1. Schweitzer, "Die Philosophie und die allgemeine Bildung im neunzehnten Jahrhundert," pp. 61ff.
2. See Immanuel Kant, *Fundamental Principles of a Metaphysic of Morals*, Part I.
3. *CE*, p. 108.
4. *Ibid.*, pp. 108-109.
5. *Ibid.*, p. 109.
6. *Ibid.*, pp. 107-108.
7. *Ibid.*, pp. 110ff.
8. *Ibid.*, p. 127.
9. *Ibid.*, p. 131.
10. *Ibid.*, pp. 137ff.
11. Schweitzer, "Die Philosophie und die allgemeine Bildung im neunzehnten Jahrhundert," pp. 63-64.
12. *CE*, p. 162.
13. *Ibid.*
14. *Ibid.*, pp. 153-155; cf. p. 147.
15. Schweitzer, "Religion in Modern Civilization," pp. 1519-1520.
16. *CE*, p. 163.
17. *Ibid.*, pp. 175-176.
18. I. Kant, *op. cit.*, p. 5.
19. *Ibid.*, p. 7.
20. I. Kant, *Religion Within the Bounds of Reason Alone* (Abbott edition), p. 248.
21. *Ibid.*, p. 250.
22. *Ibid.*, p. 252.
23. *Ibid.*, pp. 252-253.
24. *Ibid.*, p. 254.
25. R. Eisler, ed., *Wörterbuch der Philosophischen Begriffe*, 4th ed., Band 3 (Sci - Z), pp. 429-435.
26. *CE*, p. 164.
27. *Ibid.*, pp. 165-166.
28. *Ibid.*, p. 170.
29. *Ibid.*, p. 174.
30. *Ibid.*, p. 175.
31. For an even more penetrating and sympathetic interpretation of Nietzsche, see Walter Kaufmann, *Nietzsche*, especially pp. 182-222. In his discussion of "The Nietzsche Legend" (pp. 15-28), Kaufmann blames Nietzsche's sister for editing her brother's works in such a way as to emphasize the "proto-Nazi elements" which so many critics profess to find in Nietzsche. Kaufmann holds that *The Will to Power*, in particular, is a betrayal of Nietzsche's genuine message, and that Nietzsche himself should not be held responsible for this book.
32. Simmel's influence on Schweitzer while the latter was his student is emphasized by Professor Martin Werner of the University of Berne in his lectures on Schweitzer's thought.

33. Kurt Leese, *Die Krisis und Wende des Christlichen Geistes*, p. 287.

34. Henri Bergson, *Creative Evolution*, p. 270.

35. *CE*, p. 185.

36. *Ibid*.

37. *Ibid*., p. 186.

38. *Ibid*.

39. Schweitzer, *Goethe: His Personality and His Work*, p. 5.

40. From an unpublished essay by Lee Ellerbrock, Founder and Chairman of Fellows For Schweitzer, Sierra Madre, California and Counselor of the Albert Schweitzer Education Foundation, Chicago, Illinois.

41. *Ibid*.

42. *Ibid*. See *Verfall und Wiederaufbau der Kultur*, pp. 3-8.

43. Oskar Kraus, *Albert Schweitzer: His Work and His Philosophy*, pp. 38-39, agrees that Schweitzer rejects only the idea of a total world-view, not that of a world-view which is a "mysticism of the will."

44. *Indian*, pp. 1f., 6f.; cf. *Out*, pp. 176ff., where Schweitzer speaks of the "will-to-civilization" as a part of world-affirmation.

45. *Out*, pp. 119, 121, 127-128, 155, 170-171; *CE*, p. 267.

46. *Out*, p. 128.

47. *Decay*, p. 92; *Out*, p. 187.

48. *KEL*, XLVIII (August 2, 1919), p. 126.

49. *Out*, p. 127.

50. *Ibid*., p. 187.

51. Schweitzer, *The Problem of Peace in the World Today*, p. 16.

52. *Ibid*., p. 19.

53. Schweitzer, *Rundbrief*, XV (January 14, 1960), 58-59.

54. Quoted from lecture notes for March 27, 1957.

55. *CRW*, p. 88.

56. *Out*, p. 186.

57. *CRW*, p. 81.

58. *Theology*, p. 107.

III

CHAPTER 5

1. *Out*, p. 260.

2. *CE*, p. xiii.

3. *Ibid*., pp. xiv-xv.

4. *Ibid*., p. xv. Further comments on the mystery of evil in the world are to be found on pp. 210-212, 222, 233, 245-246, and *Out*, pp. 157, 185.

5. *Ibid*. Schweitzer considers himself the first among Western thinkers to recognize this fact.

6. *CE*, pp. xvi-xvii; cf. pp. 207-208.

7. *Ibid*.

8. Schweitzer, *Goethe: Four Studies*, p. 79.

9. Schweitzer, *Selbstdarstellung*, p. 38; cf. *Reverence*, pp. 229ff.

10. *CE*, p. 242.

11. *Ibid*., p. 210.

12. *Reverence*, p. 227.

13. *CE*, p. xviii: cf. *Selbstdarstellung*, p. 38 and *CE*, p. 242.

14. *Reverence*, p. 230.

15. *CE*, p. xviii.

16. *Reverence*, p. 231.

17. *Ibid*., pp. 230-231.

18. *Ibid*., p. 232.

19. Schweitzer condemns not only the failure of past philosophers to demand humane treatment of animals, but also any argument for humane treatment based on the motive of human self-interest. He criticizes Kant's argument that callousness to animals is to be avoided merely because it causes "a weakening of a natural disposition which is very helpful to our morality in relation to other men."

20. *Reverence*, p. 233.

21. *CE*, p. 213.

22. *Ibid*., p. 246.

23. *Reverence*, pp. 233ff.

24. *Out*, p. 158.

25. *CE*, p. xviii.

CHAPTER 6

1. *CE*, pp. 169-171; *Indian, passim.*
2. *Ibid.*, p. 176.
3. *Ibid.*, pp. 176-177.
4. *Ibid.*, p. 177.
5. *Ibid.*, p. 178.
6. Hagedorn, *op. cit.*, p. 137.
7. Schweitzer, "The Tornado and the Spirit," *The Christian Register* (September, 1947), p. 328.
8. Schweitzer, *Goethe: Four Studies*, p. 97.
9. *CE*, pp. 213-214.
10. *Ibid.*, p. 222.
11. *Ibid.*, p. 246.
12. *Ibid.*
13. Allan Hunter, "Schweitzer at Aspen," *CC*, LXVI (July 27, 1949), 890.
14. *CE*, p. 254.
15. *KEL*, XLVIII (February 9, 1919), 22. In connection with this, see Pierhal, *op. cit.*, p. 151, for an interesting account of the joy occasioned by a bowl of roast potatoes at Lambarene.
16. *CE*, p. 255; cf. *Out*, p. 187. A countervailing tendency in Schweitzer's thought asserts itself in his regret that he gave up the Goll scholarship to another person who did not make full use of it! (*Out*, p. 24.)
17. *Decay*, p. 17.
18. *Childhood*, pp. 71-72.
19. Obviously, these virtues cannot be isolated in any rigid way from the social dimension of a person's experience; however, I have chosen to discuss these particular traits in connection with the personal dimension because it seems to me that Schweitzer emphasizes their relationship to the self which is seeking to approach perfection.
20. *Out*, pp. 45, 173-174.
21. *Ibid.*, p. 93.

22. *Ibid.*, pp. 113-114.
23. *Ibid.*, p. 130.
24. From conversation with an American friend of Schweitzer.
25. *Childhood*, pp. 34-35. Schweitzer testifies that he got his temper from his mother.
26. *Ibid.*
27. *Out*, pp. 112-113.
28. See ch. 7.
29. *Childhood*, p. 16.
30. *Out*, p. 75.
31. *Ibid.*, p. 131.
32. *Edge*, pp. 33, 43, 62, 117.
33. *Out*, pp. 75, 87-88, 128; *CE*, pp. 255-256.
34. Quoted by Pastor Karl Zimmermann in his funeral sermon for Mme. Schweitzer, *Rundbrief*, XI (August 1, 1957), 9. For more information concerning Schweitzer's conception of what is involved in gratitude, see his sermon on this subject, which is printed in *KEL*, XLVIII (September 27, 1919), 158, *et seq.*
35. Schweitzer, "Forgiveness," *The Christian World* (November 1, 1934), p. 11. Cf. Cousins, *Dr. Schweitzer of Lambarene*, p. 217.
36. *CE*, p. 248.
37. *Out*, p. 71.
38. Fritz Wartenweiler, "Eine Wenig Bekannte Seite in Schweitzers Wirken," *Ehrfurcht*, p. 106.
39. Charles Hauter, "Albert Schweitzer, Professor de Theologie a Strasbourg," *Hommage à Albert Schweitzer*, pp. 53-54, 55, 57-58.
40. Archibald T. Davison, "The Transcendentalism of Albert Schweitzer," *The Albert Schweitzer Jubilee Book*, p. 201.
41. *SR*, XL (January 5, 1957), 25-26.
42. *CC*, LXX (November 18, 1953), 1316.
43. *Out*, pp. 74-75, 91, 110; *CE*, p. 269.

44. Hauter, *op. cit.*, pp. 55-56.

45. *Out*, pp. 95-96.

46. *Edge*, p. 149.

47. *CE*, p. 240.

48. *Decay*, pp. 104-105.

49. Schweitzer, "Religion in Modern Civilization," p. 1484. Copyright 1934 Christian Century Foundation. Reprinted by permission.

50. *Out*, p. 175.

51. *Ibid.*, pp. 113, 155; *CE*, p. 240; *Decay*, pp. 17-32.

52. The noted English music critic, D. F. Tovey, has remarked, "To disagree with Schweitzer is dangerously like disagreeing with Bach." (*Essays in Musical Analysis*, V, 34, as cited by Davison, *op. cit.*, p. 210.)

53. *Out*, pp. 58-68.

54. Seaver, *op. cit.*, p. 29.

55. Schweitzer, *J. S. Bach*, I, 338ff.

56. *Ibid.*, p. 167.

57. *Ibid.*

58. *Out*, p. 57.

59. Schweitzer, *J. S. Bach*, I, 166.

60. *Out*, pp. 127, 171-172.

61. *CRW*, p. 56.

62. *CE*, p. 215.

63. *Out*, p. 179.

64. *Reverence*, p. 229.

65. *CE*, p. 247.

66. *CRW*, p. 51.

67. *Indian*, p. 118; cf. p. 116.

68. *Decay*, p. 79.

69. *Out*, p. 186.

70. Everett Skillings, *ibid.* (Postscript), p. 191 (author's italics).

71. *Out*, pp. 80, 87.

72. Schweitzer, *Eight Year Report on Lambarene Hospital*, p. 3; Seaver, *op. cit.*, p. 162; Karl Budde, "Brief von Albert Schweitzer," *Christliche Welt* (1925), p. 647.

73. Schweitzer, *Eight Year Report on Lambarene Hospital*, p. 10.

74. *More*, pp. 64-65, 67, 94; *Tagebuch*, p. 935; *Edge*, p. 85.

75. *Out*, p. 195.

76. *Ibid.*, pp. 71, 72, 74.

77. *Ibid.*, pp. 153-154; cf. *Selbstdarstellung*, p. 34. Schweitzer counts it as one of his greatest blessings that the interest and generosity of friends made it so that these renunciations turned out to be neither absolute nor permanent.

78. *Edge*, p. 92.

79. *CE*, p. 222.

80. *Out*, pp. 74-75.

81. *CE*, p. 246.

82. *Infra*, ch. 8.

83. *Out*, p. 186.

84. Schweitzer, *Von Mensch zu Mensch*, p. 48.

85. *CE*, pp. 255-256.

86. *Tagebuch*, p. 943.

87. *Out*, pp. 69-70, 188. The theme of obligation because of one's blessings is also echoed in an Advent sermon on Amos recorded in *KEL*, XLVIII (January 5, 1919), 1-2.

88. *Childhood*, pp. 17-19.

89. *Ibid.*

90. *Ibid.*

91. From a personal conversation at Günsbach during the summer of 1958. Paul Schweitzer, who is in his late seventies, looks as though he were about fifty. He remarked with a grin that the entire family has "iron in its veins."

92. *Out*, p. 152. Very striking in this connection is Gunther's opinion that "As a whole the hospital gives a curious atmosphere of being a kind of abstraction, almost an exercise in penance" (*op. cit.*, p. 714).

93. *CE*, pp. 252-253.

94. *Ibid.*, p. 185.

95. *Out*, pp. 70, 75, 179.

96. *Ibid.*, p. 179; cf. *More*, pp. 162, 168 and *Edge*, p. 43, where

Schweitzer speaks of the satisfactions of his work in Africa.

CHAPTER 7

1. *CE*, p. 218.
2. *Ibid.*, p. 226.
3. *Ibid.*, p. 224.
4. *Ibid.*
5. *Ibid.*, pp. 224-225.
6. *Ibid.*, p. 157.
7. *Ibid.*, pp. 262-263.
8. *Ibid.*, p. 224.
9. *Ibid.*, p. 225.
10. *Ibid.*, p. 231.
11. *Decay*, p. 94.
12. Schweitzer, "Religion in Modern Civilization," as cited by Seaver, *op. cit.*, p. 342. Copyright 1934 Christian Century Foundation. Reprinted by permission.
13. *CE*, p. 183, and Schweitzer, *Goethe: Four Studies*, p. 97.
14. *CE*, pp. 76-79.
15. Schweitzer, *Goethe: Four Studies*, pp. 98-99.
16. Schweitzer, "Religion in Modern Civilization," as cited by Seaver, *op. cit.*, pp. 338-339. Copyright 1934 Christian Century Foundation. Reprinted by permission.
17. *CE*, p. 181.
18. *Ibid.*, p. 227.
19. *Out*, p. 122; cf. *Decay*, pp. 88ff.
20. *CE*, p. 181.
21. Schweitzer, "Religion in Modern Civilization," as cited by Seaver, *op. cit.*, p. 335; cf. *Decay*, pp. 78-79.
22. *Childhood*, p. 98.
23. *Out*, p. 171.
24. See *Quest*, pp. 27ff., 57; *Indian*, p. 119. Babel reports that Schweitzer thought the Nobel Prize was given to him for his discovery of reverence for life as the outcome of elemental thinking, and cites a letter from Schweitzer to prove the point (Henry Babel, *La Pensée d'Albert Schweitzer*, p. 206).

25. "Religion in Modern Civilization," as cited by Seaver, *op. cit.*, p. 340.
26. *Out*, p. 173.
27. *Ibid.*, pp. 173-174.
28. *CE*, p. 184.
29. *Ibid.*, p. 245.
30. *Ibid.*, p. 261.
31. *Indian*, p. 106.
32. *Ibid.*, p. 153.
33. *Paul*, p. 297.
34. *CE*, p. 235.
35. *Ibid.*, p. 169.
36. Reinhold Planck, "Der sittliche Wille in seinem Verhältnis zur Natur," *Christliche Welt* (1935), p. 306.
37. *Out*, p. 72.
38. Roland Schütz, "Albert Schweitzers Christentum und Theologische Forschung," *Rundbrief*, IX (January 1, 1956), 16.
39. Marie Woytt-Secretan, "A l'Hôpital de Lambarene," *Hommage à Albert Schweitzer*, p. 119.
40. Kurt Reuber, "Albert Schweitzer und Goethe," *Christliche Welt* (1932), p. 686; Rudolph Grabs, "Sinngebung des Lebens," *Albert Schweitzer: Genie der Menschlichkeit*, pp. 215-216.
41. *Decay*, p. 28.
42. *CE*, p. 279.
43. *Ibid.*, p. 226.
44. Pierhal, *op. cit.*, p. 146.
45. *Ibid.*
46. Hunter, *Three Trumpets Sound*, p. 146.
47. Pierhal, *op. cit.*, p. 160.
48. Gunther, *op. cit.*, p. 716.
49. Reuber, *op. cit.*, p. 682.
50. *CE*, pp. 157-158.
51. *Ibid.*, p. xxi.
52. *Ibid.*, p. 254.
53. *Edge*, p. 53.
54. *Ibid.*, p. 114.
55. *Ibid.*, p. 115.
56. *Ibid.*, p. 117.
57. *CE*, p. 245.
58. *Decay*, pp. 24-25.

59. *Out*, pp. 76-77.

60. *CE*, p. 257.

61. Grabs, *op. cit.*, p. 210.

62. Gunther, *op. cit.*, p. 731.

63. See ch. 8.

64. Fritz Wartenweiler, "Eine Wenig Bekannte Seite in Schweitzers Wirken," *Ehrfurcht*, p. 104.

65. *Decay*, p. 20.

66. *Ibid.*, pp. 74-75.

67. From a conversation with an intimate friend of Schweitzer.

68. *Childhood*, pp. 75-76; 95-97.

69. Wartenweiler, *op. cit.*, p. 105.

70. *Out*, pp. 73-74.

71. *Childhood*, p. 93.

72. Ernst Barthel, *Elsässische Geistesschicksale*, pp. 226-227.

73. Everett Skillings, *Out* (Postscript), p. 192.

74. *Ibid.*, pp. 197-198.

75. Siebert, "Unerwartete Begegnung im Elsass," pp. 46-53.

76. Hunter, "Schweitzer at Aspen," p. 890.

77. Gunther, *op. cit.*, pp. 713-714.

78. *Ibid.*, p. 714. Later on in his chapter on Schweitzer Gunther notes a probable reason for Schweitzer's silence; namely, his fatigue (p. 729).

79. *Out*, p. 70.

80. *More*, p. 23.

81. *Out*, pp. 80, 87.

82. Hunter, *Three Trumpets Sound*, p. 121; *Out*, p. 84.

83. *Out*, p. 71.

84. *KEL*, XLIX (December 25, 1920), 264.

85. *Out*, p. 71.

86. Bach, *op. cit.*, p. 176.

87. Hunter, "Schweitzer at Aspen," p. 176.

CHAPTER 8

1. *CE*, p. 236.

2. *Indian*, pp. 259-260.

3. *CE*, p. 231.

4. *Ibid.*, p. 232.

5. *Ibid.*

6. *Ibid.*, p. 237.

7. *Ibid.*

8. *Ibid.*

9. *Ibid.*, p. 238.

10. *Ibid.*

11. Quoted from *The Humanist*, XI (October-November, 1951), 197, with the kind permission of The American Humanist Association, Yellow Springs, Ohio.

12. Kraus, *op. cit.* (German edition), pp. 38-39.

13. *CE*, p. xv.

14. *Ibid.*, p. 242.

15. *Out*, pp. 184-185.

16. *CRW*, p. 66.

17. *Ibid.*, p. 83.

18. *Ibid.*, p. 84.

19. *Out*, p. 184.

20. Schweitzer, *Die Religionsphilosophie Kants*, p. 323.

21. Schweitzer, *Goethe: Four Studies*, p. 76.

22. *CRW*, pp. 84-85.

23. *Paul*, pp. 378-379.

24. *Ibid.*

25. Wartenweiler, *op. cit.*, p. 113.

26. *Out*, p. 126.

27. *CE*, p. 246.

28. *Ibid.*, p. xviii.

29. *Goethe*, p. 78.

30. *CE*, p. 239.

31. *Out*, p. 126.

32. See ch. 9.

33. *Out*, pp. 126-127.

34. Wartenweiler, *op. cit.*, pp. 113-114.

CHAPTER 9

1. *Deutsches Pfarrblatt*, XXXV (December 30, 1931), 824.

2. *Ibid.*, XXXV (April 28, 1931), 289-290.

3. *Ibid.*, XXXV (December 30, 1931), 824.

4. Pierhal, *op. cit.*, p. 67.

5. *Edge*, pp. 1-2.

6. *Ibid.*, p. 93.

7. *Out*, p. 72.

8. *Ibid.*, p. 73.

9. *Theology*, p. 104.

10. *Quest*, p. 397.

11. This fact is noted also by Fritz Buri, "Albert Schweitzer als Forscher, Denker und Christ," *STU*, XXV (February, 1955), 9.

12. *Quest*, pp. 368-369. Note that there is no mention of the Resurrection of Jesus. Nor is there any mention of resurrection in Steere's account of a burial at Lambarene (*SR*, XXXVI, 11-12).

13. *Ibid.*, pp. 352-356.

14. *Ibid.*, pp. 386-388; cf. *Paul*, 58, 61.

15. *Ibid.*, pp. 352ff.

16. *Ibid.*, p. 353.

17. *Ibid.*

18. *Quest*, p. xvi.

19. *Mystery*, pp. 248-250.

20. *Quest*, p. 399.

21. *Ibid.*

22. *Ibid.*

23. *Ibid.*, p. 397.

24. *Ibid.*, p. 396.

25. *Ibid.*, p. 398.

26. *Theology*, p. 104. In his 1950 preface to *Quest*, Schweitzer says that "the situation" created by the failure of the Kingdom to come "compelled believers to take a more and more spiritual view of [it]." (p. xv.)

27. *Out*, p. 46.

28. Schweitzer, "Der Recht der Wahrhaftigkeit in der Religion," *Christliche Welt* (1932), p. 941.

29. *Out*, p. 46.

30. *Ibid.*, p. 180.

31. *Ibid.*, p. 89.

32. *Ibid.*, p. 50; cf. *KEL*, XLVIII (January 19, 1919), 11.

33. *CE*, p. 25.

34. *Out*, p. 47.

35. Schweitzer, "Religion in Modern Civilization," quoted by Seaver, *op. cit.*, p. 337.

36. *Quest*, pp. 355-356.

37. *Theology*, pp. 107-108.

38. *Indian*, p. 4.

39. *Ibid.*, pp. 4-5.

40. *CE*, pp. 65-66.

41. *Ibid.*, pp. 66-67.

42. *Ibid.*, p. 29.

43. Schweitzer, *J. S. Bach*, I, 15, 17-18.

44. *Ibid.*, p. 29.

45. *Ibid.*, pp. 37-38.

46. *Ibid.*, p. 41.

47. *Ibid.*

48. Leo Schrade, "Schweitzer's Aesthetics," *The Albert Schweitzer Jubilee Book*, pp. 189-190; 193-194.

49. *Ibid.*, pp. 194-195.

50. *Quest*, p. 397.

51. *Ibid.*

52. *CE*, p. 67.

53. *Quest*, p. 250.

54. *Out*, p. 50.

55. *Ibid.*

56. *Theology*, p. 105.

57. *Out*, p. 50.

58. *Mystery*, p. 251.

59. *Theology*, p. 105.

60. *Quest*, pp. xv-xvi.

61. *Ibid.*, p. 396.

62. *Paul*, p. 385.

63. *CRW*, p. 90.

64. *Quest*, p. 399.

65. *Ibid.*, p. 400.

66. *Ibid.*

67. *Ibid.*, p. 401.

68. *Mystery*, pp. 274-275.

69. Schweitzer, from an unpublished sermon quoted by Wartenweiler, *op. cit.*, p. 109.

70. *Theology*, pp. 89-90.

71. D. Roland Schütz, *op. cit.*, pp. 12-13.

72. *Paul*, p. 388.

73. Schweitzer, as quoted in Seaver, *op. cit.*, p. 121.

74. Schweitzer, quoted by Wartenweiler, *op. cit.*, p. 113 (author's italics).

75. Schütz, *op. cit.*, p. 13 (quoting Schweitzer himself).

76. *Ibid.*, p. 14.

77. Schweitzer, "How Can We Attain the Kingdom of God?" *CC*, LXXII (September 7, 1955), 1022.

78. Schweitzer, quoted by Seaver, *op. cit.*, p. 122.

79. *Paul*, p. 388.

80. Schweitzer, personal letter quoted by Emil Lind, *Albert Schweitzer: Aus seinem Leben und Werk*, pp. 158-159.

81. *Paul*, p. 396.

82. *Ibid.*, p. 378. Note the parallels between this passage and the famous closing paragraph of the *Quest*.

83. See ch. 8.

84. *Paul*, pp. 17, 118, 123, 125, 127.

85. *Ibid.*, 123.

86. *Ibid.*, p. 118.

87. *Ibid.*, p. 378.

88. *Ibid.*, pp. 385-386.

89. *Ibid.*, pp. 16-17.

90. *Ibid.*, pp. 17, 385.

91. *Ibid.*, p. 333.

92. *Ibid.*

93. *Ibid.*, p. 379.

94. *Out*, p. 184.

95. *Paul*, p. 379.

96. Beintker, *op. cit.*, p. 242.

97. *Out*, p. 48.

98. *Ibid.*

99. *Ibid.*, p. 49.

100. Albert Schweitzer, "Die Idee des Reiches Gottes," *STU*, XXIII (January-February, 1953), 19.

101. *Out*, p. 49.

102. *Quest*, p. 401.

103. *Ibid.*, pp. 399-400.

IV

CHAPTER 10

1. H. Richard Niebuhr, *Radical Monotheism and Western Culture*, p. 37.

2. *CE*, p. 213; *Reverence*, p. 237.

3. Kraus, *op. cit.*, pp. 47-48.

4. Hans Leisegang, *Religionsphilosophie der Gegenwart*, pp. 87-89.

5. J. M. Murry, *Love, Freedom and Society*, pp. 199-201.

6. *Out*, p. 162.

7. *CE*, p. 243.

8. *Reverence*, p. 233.

9. *CE*, p. 246.

10. So Carl Dyrssen, "Die Lebensethik Albert Schweitzers," *Christistliche Welt* (1925), p. 542; cf. Babel, *op. cit.*, pp. 209-210.

11. *Edge*, p. 92.

12. *Indian*, pp. 83-84.

13. *CE*, pp. 251-252; cf. pp. 259-260.

14. *Out*, p. 181.

15. *CE*, p. 257. Other commentators on Schweitzer who have reached similar conclusions are Georges Marchal, "Paradox et Respect de la Vie dans la Pensée d'Albert Schweitzer," *Hommage*, pp. 70-72; Fritz Medicus, *Wissen und Leben*, XVIII (August 1, 1925), 832-833; August Messer, "Albert Schweitzers Kulturphilosophie," *Philosophie und Leben*, I (March, 1925), 93; William Montgomery, "Schweitzer's Ethic," *Hibbert Journal*, XXIII (July 1925), 699.

16. *CE*, p. 252.

17. *Reverence*, p. 233.

18. H. Babel, *La Pensée d'Albert Schweitzer*, pp. 210-211. For a stimulating discussion of several issues of this sort, see Joseph Fletcher, *Morals and Medicine*.

CHAPTER 11

1. Letter to the *London Daily Herald*, quoted in *SR*, XXXVII (July 17, 1954), 23.

2. Quoted by Norman Cousins in an introductory article to Schweitzer's radio appeal for an end to testing of atomic weapons, *SR*, XL (May 18, 1957), 14.

3. Gunther, *op. cit.*, p. 732.

4. Schweitzer, *The Problem of Peace in the World Today*, p. 13.

5. *Ibid.*

6. *KEL*, L (January 29, 1921), pp. 37-38.

7. *Indian*, pp. 233-234.

8. Hunter, *Three Trumpets Sound*, pp. 145-146.

9. *Indian*, p. 233.

10. *Ibid.*, p. 84.

11. Schweitzer, *Peace or Atom War*, 28 pp. All statements made in the paragraph are based on arguments advanced in the booklets; indeed, I have not varied the progression of the arguments very much.

12. *Ibid.*, p. 28.

13. *Ibid.*, p. 23 (author's italics).

14. This report of Schweitzer's thinking illustrates extraordinarily well his bias against collective action. Even the United Nations—which most political scientists regard as too idealistic in structure to be effective unless the big powers choose to allow it — is not sufficiently pure for Schweitzer.

15. *KEL*, XLVIII (August 2, 1919), 126. Schweitzer's opinions concerning colonialism are contained mainly in his chapter called "The Book of African Reminiscences" in his autobiography (pp. 146-151) and in his article "Relations of the White and Colored Races," *Contemporary Review*, CXXXIII (January, 1928), 65-70. George Seaver has done a great service to students of Schweitzer by weaving these two sources together in an appendix to his major work on Schweitzer (*op. cit.*, pp. 317-328). Schweitzer has also written a six-page article entitled "Our Task in Colonial Africa," which appears at the conclusion of Charles R. Joy, *The Africa of Albert Schweitzer* (pages unnumbered). This third article says nothing new; its chief interest consists in the fact that it reveals how little Schweitzer's opinions on the subject have changed.

16. "Relations," quoted by Seaver, *op. cit.*, p. 319.

17. *Decay*, pp. 25-26.

18. "Relations," quoted by Seaver, *op. cit.*, pp. 317-319.

19. *Ibid.*, p. 320.

20. *Ibid.*

21. *Ibid.*, pp. 322-323.

22. *Ibid.*, pp. 325-326; cf. *More*, pp. 81-82, 103.

23. *Edge*, p. 123.

24. Seaver, *op. cit.*, p. 323; cf. *Out*, p. 149.

25. *Ibid.*

26. *Edge*, pp. 24-25, 44, 125; *Out*, p. 151.

27. *Edge*, pp. 24-25.

28. *Ibid.*, pp. 113-114; Schweitzer, *The Hospital at Lambarene During the War Years*, p. 4.

29. *KEL*, XLVIII (January 12, 1919), 6; cf. *Edge*, p. 154 and *More*, pp. 153-155.

30. *More*, pp. 57-62; *Out*, p. 113; Elsa Lauterbourg-Bonjour, *Lambarene*, pp. 90-91.

31. Seaver, *op. cit.*, pp. 323-324.

32. *Edge*, pp. 126ff., 162ff.; Seaver, *op. cit.*, p. 63.

33. Seaver, *op. cit.*, p. 326.

34. *More*, pp. 18, 142.

35. *Out*, pp. 147-148.

36. *Ibid.*, p. 147.

37. *Ibid.*, pp. 147-148.

38. Grabs, *Denken und Tat*, p. 243.

39. Siebert, *op. cit.*, p. 50.

40. Gunther, *op. cit.*, p. 714.

41. *Ibid.*, pp. 726-727; cf. *More*, p. 109.

42. *More*, pp. 133-134, 165.

43. *Edge*, pp. 130-131.

44. *Ibid.*, p. 131.

45. *Ibid.*, pp. 131, 132, 134.

46. Schweitzer, as quoted by Seaver, *op. cit.*, p. 157.

47. *Edge*, pp. 44, 133; *Tage-buch*, p. 933; *More*, pp. 26, 93; cf. Pierhal, *op. cit.*, p. 132.

48. Schweitzer, "Ich muss wieder Bauunternehmer sein," *Universitas*, X (1955), 349.

49. *Tagebuch*, p. 931; cf. *More*, p. 14.

50. Feschotte, *op. cit.*, p. 114 (*sic*).

51. Bach, *op. cit.*, p. 164.

52. Fritz Buri, "The Belief in the Power of the Spirit," *To Dr. Albert Schweitzer*, p. 20.

53. Robert McGregor, "Schweitzer's Birthday at Lambarene," *SR*, XXXVIII (April 9, 1955), p. 24.

54. *Ibid.*

55. Hunter, *Three Trumpets Sound*, pp. 145-146.

56. C. W. M. Gell, "Dr. Schweitzer—a Reassessment," *The Hibbert Journal*, LV (1956-1957), 334.

57. Gunther, *op. cit.*, pp. 714, 733.

58. Gell, *loc. cit.*

59. Gunther, *op. cit.*, p. 714.

60. See chapter 14.

61. Cecil Northcott, "Schweitzer—Spiritual Adventurer," *CC*, LXXII (January 12, 1955), 42.

62. Cousins, *Dr. Schweitzer of Lambarene*, p. 22.

63. Jack, "With Schweitzer in Africa," *CC*, LXIX (July 16, 1952), 824.

64. Gunther, *op. cit.*, p. 714.

65. Jack, *loc. cit.*

66. *Ibid.*

67. Cousins, "Lambarene and the Image of Schweitzer," *SR*, XL (December 28, 1957), 18.

68. Gell, *op. cit.*, p. 332.

69. Schweitzer's opinions on this issue are vouched for by Seaver, *op. cit.*, p. 328.

70. Gunther, *op. cit.*, p. 724.

71. Cousins, *op. cit.*, pp. 19-20.

72. *Ibid.*, p. 20.

73. *Ibid.*

74. Schweitzer, "Ich muss wieder Bauunternehmer sein," *Universitas*, X (1955), 349.

V

CHAPTER 12

1. *Out*, p. 122.

2. *Ibid.*, p. 124.

3. *Ibid.*, p. 125.

4. *CE*, p. 106.

5. According to the bulletin issued by the Albert Schweitzer Education Foundation upon the occasion of an essay contest on Schweitzer's thought which it sponsored in 1959, the doctor urges every thoughtful person to subject him, or any other thinker, to "ruthless" criticism.

CHAPTER 13

1. Lewis Mumford, *The Conduct of Life*, pp. 207-215.

2. Schweitzer, *J. S. Bach*, I, 166.

3. A doctrine of essential manhood is to be found in countless philosophers, ancient and modern. The concept takes on new interest in our own day because of the theories of personality development expounded by social scientists and the theories of authentic existence developed by existentialist thinkers. One of the most provocative analyses of selfhood to appear in recent years is that of Riezler in his *Man: Mutable and Immutable*, pp. 74-92.

4. *Out*, p. 186.

5. Robert Minder, "Schweitzer, Professeur de Piano," *Hommage à Schweitzer*, p. 78.

6. Schütz, *op. cit.*, pp. 12-13.

7. From personal conversation with a student at the University of Bern, a former lawyer who had

just commenced his academic preparation for the ministry.

8. M. Werner, *Das Weltanschauungsproblem bei Karl Barth und
Albert Schweitzer*, pp. 125-127.

9. Hogg, "The Ethical Teaching of Dr. Schweitzer," *The International Review of Missions*, XIV
(April, 1925), 247.

10. Planck, *op. cit.*, p. 382.

11. *Out*, p. 187.

12. *Reverence*, p. 230.

13. *CE*, pp. 213-214.

CHAPTER 14

1. Cousins, "The Point About
Schweitzer," *SR*, XXXVII (October
2, 1954), 22.

2. Zimmermann, *loc. cit.*

3. Cf. August Messer, "Albert
Schweitzers Kulturphilosophie," pp.
90 ff.; Hogg, "To the Rescue of
Civilization," p. 55; J. M. Murry,
The Challenge of Schweitzer, p. 167.

4. Gell, *op. cit.*, p. 332.

5. *Ibid.*

6. Schweitzer, *The Problem of
Peace in the World Today*, p. 9.

7. *New Republic*, CXLIII
(July 25, 1960), 7-8; *The Reporter*,
XXIII (September 1, 1960), 16-19
and XXIII (October 13, 1960), 25-
28.

8. *The Reporter*, XXIII (September 1, 1960), 18.

9. *Christianity and Crisis*, XX
(September 19, 1960), 132.

10. *Decay*, p. 28.

11. *Edge*, p. 53, 114, 117.

12. See Max Weber, *The Protestant Ethic and the Spirit of Capitalism* and R. H. Tawney, *Religion
and the Rise of Capitalism*.

13. *Edge*, p. 115.

14. *CE*, p. 254; cf. pp. 157-158.

15. Ernest Lefever, *Ethics and
United States Foreign Policy*, pp.
65-72; cf. Hans J. Morgenthau,
Politics Among Nations, pp. 519ff.

16. Lefever, *op. cit.*, pp. 70-71.

17. This very excellent definition of justice was given by Professor John C. Bennett of Union Theological Seminary in a lecture on October 23, 1958. Schweitzer explicitly
rejects justice as an ideal for social
ethics (*CRW*, pp. 18f.).

18. See especially Reinhold Niebuhr, *Moral Man and Immoral Society* and Donald Meyer, *The Protestant Search for Political Realism*.

19. Kraus, *op. cit.*, pp. 47-48.

20. Hunter, "Schweitzer at Aspen," p. 841.

21. Bertrand Russell, "The Ele-
ments of Ethics," *Readings in Ethical
Theory*, eds. Wilfrid Sellars and John
Hospers, p. 14.

22. Messer, *op. cit.*, pp. 91-92.

23. See Murry, *op. cit.*, pp.
138-145, 164 for a rather intemper-
ate attack on reverence for life and
Schweitzer's motives and attitude in
proclaiming it.

24. Barth, *op. cit.*, III, 4, p.
403.

25. "And the fear of you and
the dread of you shall be upon every
beast of the earth, and upon every
fowl of the air, upon all that moveth
upon the earth . . . ; into your hand
are they delivered."

26. Barth, *op. cit.*, III, 4, 398.

27. Boris Pasternak, *Doctor
Zhivago* (Signet edition), p. 417.

CHAPTER 15

1. Barthel, *op. cit.*, p. 278.

2. F. Sawicky, *Literarischer
Handweiser*, LX (1924), 22.

3. Theodor Steinbuchel, "Zur
Problematik der Ethik in der Gegenwart," p. 297.

4. R. P. Jeschke, *Reverence
for Life as an Ethical Ideal*, pp.
174-175; Hans Wegmann, *Albert
Schweitzer als Führer*, p. 33; Fritz
Buri, "Albert Schweitzer als Forscher,
Denker und Christ," *STU*, XXV
(February, 1955), 8.

5. Reinhold Niebuhr, "Can Schweitzer Save Us From Russell?" *CC*, XLII (September 3, 1925), pp. 1093-1094.

6. *Out*, p. 170.

7. See Jean-Paul Sartre, *L'Existentialisme est un Humanisme*, and Albert Camus, *The Rebel*.

8. Georg Simmel, *Lebensanschauung*, pp. 20, 27, cited by Kurt Leese, *Die Krisis und Wende des Christlichen Geistes*, pp. 285ff. Simmel made his idea even more explicit with a second definition of life ("Mehr-als-Leben") and with his dictum to the effect that the unifying factor in personality is its "sich-über-sich-selbst-Erhebens" quality.

9. Hogg, "To the Rescue of Civilization," pp. 55ff.

VI

CHAPTER 16

1. See especially A. J. Ayer, *Language, Truth and Logic*, ch. 6; P. H. Nowell-Smith, *Ethics*; C. L. Stevenson, *Ethics and Language*.

2. Ruth Benedict's *Patterns of Culture* is justly acclaimed as a good introduction to this point of view. In her opinion, "Social thinking at the present time has no more important task before it than that of taking adequate account of cultural relativity" (pp. 256-257).

3. An especially provocative statement of the popular interpretation of Freud's ethical thinking is contained in Philip Rieff's *Freud: The Mind of the Moralist*.

4. See Sartre, *Existentialism*, and Norman Greene, *Jean-Paul Sartre: The Existentialist Ethic*.

5. These terms were coined in two of the most readable as well as thought-provoking analyses of American society today: David Riesman's *The Lonely Crowd*, and William Whyte's *The Organization Man*.

6. Whyte, *op. cit.*, pp. 173-185.

7. Quoted in George Forell, *Faith Active in Love*, p. 64.

8. C. G. Jung, *Answer to Job*.

9. Westminster Confession, Article III, quoted in Waldo Beach and H. Richard Niebuhr, *Christian Ethics*, p. 299.

10. Ludwig Feuerbach, *The Essence of Christianity*, ch. 26.

11. Erich Fromm, *Man For Himself*, pp. 141-172.

12. *Ibid.*, p. 148.

13. *Ibid.*, p. 149.

14. *Ibid.*, p. 150.

15. *Ibid.*, pp. 150-151.

16. *Ibid.*, p. 151.

17. *Ibid.*, p. 155.

18. *Ibid.*

19. *Ibid.*, p. 126.

20. See especially Barth, *Church Dogmatics*, II, 2, 1-563.

21. Beach and Niebuhr, *op. cit.*, p. 302.

22. I John 4:19 (RSV).

23. Barth, *Church Dogmatics*, II, 2, p. 522. "The freedom of God" is a shibboleth that is constantly reiterated by Barthians. Cf. Rudolph Bultmann, *Primitive Christianity*, p. 73.

24. Fromm, *op. cit.*, p. 155.

25. Barth, *Church Dogmatics*, II, 2, p. 533.

26. Brunner, *Reason and Revelation*, p. 83.

27. Luther, quoted in Forell, *op. cit.*, p. 65; cf. Barth, *Romans*, p. 455.

28. Barth, *Romans*, p. 452.

29. Thomas J. Bigham, "A Christian Philosophy of Social Work and Psychotherapy," *Pastoral Psychology*, VI, pp. 27-28.

30. The definitive treatment of this quite valid point is to be found in Reinhold Niebuhr's *The Nature and Destiny of Man*, vol. I.

31. Barth, *The Word of God and the Word of Man*, pp. 179ff.;

Romans, p. 431; Brunner, *The Divine Imperative*, pp. 162-163.

32. Barth, *Romans*, p. 436.

33. Charles West, *Communism and the Theologians*, p. 209; Brunner, *The Divine Imperative*, p. 162; Barth, *Romans*, p. 431.

34. Brunner, *The Divine Imperative*, p. 162; cf. Anders Nygren, *Agape and Eros, passim*. Nygren contends that man cannot *love* God, in the Christian sense of that word: only God can love, and the word which describes man's proper activity toward God is *faith*. It follows that Nygren shares the opinion of Barth and Brunner that man can do no more than be a pipe through which God's love flows.

35. Soren Kierkegaard, *Fear and Trembling*, p. 80. (Anchor edition.)

36. *Ibid*.

37. Barth, *Romans*, pp. 482-483; *Church Dogmatics* II, 2, 782ff.

38. Barth, *Kirchliche Dogmatik*, III, 4, 1-10; cf. *Church Dogmatics*, II, 2, 537-538.

39. See Luther's *Treatise on Christian Liberty* and his *Treatise on Good Works, passim*.

40. *Institutes*, Bk. II, ch. 8, para. 11.

41. E. C. Gardner, *Biblical Faith and Social Ethics*, p. 178.

42. Nicolai Hartmann, *Ethics*, I, p. 291.

43. Nels Ferre's *The Sun and the Umbrella* is a popular treatment of this theme; judging from his lectures and seminar comments, H. Richard Niebuhr's forthcoming work on Christian ethics will probably contain a systematic statement of it.

44. Paul Tillich, *The Protestant Era*, pp. 62ff. and *The Courage to Be*, pp. 182ff., contain concise statements of this thesis. For a more systematic defense of it, see the introductory section of Tillich's *Systematic Theology*, vol. II.

45. Reinhold Niebuhr, *Applied Christianity*, p. 193.

46. *Ibid*., p. 149; cf. *The Nature and Destiny of Man*, II, p. 196.

47. Reinhold Niebuhr, "The Relations of Christians and Jews in Western Civilization," *Pious and Secular America*, pp. 86-112.

48. Roger Shinn, "Some Ethical Foundations of Christian Theology," *The Union Seminary Quarterly Review*, XV (January, 1960), 110.

49. Matthew 21:28ff.

50. Any thinker who states his views with conviction may be accused of arrogance, of course, and this kind of *ad hominem* argument is as unprovable as it is irrefutable. But religious thinkers, especially those who believe strongly in exclusive revelation, are more prone to this failing than they like to admit. Karl Jaspers, a leading European philosopher who has attempted to maintain genuine dialogue with religious thinkers, has this to say of his contact with European theologians:

It is among the sorrows of my life spent in the search for truth, that discussion with theologians always dries up at crucial points; they fall silent, state an incomprehensible proposition, speak of something else, make some categoric statement, engage in amiable talk, without really taking cognizance of what one has said—and in the last analysis they are not really interested. For on the one hand they are certain of their truth, terrifyingly certain; and on the other hand they do not regard it as worth while to bother about people like us, who strike them as merely stubborn. (*The Perennial Scope of Philosophy*, p. 77.)

51. Reinhold Niebuhr, *Applied Christianity*, pp. 172-173.

52. Kierkegaard, *Stages on Life's Way.*

53. Shinn, *op. cit.*, p. 104.

54. Arnold Toynbee argues that claims to exclusive possession of truth are also a serious barrier to international understanding and peace. His analysis of this problem is worthy of serious attention. (See *An Historian's Approach to Religion*, pp. 261-297.)

55. Kraus, *op. cit.*, pp. 38-39.

56. *CE*, pp. 176, 185.

CHAPTER 17

1. Rudolph Otto, *The Idea of the Holy*, pp. 173, 175-178.

2. *Ibid.*, p. 178.

3. *Childhood*, p. 90.

4. I venture this assertion for two reasons: First, the attempt to deny the futurist aspect of Jesus' eschatology has been "amply refuted" (Clarence T. Craig, "The Proclamation of the Kingdom," *The Interpreter's Bible*, VII, 153). Secondly, the argument that certain signs of the inbreaking power of God were already visible to the eyes of the New Testament writers merely reinforces Schweitzer's point of view, for he emphasized the same finding, especially in his interpretation of Paul. The healing power and the teaching authority of Jesus were signs that the power of the demons was *beginning* to be broken, but the decisive event was the expected coming of the Son of Man, and the signs merely increased the expectation of this event.

5. Donald Baillie, *God Was in Christ*, quoted in D. D. Williams, *What Present-Day Theologians Are Thinking*, pp. 101-102.

6. Robinson, *A New Quest of the Historical Jesus*, p. 35.

7. The story of the Slaughter of the Innocents and those of the Descent into Egypt and the Temptation serve this function. See also Benjamin Bacon, *Studies in Matthew* for the New Law parallel.

8. Robinson, *op. cit.*, pp. 35-36.

9. *Ibid.*, p. 36.

10. For a concise yet authoritative summary of the form critical approach, see Bultmann's *Form Criticism.*

11. John Knox, *Christ the Lord*, quoted in Williams, *op. cit.*, p. 101.

12. Ernst Heitsch, quoted in Robinson, *op. cit.*, p. 80.

13. Grässer, *Das Problem der Parusieverzögerung*, pp. 137-141.

14. Bultmann, *Die Geschichte der synoptischen Tradition*, pp. 278ff.

15. See Grässer, *Das Problem der Parusieverzögerung.*

16. Barth, quoted in Robinson, *op. cit.*, p. 44 (author's italics).

17. *Ibid.*, p. 45.

18. See especially Bultmann, *Theology of the New Testament.*

19. Robinson, *op. cit.*, p. 81.

20. Robinson, "The Historical Question," *CC*, LXXVI (Ocober 21, 1959), 1210. Copyright 1959 Christian Century Foundation. Reprinted by permission.

21. Robinson, *A New Quest of the Historical Jesus*, pp. 28-29.

22. *Ibid.*, p. 24.

23. *Ibid.*, pp. 67-68.

24. *Ibid.*, p. 72.

25. *Ibid.*, p. 68.

26. Schweitzer, *Geschichte der Leben-Jesu-Forschung*, p. 636.

27. *Quest*, p. 399.

28. *Ibid.*

29. *Theology*, p. 104.

30. See, for example, Frederick C. Grant, "The Jesus of History," *The Union Seminary Quarterly Review*, XIV (March, 1959), 1-16.

31. Günther Bornkamm, *Jesus von Nazareth*, pp. 142-143.

32. *Out*, p. 49.

33. This charge has recently been articulated by William W.

Bartley III, "I Call Myself a Protestant," *Harper's*, CCXVIII (May, 1959), 49-56.

34. The resentment and scoffing which greeted Bartley's article were similar to that given Fromm by many theological students. It is unfortunate that the polemical tone of the article obscured the substantial element of truth it was intended to convey. For a thought-provoking essay on this problem, see J. Milton Yinger (ed.), *Religion, Society and the Individual*, pp. 599ff.

35. See Houston Smith's reply to Bartley in the special "letters to the editor" section of the July, 1959 issue of *Harper's*.

CHAPTER 18

1. From a television program entitled "The Theological Significance of Schweitzer." Script made available through the kindness of The Albert Schweitzer Education Foundation, Chicago, Illinois.

2. Tillich, *Love, Power and Justice*, pp. 112ff.

3. CE, pp. 176-177.

4. *Out*, p. 126.

5. *Ibid.*, p. 121.

6. CE, p. 184.

7. Alfred North Whitehead, as quoted by Lucien Price, *The Dialogues of Whitehead*, p. 389. The theological implications of Whitehead's thought are developed further in the very distinguished work of Charles Hartshorne.

8. Tillich, *op. cit.*, p. 56.

9. *Ibid.*, p. 82.

10. *Ibid.*, p. 71.

11. I am greatly intrigued by Camus' suggestion that if God is declared to be dead, then man is apt to put himself in God's place and metaphysical rebellion is apt to lead to political rebellion that ends as murder (*op. cit., passim*). It is not without significance that this Nobel Prize-winning humanist finds himself in agreement on this important point with the biblical insights as to the nature of man, as interpreted by Reinhold Niebuhr (*The Nature and Destiny of Man, passim*) and John Bennett (*Christian Realism*, pp. 46-73).

12. Reinhold Niebuhr, "Can Schweitzer Save Us From Russell?" CC, XLII (September 3, 1925), p. 1095.

13. See Toynbee, *A Study of History*, I, especially pp. 60ff.

14. Williams, *God's Grace and Man's Hope*, p. 55. The phrase in the preceding sentence is from the same page.

15. *Ibid.*, p. 57.

16. *Ibid.*, p. 148. The preservation of some kind of genuine selfhood in the universal community is insured by the fact that it is elsewhere defined as "an order of mutuality" in which "each gives itself to the whole, each has its own claim on the whole" (*ibid.*, p. 79).

Bibliography*

I. Primary Sources

A. Books written entirely by Schweitzer.

1899

Die Religionsphilosophie Kants (Tübingen: J. C. B. Mohr).

1901

Das Abendmahl im Zusammenhang mit dem Leben Jesu und der Geschichte des Urchristentums. Vol. I. *Das Abendmahlsproblem auf Grund der Wissenschaftlichen Forschung des 19. Jahrhunderts und der Historischen Berichte.* Vol. II. (Tübingen: J. C. B. Mohr). Vol. II has been translated under the title *The Mystery of the Kingdom of God.* Translated by Walter Lowrie (London: A. & C. Black, 1925, and New York: Macmillan Co., 1950).

1906

Von Reimarus zu Wrede (Tübingen: J. C. B. Mohr). Translated by W. Montgomery as *The Quest of the Historical Jesus* (London: A. & C. Black, 1910, and New York: Macmillan Co., 1957).

1908

J. S. Bach (Leipzig: Breitkopf & Härtel). Translated by Ernest Newman as *J. S. Bach* (London: A. & C. Black, 1911).

1913

Geschichte der Leben–Jesu–Forschung (Tübingen: J. C. B. Mohr).
Die Psychiatrische Beurteilung Jesu (Tübingen: J. C. B. Mohr). Translated by Charles R. Joy as *The Psychiatric Study of Jesus* (Boston: Beacon Press, 1948).

1920

Zwischen Wasser und Urwald (Bern: Paul Haupt). Translated by C. T. Campion as *On the Edge of the Primeval Forest* (London: A. & C. Black, 1922, and New York: Macmillan Co., 1948).

1923

Christianity and the Religions of the World. Translated by Joanna Powers (London: Allen & Unwin, and New York: Henry Holt and Co., 1939).

* For a more complete bibliography see Charles R. Joy, *Schweitzer: An Anthology* (Boston: Beacon Press, Enlarged Edition, 1956).

Kulturphilosophie I: Verfall und Wiederaufbau der Kultur and *Kulturphilosophie II: Kultur und Ethik* (Bern: Paul Haupt). Translated by C. T. Campion (London: A. & C. Black). Both volumes published together under the title *The Philosophy of Civilization* (New York: Macmillan Co., 1950).

1924

Aus Meiner Kindheit und Jugendzeit (Munich: C. H. Beck). Translated by C. T. Campion as *Memoirs of Childhood and Youth* (London: Allen & Unwin, and New York: Macmillan Co., 1931).
Mitteilungen aus Lambarene, I (Bern: Paul Haupt).

1925

Mitteilungen aus Lambarene, II (Bern: Paul Haupt).

1928

Mitteilungen aus Lambarene, III (Bern: Paul Haupt).

1929

Selbstdarstellung (Leipzig: Felix Meiner).

1930

Die Mystik des Apostels Paulus (Tübingen: J. C. B. Mohr). Translated by W. Montgomery as *The Mysticism of Paul the Apostle* (London: A. & C. Black, and New York: Macmillan Co., 1955).

1931

Aus Meinem Leben und Denken (Leipzig: Felix Meiner). Translated by C. T. Campion as *Out of My Life and Thought* (New York: Henry Holt and Co., 1933. Published as a Mentor Book with a postscript on Schweitzer's life since 1931 by Everett Skillings, 1953).
Das Urwaldspital zu Lambarene (Munich: C. H. Beck). Translated by C. T. Campion as *More from the Primeval Forest* (London: A. & C. Black). Published in the United States as *The Forest Hospital at Lambarene* (New York: Macmillan Co., 1948).

1935

Die Weltanschauung der Indischen Denker (Munich: C. H. Beck). Translated by Mrs. C. E. B. Russell as *Indian Thought and its Development* (Boston: Beacon Press, 1936).

1938

Afrikanische Geschichten (Leipzig: Felix Meiner). Translated by Mrs. C. E. B. Russell as *From My African Notebook* (London: Allen & Unwin).

1947

Albert Schweitzer: An Anthology. Edited by Charles R. Joy (Boston: Beacon Press).
The Hospital at Lambarene during the War Years (New York: The Albert Schweitzer Fellowship).

1949

Goethe: Four Studies. Translated by Charles R. Joy (Boston: Beacon Press).
The Wit and Wisdom of Albert Schweitzer. Edited by Charles R. Joy (Boston: Beacon Press).
Goethe: His Personality and His Work (Chicago: Albert Schweitzer Education Foundation).

1950

The Animal World of Albert Schweitzer. Translated and edited by Charles R. Joy (Boston: Beacon Press).

1951

Music in the Life of Albert Schweitzer. Edited by Charles R. Joy (New York: Harper & Bros., and Boston: Beacon Press).

1952

Le Pelican du Docteur Schweitzer (Paris: Editions Sun).

1954

The Problem of Peace in the World Today (New York: Harper & Bros.).

1955

Eight Year Report on Lambarene Hospital (New York: Harper & Bros.).

1958

Friede oder Atomkrieg? (Bern: Paul Haupt).
Peace or Atom War? (New York: Henry Holt & Co.)

B. *Books containing an essay or letters of Schweitzer.*

Das Neunzehnte Jahrhundert, 24 Aufsätze zur Jahrhundertwende (Strasbourg: Georg Wolf, 1900), pp. 61-68.
Joy, Charles R. *The Africa of Albert Schweitzer* (New York: Harper & Bros., 1948).
Mozley, E. N. *The Theology of Albert Schweitzer for Christian Inquirers* (London: A. & C. Black, 1950), pp. 79-108.
Kik, Richard, ed. *Von Mensch zu Mensch* (Freiburg in Br.: Hyperion Verlag, 1956).

C. *Articles written by Schweitzer in periodicals.*

Evangelisch-Protestantischer Kirchenbote für Elsass und Lothringen, vol. 47, no. 50–vol. 50, no. 5, *passim.* (Schweitzer was the editor of this periodical from December 1918 to February 1921.)
"Relations of the White and Colored Race," *Contemporary Review,* CXXXIII (January, 1928), 65-70.
(Letter) *Deutsches Pfarrblatt,* XXXV (December 30, 1931), 824.
"Der Recht der Wahrhaftigkeit in der Religion," *Christliche Welt* (1932), pp. 941-942.
"Religion in Modern Civilization," *The Christian Century,* LI (November 21 and 28, 1934), 1483-1484 and 1519-1521.
"Forgiveness," *The Christian World* (November 1, 1934), p. 11.

"Reverence for Life," *The Animal Magazine* (October, 1935), pp. 3-4.
"The Ethics of Reverence for Life," *Christendom*, I, (Winter, 1936), 222-239.
"Afrikanisches Tagebuch," *Universitas*, I (November, 1946), 931-943.
"The State of Civilization," *Christian Register* (September, 1947), pp. 320-323.
"The Tornado and the Spirit," *Christian Register* (September, 1947), p. 328.
"Schweitzer Sees the End of Civilization," *The Christian Century*, LXIV (October 1, 1947), 1165.
"Die Idee des Reiches Gottes," *Schweizerische Theologische Umschau*, XXIII (January-February, 1953), 2-20.
"The H-Bomb," *London Daily Herald*, April 14, 1954, reprinted in *The Saturday Review*, XXVII (July 17, 1954), 23.
"How Can We Attain the Kingdom of God?" *The Christian Century*, LXXII (September 7, 1955), 1021-1022.
"Ich muss wieder Bauunternehmer sein," *Universitas*, X, (1955), 337-353.
"An Obligation to Tomorrow," *The Saturday Review*, XLI (May 24, 1958), 21-28. (This article is an early translation of Schweitzer's radio broadcasts on the problem of atomic testing.)
"Haltet den Glauben an den Menschen fest!" *Rundbrief für den Freundeskreis von Albert Schweitzer* (January 14, 1960), pp. 58-59. (Almost every issue of this privately printed magazine has a letter from Schweitzer or an article by a friend who has recently seen him or heard from him.)

II. Secondary Sources Which Deal Directly with Schweitzer

A. Books.

Amadou, Robert. *Albert Schweitzer: Etudes et Témoinages* (Paris: L'Arche, 1952).
Anderson, Erica and Exman, Eugene. *The World of Albert Schweitzer* (New York: Harper & Bros., 1955).
Babel, Henry. *La Pensée d'Albert Schweitzer* (Neuchatel: Editions H. Messeiller, 1956).
Bach, Marcus. *The Circle of Faith* (New York: Hawthorn, 1956).
Barthel, Ernst. *Elsässische Geistesschicksale* (Heidelberg: Carl Winters Universitätsbuchhandlung, 1928).
Baruk, Henri and others. *Hommage à Albert Schweitzer* (Paris: Le Guide, 1955).
Bremi, Willy. *Der Weg des Protestantischen Menschen* (Zürich: Artemis Verlag, 1953).
Buri, Fritz. *Albert Schweitzer als Theologe Heute* (Zürich: Artemis Verlag, 1955).
————. *Albert Schweitzer und Karl Jaspers* (Zürich: Artemis Verlag, 1950).
————. *Albert Schweitzer und Unsere Zeit* (Zürich: Artemis Verlag, 1947).
————. *Albert Schweitzers Wahrheit in Anfechtung und Bewährung* (Zürich: Artemis Verlag, 1960).

————. *Christentum und Kultur bei Albert Schweitzer* (Bern and Leipzig: Paul Haupt, 1941).

————. (ed.). *Ehrfurcht vor dem Leben* (Bern: Paul Haupt).

Cousins, Norman. *Dr. Schweitzer of Lambarene* (New York: Harper & Bros., 1960).

Daniel, Anita. *The Story of Albert Schweitzer* (New York: Random House, 1957).

Feschotte, Jacques. *Albert Schweitzer: An Introduction* (Boston: Beacon Press, 1955).

Franck, Frederick S. *Days with Albert Schweitzer* (New York: Henry Holt & Co., 1959).

Furr, Lester S. "The Philosophy of Dr. Albert Schweitzer" (unpublished B. D. thesis, Duke Divinity School, 1936).

Grabs, Rudolph. *Albert Schweitzer: Die Erste Deutsche Biographie* (Berlin: Steuben-Verlag Paul G. Esser, 1949).

————. *Albert Schweitzer: Denken und Tat* (Hamburg: Robert Meiner, 1950).

————. "Sinngebung des Lebens" in *Albert Schweitzer: Genie der Menschlichkeit* (Frankfort & Hamburg: Fischer, 1955).

Grässer, Erich. *Das Problem der Parusieverzögerung* (Berlin: Töpelmann Verlag, 1957).

Gunther, John. *Inside Africa* (New York: Harper & Bros., 1955).

Hagedorn, Hermann. *Prophet in the Wilderness* (New York: Macmillan Co., 1947).

Heisler, August. (ed.). *Albert Schweitzer: Zeitliches und Überzeitliches* (Hamburg: Johann Trautmann, 1947).

Hunter, Allan A. *Three Trumpets Sound* (New York: Association Press, 1939).

Jack, Homer A. (ed.). *To Dr. Albert Schweitzer* (New York: The Profile Press, 1955).

Jeschke, Reuben P. "Reverence for Life as an Ethical Ideal" (unpublished Ph.D. dissertation, Columbia University, 1951).

Kraus, Oskar. *Albert Schweitzer: His Work and His Philosophy* (London: A. & C. Black, 1944).

Langfeldt, Gabriel. *Albert Schweitzer* (London: Allen & Unwin, 1960).

Lauterbourg-Bonjour, Elsa. *Lambarene* (Bern: Paul Haupt, 1931).

Leisegang, Hans. *Religionsphilosophie der Gegenwart* (Berlin: Junker & Dünnhaupt Verlag, 1930).

Lind, Emil. *Albert Schweitzer: Aus seinem Leben und Werk* (Bern: Paul Haupt, 1948).

Mumford, Lewis. *The Conduct of Life* (New York: Harcourt, Brace & Co., 1951).

Murry, John Middleton. *The Challenge of Schweitzer* (London: Jason Press, 1948).

————. *Love, Freedom and Society* (London: J. Cape, 1957).

Phillips, Herbert M. *Safari of Discovery* (New York: Twayne Publishers, 1958).

Pierhal, Jean. *Albert Schweitzer* (London: Lutterworth Press, 1956).

Raab, Karl. *Albert Schweitzer: Persönlichkeit und Denken* (Düsseldorf: Dissertations-Verlag G. H. Nolte, 1937).

Ratter, Magnus C. *Albert Schweitzer* (London: Allenson & Co., 1935).

Rees, Theophil. *Albert Schweitzer: Ehrfurcht vor dem Leben* (Karlsruhe: Verlag G. F. Miller, 1947).

Regester, John D. *Albert Schweitzer: The Man and His Work* (New York: The Abingdon Press, 1931).

Roback, A. A. (ed.). *The Albert Schweitzer Jubilee Book* (Cambridge: Sci-Art Publishers, 1945).

Russell, Lillian M. *The Path to Reconstruction* (New York: Henry Holt & Co., 1941).

Seaver, George. *Albert Schweitzer: The Man and His Mind* (New York: Harper & Bros., 1947).

————. *Albert Schweitzer: Christian Revolutionary* (London: James Clarke & Co., Ltd., 1944).

————. *A Vindication* (Boston: Beacon Press, 1951).

Sorokin, Pitrim. *Social Philosophies of an Age of Crisis* (Boston: Beacon Press, 1950).

Strege, Martin. *Zum sein in Gott durch Denken* (Bern: Paul Haupt, 1937).

Wartenweiler, Fritz. *Der Urwalddoktor Albert Schweitzer* (Aargau, Schweiz: Freunden Schweitzer Volksbildungsheime, n. d.).

Wegmann, Hans. *Albert Schweitzer als Führer* (Zürich: Beer & Cie., 1928).

Werner, Martin. *Albert Schweitzer und das Freie Christentum* (Zürich: Beer & Cie., 1924).

————. *Glaube und Aberglaube* (Bern: Paul Haupt, 1957).

————. *Das Weltanschauungsproblem bei Karl Barth und Albert Schweitzer* (Munich: C. H. Beck, 1924).

Wolfram, Aurel. *Albert Schweitzer und die Krise des Abendlandes* (Vienna: Gerold & Co., 1947).

B. Articles in Periodicals.

Barthel, Ernst. "Dr. Albert Schweitzer as Theologian," *The Hibbert Journal*, XXVI (July, 1928), 720-735.

Beintker, H. "Albert Schweitzers Theologische Bedeutung," *Wissenschaftliche Zeitschrift der Ernst-Moritz-Arndt Universitat*, IV (1954-1955), 233-244.

Bergholz, Harry. "Albert Schweitzer's Message," *The Midwest Journal*, VI (Winter, 1954-1955), 9-15.

Bixler, J. S. "Portrait of an Internationalist," *Christendom*, I (Winter, 1944), 35-39.

————. "Interpreter of Jesus and Bach," *The Christian Century*, XLV (November 15, 1928), 1395-1396.

————. "The Miracle of Lambarene," *The Saturday Review*, XXXVIII (January 15, 1955), 24.

Bowman, John W. "From Schweitzer to Bultmann," *Theology Today*, XI (July, 1954), 160-178.

Brock, Erich. Review of *Verfall und Wiederaufbau der Kultur*, in *Logos*, XII (1924), 415-418.

Budde, Karl. "Brief von Albert Schweitzer," *Christliche Welt* (1925), p. 647.

Buri, Fritz. "Albert Schweitzer als Forscher, Denker und Christ," *Schweizerische Theologische Umschau*, XXV (February, 1955), 4-11.

————. "Das hermeneutische Problem in der Protestantischen Theologie der Gegenwart," *Schweizerische Theologische Umschau*, XXVII (June, 1957), 29-37.

Clausen, Bernard C. "Baffled Kindness," *The Christian Century*, LVI (September 27, 1939), 1166-1167.

Cousins, Norman. "The Point About Schweitzer," *The Saturday Review*, XXXVII (October 2, 1954), 22-23.

———. "A Movie on Albert Schweitzer," *The Saturday Review*, XL (January 5, 1957), 25-26.

———. "Lambarene and the Image of Schweitzer," *The Saturday Review*, XL (December 28, 1957), 18-20.

Dodd, E. M. "Kierkegaard and Schweitzer," *London Quarterly Review*, CLXX (April, 1945), 148-153.

Dryssen, Carl. "Die Lebensethik Albert Schweitzers," *Christliche Welt* (1925), pp. 542-545.

Emmel, Felix. (Review of *Kulturphilosophie*, I and II) *Preussischen Jahrbücher*, CLXXXXV (March, 1924), 293-296.

Friedmann, K. "Albert Schweitzer's Irrtum," *Neues Abendland*, XXXIV (July, 1953), 437-440.

Gell, C. W. M. "Dr. Schweitzer—a Reassessment," *The Hibbert Journal*, LV (1956-1957), 330-334.

———. "Schweitzer and Radhakrishnan," *The Hibbert Journal*, LI (1951-1952), 234-241, 255-265.

Hess, M. W. "The Apotheosis of Albert Schweitzer," *Catholic World*, CLXXIV (1952), 425-429.

Hogg, A. G. "To the Rescue of Civilization," *The International Review of Missions*, XIV (January, 1925), 45-58.

———. "The Ethical Teaching of Dr. Schweitzer," *The International Review of Missions*, XIV (April, 1925), 237-251.

Holz, Karl. "Die Botschaft Albert Schweitzers," *Neue Schweizer Rundschau*, IX (June, 1941), 77-88.

Hunter, Allan A. "Schweitzer at Aspen," *The Christian Century*, LXVI (July 27, 1949), 890-891.

Jack, Homer A. "With Schweitzer in Africa," *The Christian Century*, LXIX (July 16, 1952), 823-825.

———. "Twenty Questions About Albert Schweitzer," *The Christian Century*, LXXV (October 29, 1958), 1243-1244.

Kendon, Frank. "Albert Schweitzer," *The Fortnightly*, CLXIII (January, 1948), 59-64.

Kleine, H. O. "Religiöse Duldsamkeit," *Rundbrief für den Freundeskreis von Albert Schweitzer*, IX (January 1, 1956), 41-43.

McGregor, Robert. "Schweitzer's Birthday," *The Saturday Review*, XXXVI (April 9, 1955), 24.

Medicus, Fritz. (Review of *Kultur und Ethik*) *Wissen und Leben*, XVIII (August 1, 1925), 829-834.

Messer, August. "Albert Schweitzer's Kulturphilosophie," *Philosophie und Leben*, I (March, 1925), 77-98.

Montgomery, William. "Schweitzer's Ethic," *The Hibbert Journal*, XXIII (July, 1925), 695-708.

Neuenschwander, Ulrich. "Auswirken der Gedanken Albert Schweitzers in der gegenwartigen Theologie," *Schweizerische Theologische Umschau*, XXV (February, 1955), 17-23.

Niebuhr, Reinhold. "Can Schweitzer Save Us From Russell?" *The Christian Century*, XLII (September 3, 1925), 1093-1095.

Northcott, Cecil. "Schweitzer: Spiritual Adventurer," *The Christian Century*, LXXII (January 12, 1955), 42-43.

O'Brien, John A. "God's Eager Fool," *Reader's Digest*, XLVIII (March, 1946), pp. 43-47.

Pfister, Oskar. "Albert Schweitzer—Missionary, Musician, Physician," *The Living Age*, CCCXXII (August 2, 1924), 229-233.

Planck, Reinhold, "Der sittliche Wille in seinem Verhältnis zur Natur," *Christliche Welt* (1935), pp. 303-308, 380-382.

Reuber, Kurt. "Albert Schweitzer und Goethe," *Christliche Welt* (1932), pp. 682-686.

Rolffs, A. S. "Die Ethik Albert Schweitzers," *Deutsches Pfarrblatt*, XXXV (April 21 and 28, May 5 and 12, 1931), 241-245, 257-259, 271-278, 289-290.

Ross, Emory. "Albert Schweitzer, the Man and His Mind," *The International Review of Missions*, XXXVII (July, 1948), 330-333.

————. "Schweitzer, Man of Action," *The Christian Century*, LXV (January 7, 1948), 9-11.

Sawicky, F. Review of *Kultur und Ethik*, *Literarischer Handweiser*, LX (January-February, 1924), 21-22.

Schacht, Robert H. "The Greatest Living Soul in Christendom and His Stand on Free Religion," *Christian Register*, (August-September, 1949), pp. 17-19.

Schütz, D. Roland. "Albert Schweitzers Christentum und Theologische Forschung," *Rundbrief für den Freundeskreis von Albert Schweitzer*, IX (January 1, 1956), 12-31.

Siebert, Theodor. "Unerwartete Begegnung im Elsass," *Rundbrief für den Freundeskreis von Albert Schweitzer*, IX (January 1, 1956), 46-53.

Steere, Douglas. "Death at Lambarene," *The Saturday Review*, XXXVI (June 13, 1953), 11-12.

Steinbuchel, Theodor. "Zur Problematik der Ethik in der Gegenwart," *Bonner Zeitschrift für Theologie und Seelsorge*, I (March, 1924), 290-300.

Ströle, Albrecht. "Albert Schweitzer als Kulturkritiker," *Rundbrief für den Freundeskreis von Albert Schweitzer*, IX (January 1, 1956), 32-41.

Tasker, A. G. "Dr. Albert Schweitzer," *London Quarterly Review*, CXLVIII (July, 1927), 106-109.

Trueblood, D. Elton. "A Philosophy in Action," *The Christian Century*, XLVIII (April 29, 1931), 575-577.

Vogelsanger, Peter. "Albert Schweitzer als Theologe," *Reformatio*, IV (January, 1955), 8-20.

Wantz, Andre. "Albert Schweitzer," *Le Christianisme Social*, III (April, 1930), 352-357.

Wehrung, Georg. "Albert Schweitzer und sein Zeitspiegel," *Türmer*, XXVI (July, 1924), 677-681.

Werner, Martin. "Die Religiöse Botschaft Albert Schweitzers," *Schweizerische Theologische Umschau*, XXV (February, 1955), 17-23.

————. "Die heute Entwicklungen der liberalen Theologie," *Schweizerische Theologische Umschau*, XXV (July, 1955), 49-60.

Zimmermann, Karl. "Funeral Sermon for Madame Schweitzer," *Rundbrief für den Freundeskreis von Albert Schweitzer*, XI (August 1, 1957), 5ff.

III. Other Secondary Sources.

Bacon, B. W., *Studies in Matthew* (New York: Henry Holt & Co., 1930).

Barth, Karl. *Church Dogmatics*, II/1 and II/2. Trans. by T. H. L. Parker et. al. (New York: Charles Scribner's Sons, 1957).

———. *Kirchliche Dogmatik*, III/4. (Zürich: Evangelischer Verlag A. G., 1951).

———. *Romans* (London: Oxford University Press, 1933).

———. *The Word of God and the Word of Man* (New York: Harper & Bros., 1956).

Bartsch, H. W. (ed.). *Kerygma and Myth* (London: S.P.C.K., 1954).

Beach, Waldo and Niebuhr, H. Richard. *Christian Ethics* (New York: The Ronald Press Company, 1955).

Bennett, John. *Christian Ethics and Social Policy* (New York: Charles Scribner's Sons, 1946).

———. *Christian Realism* (New York: Charles Scribner's Sons, 1952).

———. *Christians and the State* (New York: Charles Scribner's Sons, 1958).

Berdyaev, Nicholas. *The Destiny of Man* (London: Geoffrey Bles, Ltd., 1955).

Bonhoeffer, Dietrich. *Ethics* (New York: Macmillan Co., 1955).

Bornkamm, Günther. *Jesus von Nazareth* (Stuttgart: Verlag W. Kohlhammer GmbH., 1956).

Brunner, Emil. *The Divine Imperative* (Philadelphia: Westminster Press, 1947).

———. *Justice and the Social Order* (New York: Harper & Bros., 1945).

———. *Reason and Revelation* (London: SCM Press, 1947).

———. *The Scandal of Christianity* (Philadelphia: Westminster Press, 1951).

———. *Theology of Crisis* (New York and London: Charles Scribner's Sons, 1929).

Bultmann, Rudolph. *Jesus and the Word* (New York: Charles Scribner's Sons, 1934).

———. *Jesus Christ and Mythology* (New York: Charles Scribner's Sons, 1958).

———. *Theology of the New Testament*. Trans. by Kendrick Grobel (New York: Charles Scribner's Sons, 1955).

———, and Jaspers, Karl. *Myth and Christianity* (New York: Noonday Press, 1958).

Buri, Fritz. *Theologie der Existenz* (Bern: Paul Haupt, 1954).

Calvin, John. *The Institutes of the Christian Religion*. Trans. by Henry Beveridge (Grand Rapids: Wm. B. Eerdmans Publishing Co., 1957).

Dodd, C. H. *The Parables of the Kingdom* (New York: Charles Scribner's Sons, 1936).

Feuerbach, Ludwig. *The Essence of Christianity.* Trans. by George Eliot (New York: Harper & Bros., 1957).

Fletcher, Joseph. *Morals and Medicine* (Princeton: Princeton University Press, 1954).

Forell, George W. *Faith Active in Love* (Minneapolis: Augsburg Publishing House, 1954).

Frankl, Viktor. *From Death-Camp to Existentialism* (Boston: Beacon Press, 1959).

———. *The Doctor and the Soul* (New York: Alfred Knopf, 1955).

Fromm, Erich. *Man for Himself* (New York and Toronto: Rinehart & Co., Inc., 1947).

Gardner, E. C. *Biblical Faith and Social Ethics* (New York: Harper & Bros., 1960).

Greene, Norman N. *Jean-Paul Sartre: The Existentialist Ethic* (Ann Arbor: University of Michigan Press, 1960).

Hartmann, Nicolai. *Ethics* (London: Allen & Unwin, 1932).

Hartshorne, Charles. *Man's Vision of God* (Chicago and New York: Willett, Clark & Co., 1941).

———. *Reality as Social Process* (Glencoe, Ill.: The Free Press, 1953).

Jung, Carl. *Answer to Job* (New York: The Bollingen Foundation, Inc., 1954).

Kaufmann, Walter. *Nietzsche* (Princeton: Princeton University Press, 1950).

Kierkegaard, Soren. *Fear and Trembling* and *The Sickness unto Death* (New York: Doubleday, Anchor Books, 1956).

Knox, John. *Christ the Lord* (Chicago: Willett, Clark & Co., 1945).

Leese, Kurt. *Die Krisis und Wende des Christlichen Geistes* (Berlin: Junker & Dunnhaupt, 1932).

Luther, Martin. *Three Treatises* (Philadelphia: Muhlenberg Press, 1947).

May, Rollo. (ed.). *Existence* (New York: Basic Books, 1958).

Niebuhr, H. Richard. *Christ and Culture* (New York: Harper & Bros., 1951).

———. *The Meaning of Revelation* (New York: Harper & Bros., 1941).

———. *Radical Monotheism and Western Culture* (New York: Harper & Bros., 1960).

Niebuhr, Reinhold. *Applied Christianity* (New York: Meridian Books, Inc., 1959).

———. *The Children of Light and the Children of Darkness* (New York: Charles Scribner's Sons, 1944).

———. *Christian Realism and Political Problems* (New York: Charles Scribner's Sons, 1953).

———. *An Interpretation of Christian Ethics* (New York: Harper & Bros., 1935).

———. *Leaves from the Notebook of a Tamed Cynic* (New York: Meridian Books, Inc., 1957).

———. *Moral Man and Immoral Society* (New York: Charles Scribner's Sons, 1932).

———. *The Nature and Destiny of Man* (New York: Charles Scribner's Sons, 1941, 1943).

———. *Pious and Secular America* (New York: Charles Scribner's Sons, 1958).

Otto, Rudolph. *The Idea of the Holy.* Trans. by John W. Harvey, 2nd ed. (London and New York: Oxford University Press, 1957).

Price, Lucien. *The Dialogues of Whitehead* (New York: Mentor, 1955).

Ramsey, Paul. *Basic Christian Ethics* (New York: Charles Scribner's Sons, 1951).

Rieff, Philip. *Freud: The Mind of the Moralist* (New York: Viking Press, 1959).

Robinson, James. *A New Quest of the Historical Jesus* (Naperville: Allenson Press, 1959).

Sartre, Jean-Paul. *Existentialism.* Trans. by Bernard Frechtman (New York: Philosophical Library, 1947).

————. *No Exit and Three Other Plays* (New York: Vintage Books, 1955).

Thomas, George. *Christian Ethics and Moral Philosophy* (New York: Charles Scribner's Sons, 1955).

Tillich, Paul. *Love, Power, and Justice* (New York: Oxford University Press, 1954).

————. *The Protestant Era* (Chicago: University of Chicago Press, 1948).

Toynbee, Arnold. *An Historian's Approach to Religion* (London: Oxford University Press, 1956).

————. *A Study of History.* Abridgement of Vols. I-VI by D. C. Somervell (London: Oxford University Press, 1946).

Werner, Martin. *Die Entstehung des Christlichen Dogmas* (Bern: Paul Haupt, 1941).

West, Charles. *Communism and the Theologians* (Philadelphia: The Westminster Press, 1958).

Whitehead, Alfred North. *Process and Reality* (Cambridge: Cambridge University Press, 1929).

————. *Science and the Modern World* (New York: Macmillan Co., 1926).

Wilder, Amos. *Eschatology and Ethics.* Rev. ed. (New York: Harper & Bros., 1950).

Williams, Daniel Day. *God's Grace and Man's Hope* (New York: Harper & Bros., 1949).

————. *What Present-Day Theologians Are Thinking.* Rev. ed. (New York: Harper & Bros., 1959).

B. Articles in Periodicals.

Bartley, William W. "I Call Myself a Protestant," *Harper's,* CCXVIII, 1308 (May, 1959), 49-56.

Carpenter, George W. "Collapse in the Congo: the Price of Paternalism," *Christianity and Crisis,* XX (September 19, 1960), 128-132.

"Collapse in the Congo," *New Republic,* CXLIII, (July 25, 1960), 7-8.

Garrison, Lloyd M. "The New Heart of Darkness," *The Reporter,* XXIII (September 1, 1960), 16-19.

Grant, Frederick C. "The Jesus of History," *Union Seminary Quarterly Review,* XIV (March 1959), 1-16.

Shinn, Roger L. "Some Ethical Foundations of Christian Theology," *Union Seminary Quarterly Review,* XV (January, 1960), 99-110.

Sterling, Claire. "Why the Belgians Failed," *The Reporter,* XXIII (October 13, 1960), 25-28.

Index